TOWARD A POST-INDUSTRIAL PSYCHOLOGY

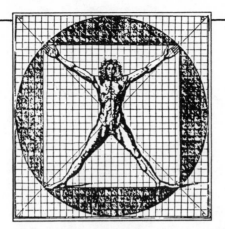

TOWARD A POST·INDUSTRIAL PSYCHOL-OGY: EMERGING PERSPECTIVES ON TECHNOLOGY, WORK, EDUCA-TION, AND LEISURE

DON MANKIN
University of Maryland
University College

JOHN WILEY & SONS
New York · Santa Barbara · Chichester ·
Brisbane · Toronto

Text and cover designed by Mark E. Safran.
Production supervised by Janet Sessa.

Library of Congress Cataloging in Publication Data:

Mankin, Don, 1942-
    Toward a post-industrial psychology.

    Bibliography: p.
    Includes index.
    1. Psychology, Industrial.   2. Personnel management.
I. Title.

HF5548.8.M36   158.7   78-5302
ISBN 0-471-02086-9 pbk.

Printed in the United States of America

10 9 8 7 6 5 4 3 2

To my parents,
Eva and Harry

Preface

The two expressions that form the main title of this book, *post-industrial* and *industrial psychology*, are probably the simplest and most direct means of conveying its purpose and themes. While each of these expressions will be dealt with in more detail in the introductory chapter, a brief comment concerning both of them at this point will help to describe the intent, scope, and point of view of this book.

The expression "post-industrial society" has been used in recent years to convey a sense of the profound changes that advanced industrialized nations are undergoing and will most likely continue to experience for the foreseeable future. This expression is most often associated with sociologist Daniel Bell (1973), who uses it to describe a society in which the majority of the labor force is engaged in providing services such as government, health care, research, education, and entertainment as compared to an "industrial society" in which the majority of the labor force is engaged in the manufacture of goods. Some of the other characteristics of post-industrial societies Bell and others have identified include the increased importance of leisure, a greater emphasis on long-range planning to guide the future of societies, the growing interdependence among the nations of the world, the development of new and important problems and opportunities, and the expanding influence of technology, particularly for storing, retrieving, processing, and transmitting information. It is in this broader sense that the "post-industrial" in the title is intended.

As society changes, so must academic and professional disciplines. This is especially true for those disciplines that deal with the institutions and phenomena central to these changes, not the least of which are work and work organizations. Industrial psychology or, as it is more frequently referred to today, *industrial and organizational (I/O) psychology,* is one such discipline, and, as we shall see in the chapters that follow, it is already responding to and shaping changes in our society. The nature of these responses and influences is the subject of this book.

To be more specific, this book broadens the traditional perspectives and scope of I/O psychology in a manner consistent with recent and anticipated societal changes and developing images of human nature. To accomplish this, past and present efforts within I/O psychology and related fields are surveyed

vii

and integrated with information and points of view from other fields, and then, after seasoning liberally with some personal speculation, the lot is brought to bear on particular issues and problems. In this context, the focus is more on present and future *societal* problems, issues, and opportunities than on those of more immediate concern to organizations except where the latter have significant consequences for the former.

Since this book is not designed as a review of the data and theories of I/O psychology, no attempt has been made to be exhaustive. On the contrary, I have tried to avoid duplicating basic material presented in other textbooks except where it is necessary for continuity, exposition or organization. I have chosen to emphasize, instead, issues that are not covered by available textbooks or that have received only limited attention. In addition, in the interests of brevity and readability, footnotes and intensive discussion of some principal issues and important but relatively peripheral topics have been kept to a minimum. For the reader who would like to examine these topics in more depth, annotated comments and suggestions for further reading can be found at the conclusion of each chapter. Teachers may want to use these comments and suggestions as the basis for class discussion, homework assignments, and examination questions. A cross-reference table is also provided to indicate where detailed presentations of the basic background material in I/O psychology can be found in several of the more widely known textbooks and references in the field (see Table 1).

This book can be used in courses on I/O psychology and organizational behavior and as a contemporary survey of these fields in courses on applied, introductory, and general psychology. It might also be used in any specialized courses dealing with the relationships between organizations, social and technological change, the individual, the processes of industrialization, and the problems that may arise from these interactions. Finally, anyone concerned with the problems and points of view presented and discussed herein should find this book to be of interest and may be able to think of other courses and contexts in which it can be effectively put to use.

Don Mankin

Table 1 Correspondence Between this Book and Other I/O Textbooks[a]

Chapters in Selected I/O Texts	Chapters in Present Text				
	1	2	3	4	5
Bass and Barrett (1972)	1, 2, 5 (pp. 110–115)	7–12, 19 (pp. 564–578)	3–6, 13–15	14 (pp. 436–442)	
Blum and Naylor (1968)	1, 10, 20 (pp. 571–582)	2–8, 17	9, 10–14, 16–20	18 (pp. 543–548)	
Gilmer (1971)	1	4, 11 (pp. 289–296) 13, 14	2, 3, 5, 6, 9–11, 15–20	11 (pp. 302–307)	
Korman (1971)	1, 2	4, 8–12, 13 (pp. 292–302) 14 (pp. 306–321), 15	3, 5–7, 13 (pp. 302–305), 14 (pp. 321–330) 15, 16		
Landy and Trumbo (1976)	1, 2	3–8, 14	9–13, 15		
Maier (1973)	1, 2	7–10, 12, 20	3–6, 11, 13–19, 21	15 (pp. 407–416)	
McCormick and Tiffin (1974)	1	2–10	11–19		
Schultz (1978)	1, 2, 11 (pp. 362–365)	2 (pp. 60–62), 3–6	7–12	10 (pp. 338–348)	
Siegel and Lane (1974)	1, 2, 11	3–7, 2 (pp. 52–60)	8–17		
Smith and Wakely (1972)	1, 13	2, 8, 9, 11, 13	1, 3–7, 10, 12, 13		
Brooks/Cole Series		Dunnette (1966) Goldstein (1974) Hunt (1974)	Lawler (1973)		

[a]The reader should consult these basic textbooks to supplement material covered in this book.

Acknowledgments

This book could not have been written without the help of many people. Acknowledging everyone's contribution would take several pages, so with two exceptions, I have limited myself to those who reviewed the most recent drafts of the entire manuscript.

Ken Brousseau, Daniel Katz, Jim O'Toole, and Robert Zajonc furnished the kind of constructive feedback that every textbook writer needs but is not always fortunate enough to receive. Fred Blum's detailed editorial comments were invaluable in helping me to identify problems with writing style, vagueness, and portions of the text that were either unnecessary or in need of further elaboration.

Without the contribution of two other individuals in the early stages of this project, I seriously doubt that it would have gone very far. By recognizing a kernel or two of quality in the early drafts and the overall worthiness of the intent, Duane Schultz provided the reassurance and incentive for me to persevere through its most discouraging phases. Nils Hovik offered continued encouragement, contributed ideas, recommended important reference material, and generally acted as a sounding board during the critical formative stages of this work. In many respects, this book grew out of the excitement and stimulation of my interactions and exchanges with Nils. His contribution is perhaps the most significant.

While the final product reflects the contribution of all these individuals, they are in no way responsible for any omissions or flaws.

The flying and essentially unerring fingers of Anita Woodcock and "Annie Oakely"/Joanne/Joy in typing the final manuscript made this phase of the project as headache-free as possible. Their good-natured acceptance of and skill in dealing with my "chicken-scratch" handwriting, last-minute revisions, and unreasonable deadlines were impressive. For this, they deserve special thanks.

Last but far from least was the support, encouragement and patient indulgence of my friends. They created the conditions that enabled me to carry the project through to completion. I cannot thank you all enough.

Venice, Calif.
July 18th, 1977

D. M.

Contents

chap. 1.   Introduction 1
A Brief History of I/O Psychology 1
Two Paradigms in the History of I/O Psychology 3
A New Paradigm? 6
A Post-Industrial Perspective 7
The Humanistic Application of Technology 8
Alternative Futures and the Idea of a System 9
   Alternative Futures 9
   The Idea of a System 10
   Conclusion 12
Some Comments Concerning Style, Content, and Organization 13
Subjectivity 13
An Interdisciplinary Emphasis 14
Organization and Content 14
Summary 16
Notes and Suggestions for Further Reading 16

**chap. 2.   Fitting the Worker to the Job:
Personnel Selection, Placement,
and Training** 19
Assumptions Underlying the Selection Process 19
Conclusion 21
Equal Employment Opportunity and Personnel Selection 22
Job-Related Validity 22
Differential Validity 23
Work Samples 24
Conclusion 25
A Systems Approach to Maximum Utilization of Human Resources 26
Programs and Initiatives by Organizations 26
   Counseling and Placement 26
   Training 29
   Support Services and Organizational Accommodation 30
   Conclusion 31

Public Programs, Services, and Policy   32
   Computerized Job-Person Matching   32
   Creating Jobs   34
Conclusion   37
An Educational System for the Post-Industrial Society   38
Educational Goals for the Future   38
   A Look at the Future of Work   39
   Implications for Educational Goals   41
   Educating for Leisure and Citizenship   43
Suggestions for Design   44
   Information Technology in Education   46
   Summarizing the Relative Advantages   49
Conclusion   51
Summary   52
Notes and Suggestions for Further Reading   52

chap. 3.   Fitting the Job to the Worker: Job Satisfaction and the Design of Work Systems

Work Systems   59
Job Dissatisfaction and Quality of Life   60
Human Needs and Contemporary Work   62
Reviewing the Evidence   65
   Extent, Trends, and Causes   65
Personal and Societal Consequences   69
   Mental and Physical Health   70
   Drug Use   71
   Non-Work Attitudes and Behavior   71
Conclusion   74
Strategies for Increasing Job Satisfaction   75
Conclusions from the Research   79
The Role of Individual Differences   82
Toward a Technology for Designing Jobs and Organizations   85
   Conclusion   88
Alternative Futures for Work   88
Rising Expectations, Decreasing Opportunities   89
Societal and Technological Change as a Catalyst for Worklife
Improvement   91
   The Impact of Technology   91

The Journey to Work   95
''Telecommuting'' as an Alternative to Travel   97
Resource Shortages   102
Conclusion   105
Summary   105
Notes and Suggestions for Further Reading   106

chap. 4.   Leisure in the Post-Industrial Society   113

The Meaning and Functions of Leisure   114
Alternative Models for Leisure   115
Comparing the Two Alternatives   118
Play as a Model for Leisure   119
   Summary   122
Work and Leisure   124
The Pragmatic Perspective   125
   Industrial Recreation   125
   Alternative Work Schedules   126
   Adjusting to Retirement   130
   Advocational Counseling and Design   133
Theoretical/Empirical Perspective   136
Normative Perspective   139
Conclusion   143
Summary   145
Notes and Suggestions for Further Reading   145

chap. 5.   Conclusion: The Sociotechnological Context for a Post-Industrial Psychology   151

The Information Utility   153
Planning the Future   155
An Emerging Model for Planning   156
Summary and Conclusions   159
Notes and Suggestions for Further Reading   160

References   165

Author Index   201

Subject Index   209

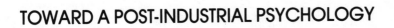

TOWARD A POST-INDUSTRIAL PSYCHOLOGY

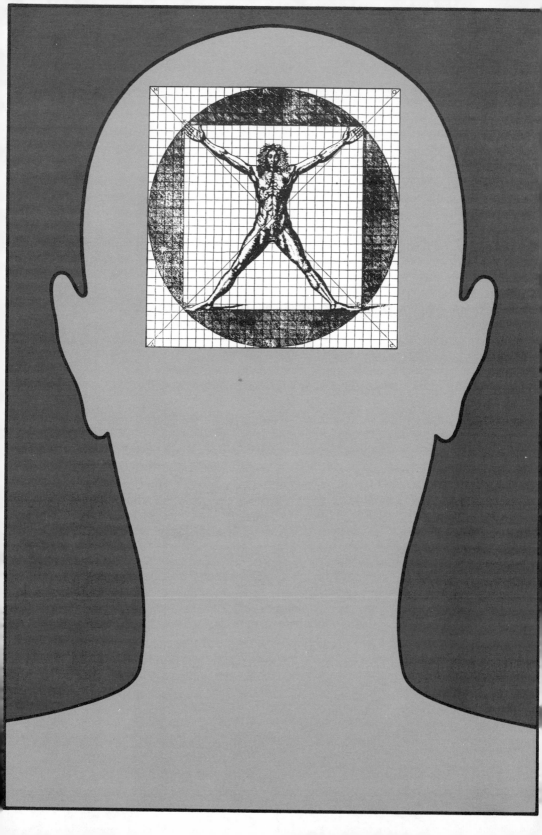

Introduction

For convenience and marketability, books intended for educational or professional use are usually classified by subject area or formal academic discipline. To be consistent with this convention, one could say that this book is about industrial and organizational (I/O) psychology, but that would only be part of the story. By the end of the book, if not by the end of this chapter, it should be clear that I/O psychology is only one of the subjects, albeit a particularly important one, we discuss. However, since I/O psychology provides the foundation for the discussion of these other, related topics, a definition of the expression is an appropriate place to begin.

Representative of the many definitions available is the one offered by Blum and Naylor in their basic textbook, *Industrial Psychology: Its Theoretical and Social Foundations* (1968). They define I/O psychology as:

> *the application or extension of psychological facts and principles to the problems concerning human beings operating within the context of business and industry. (p. 4)*

The phrase "operating within the context of business and industry" generally means that the activities of I/O psychologists relate to any organization established for the purpose of producing goods or services. This includes such organizations as hospitals and educational institutions in addition to those more typically subsumed under this expression, such as factories, businesses, or banks.

Within the scope of this definition, there are a number of specific activities in which I/O psychologists engage; some of these activities will be described in more detail throughout the book. First, however, we briefly examine the history of the field to gain a better understanding of its functions, past and present, and to see how it may develop in the future.

A Brief History of I/O Psychology

Several individuals, factors, and events contributed to the early development of industrial psychology, as I/O psychology was known throughout most of its

1

history. Among the contributions are the pioneering work of Walter Dill Scott on the application of psychological principles to advertising and Hugo Münsterberg's research on movement economy, monotony, and learning (Münsterberg, 1913; Scott, 1905). Psychologists were also quite active during World War I in constructing tests to classify recruits and select officer personnel. This early work formed the basis for the study of personnel selection, which is today one of the most important and best-known areas within I/O psychology.

During these early years, developments in the related discipline of industrial engineering profoundly affected the origins of I/O psychology. In the latter part of the nineteenth century Frederick W. Taylor systematically investigated the influence of financial incentives, tool design, and work layout on job performance. Based on these investigations, Taylor devised a system of "scientific management," which included among its primary goals the determination of "the one best way" (the one that was most efficient and least fatiguing) to do a job and the standardization of work operations to make every worker easily replaceable (Taylor, 1947). To fulfill these goals, scientific management focused on the effect of financial incentives and the physical aspects of the job on worker performance.

The limitations of this emphasis were dramatically demonstrated in the series of studies conducted at the Hawthorne Works of the Western Electric Co. by Harvard sociologist Elton Mayo and several of his associates beginning in 1924 and running into the 1930s. The purpose of the Hawthorne studies was to assess the effects of such working conditions as workroom illumination, length of working day, and rest periods on worker productivity. The researchers were surprised to find that productivity increased *regardless of the experimental manipulation.* The explanation for these findings is still very much a subject of debate, but at the time, for many years following, and to a certain extent today, the Hawthorne results have been interpreted in terms of previously unrecognized social-psychological phenomena. The implications of the Hawthorne studies will be examined in more detail shortly; here we can note that the studies precipitated a significant change in the way industrial psychologists viewed the nature of human work needs and the variables that influence work behavior.

Following World War I, other important developments within the field included the appearance of the *Journal of Applied Psychology,* the introduction of the first college courses in applied psychology, and the founding of the first psychological consulting company.

World War II was the next important event in the history of industrial psychology. Once more, psychologists made a significant contribution to the war effort. As in the previous war, emphasis was placed on the development of tests for selecting and classifying recruits. In addition, the need to consider human-machine interactions in increasingly complex military systems led to the development of engineering psychology, a separate but related discipline with concerns and methodologies overlapping those of I/O psychology.

Since World War II, I/O psychology has continued to grow. Several divisions of the American Psychological Association are devoted to various aspects of the field and many journals and organizations have been created to represent the diverse interest groups within and related to it.

The most important development of recent years has been the growth of the closely allied field of organizational psychology. Recognition that organizations are complex social systems and that human behavior and needs in organizations must be viewed in the context of the entire social system making up the organization (this awareness at least partly resulting from the Hawthorne studies) led to the development of organizational psychology. The relevance of this field to industrial psychology was formally recognized in 1970 when the Division of Industrial Psychology of the American Psychological Association (APA) officially changed its name to the Division of Industrial and Organizational Psychology. Although some differences in emphasis and function remain, the interrelationships between traditional ''industrial'' concerns and more recent ''organizational'' issues are strong, and the two expressions are frequently used in combination, as is done throughout this book.

Two Paradigms in the History of I/O Psychology

The concept of the ''paradigm'' as used by philosopher/historian Thomas Kuhn refers to the coherent traditions that define the theories, methodologies, applications, and underlying assumptions of a scientific discipline at given times in the history of that discipline (Kuhn, 1970). Individuals whose research is based on shared paradigms, he argues, follow the same rules, standards, and assumptions for scientific practice and use many of the same basic concepts. The usual developmental pattern of a ''mature'' science, according to Kuhn, is marked more by the transformations of paradigms, that is, ''scientific revolutions,'' than by the steady, continuous accumulation of knowledge.

By interpreting and applying the concept of the paradigm in a somewhat broader fashion than was probably intended by Kuhn, we can see that at least two paradigms have, at different times, characterized I/O psychology. The dominant paradigm of the first 30 or so years of the field is perhaps best represented by Taylor's scientific management and the early personnel psychology, which grew out of the work conducted during World War I.

The influence and consequences of "Taylorism" were much more profound than might at first be apparent from its role as a technique for serving the interests of production and efficiency. The inexorable effect of what Bell calls the "logic of efficiency" (Bell, 1960), was to reduce the worker to little more than a machine, "to reduce human variability, to make the work process as machinelike as possible" (Neff, 1968, p. 19). There was also a tendency to think of the average worker as "dull," having "no interests except earning more money, [and being] so stupid that earning too much [was] bad for him" (Blum and Naylor, 1968, p. 578). It has even been suggested that Taylor himself lacked consideration and sympathy with workers (e.g., Blum and Naylor, 1968), although there are those who claim that while he was well aware of and concerned with the consequences of overly restrictive work, his ideas were frequently misunderstood and misused (Walker, 1968). Whatever the case, there is little disagreement concerning some of the negative consequences of Taylorism.

Focusing on the activities of psychologists during and following World War I, organizational psychologist Edgar Schein argues that the early industrial psychologists

> *started with questions which deal with the <u>assessment and selection of individual workers</u> and ignored those questions which involve the organization as a whole. . . . Selection was made more scientific by <u>measuring</u> in individuals those characteristics which the organization required of its new members. The organization itself, however, was merely a source of information and of questions to be answered. It supplied the goals to be achieved; the psychologists worked to help fulfill them. (1970, p. 2)*

According to Schein, this tradition was further reinforced by "time-and-motion" study, the eventual outgrowth of Taylor's scientific management.

> *Psychologists soon found themselves moving closer to organizational problems in a growing attempt to put order into the process of <u>designing and organizing work itself</u>. . . . Still, however, the organization served only as the environment; it defined the ultimate products or services to be obtained and enlisted psychologists to help them study human performance with the aim of making it more effective. (p. 2)*

In sum, we can see that the dominant paradigm of early industrial psychology included the following characteristics:

1. A primary focus on the individual worker as the relevant unit of analysis.

2. The assumption that the average worker was motivated almost exclusively by financial incentives.

3. The tendency to treat the worker as little more than a machine whose inherent "inefficiencies" could be compensated for by the appropriate design of tools and work processes.

4. A view of the worker as a factor to be manipulated to increase productivity.

The Hawthorne studies marked the beginning of the "revolution" that eventually led to the transformation of the existing paradigm into one that was profoundly different. These studies drew attention to the motivational and affective importance of the informal network of social relationships that usually develop in formal organizations.

> *What both [the classical industrial-engineering, or scientific management, approach and the early personnel psychology approach] have failed to recognize is that formal organizations tend to breed informal organizations within them, and that <u>in the informal organization, workers and managers are likely to establish relationships with each other which will influence the manner in which they carry out their jobs or fulfill their roles</u>. (Schein, 1970, p. 31)*

The concern for "human relations" in organizations eventually broadened into the more general recognition of the importance of such factors as managerial philosophies, leadership styles, organizational policies and structures, incentive systems, and the design of work processes. In other words, the organization is a complex system of social relationships, structures, and procedures, and individual behavior can only be fully understood by examining it as an integral part of this total system.

The important differences between the two paradigms can now be identified. In contrast to the first characteristic of the earlier paradigm, the primary focus has shifted from individual workers as separate, distinct entities to individual workers as members of a complex social and organizational system. In addition, the assumption underlying the second and third characteristics are now considered to be naively simplistic, as psychologist Walter Neff's assessment of the net effect of the Hawthorne studies so aptly illustrates.

> *The Hawthorne studies have served the purpose of calling it to our attention that the human worker brings far more to his task than a variable ability to follow instructions and carry out a prescribed series of move-*

ments. He also brings his momentary moods, as well as more enduring emotions and feelings, his social beliefs and attitudes, his entire personality. Although they have been less studied, these aspects of human work are now believed to be of crucial importance. (Neff, 1968, p. 25)

Workers are no longer viewed as being motivated almost entirely by economic considerations. Neither are they thought of as automatons. In fact, the very human complexity that produced the variability and "inefficiencies" that so vexed the early proponents of scientific management is now treated by modern I/O psychologists as an opportunity and challenge for devising new and varied means for the improvement of job performance.

With this last point we can also begin to see the ways in which the two paradigms are similar. First and foremost, the overriding goal of both the early and the more modern approaches to I/O psychology has been to improve job performance. It is true that the emphasis has begun to shift in recent years to other, less utilitarian goals, as we will see in the pages to come. It is also true that the degree to which this goal has guided theory, research, and practice in contemporary I/O psychology is far less now than it was in the early days of the discipline. Nonetheless, if one had to describe a single goal that best characterized I/O psychology today, the fourth statement in our list of paradigmatic assumptions, with some qualifications, would be reasonably accurate.

Even the first paradigmatic difference described several paragraphs back is not as great as one might imagine; that is, although the primary focus of I/O psychology has been broadened to include the individual within the context of the organization, both paradigms are similar in that they generally limit themselves to the processes that occur *within* the organization. While there is a difference of degree between the two paradigms and there are important exceptions with respect to the later paradigm, for all intents and purposes, *intra*-organizational processes are still the main concern of most I/O psychologists today.

A New Paradigm?

Many social critics argue that we are living in an era of unprecendented change. While one can reasonably claim that certain earlier times were also marked by extraordinary change (e.g., the industrial revolution), there is a growing consensus that either the rapid pace or unique nature of change today, or both, coupled with present levels of public awareness of and sensitivity to this change has produced a situation unparalleled in this century, if not in the history of humankind.

6

Societal change and the anticipatory, correlative, and reactive processes it engenders have played important roles in the shaping of our social institutions in the past and will no doubt continue to do so in the future. The work organization, being one of the dominant social institutions of contemporary society, is no exception. To be sensitive and responsive to their changing environments, organizations will increasingly have to anticipate and adapt to forces for change external to, as well as arising within the organizations themselves.

The implications for I/O psychology are clear. As a manifestation of the industrial society, in general, and the work organizations that are so important within this society, in particular, I/O psychology will have to change along with society and its organizations. In fact, there is no reason why the field cannot act as an agent of societal change in its own right by consciously transforming its paradigms and, in the process, spur rather than follow the forces shaping the future of our society.

We must begin to prepare I/O psychology today to meet the needs of tomorrow. In a sense, the future is with us already, and, as the following chapters demonstrate, the processes of adaptation and innovation indicative of a shift toward a new, post-industrial paradigm have already begun. An impression of and prescription for this emerging paradigm form the perspective of this book, the salient characteristics and nature of which is the subject of the section to follow.

A Post-Industrial Perspective

The overall perspective of this book is composed of three related themes; the humanistic application of technology, the consideration of alternative futures, and understanding the idea of a system. As we will see shortly, the second and third themes are inherently related; that is, each implies the other. This is true in any context and is not just a reflection of the particular point of view of this book. Although the first theme does not necessarily follow *logically* from the other two, the moral and pragmatic relevance of humanistic values to futuristic and systemic issues has become increasingly apparent (e.g., see Boguslaw, 1965, and "Humanist Manifesto II," 1973). One can view the first theme as the goal toward which the approaches defined by the second and third themes are directed.

Because of the inherent relationship between the second and third themes, they are discussed in a single section separate from our discussion of the first. In spite of the form of this discussion, the reader should keep in mind that the perspective of this book is the "Gestalt" created by the integration of all three and all are equally important.

7

The Humanistic Application of Technology

The word "humanistic" has been used so widely and in so many contexts in recent years that a good portion of this book could be taken up with an effort to define it. We are, therefore, forced to limit our discussion to its use in describing the perspective of this book. Before attempting this definition, however, it is important that we understand the reason why a humanistic technology is so important. Admiral Hyman Rickover presents this argument in a particularly cogent and succinct form.

> *Unless [technology] is made to adapt itself to human interests, needs, values, and principles, more harm will be done than good. Never before, in all his long life on earth, has man possessed such enormous power to injure himself, his human fellows, and his society as has been put into his hands by modern technology. (1969, p. 24)*

Preliminary to defining the total expression, the meaning of "technology" as used throughout this book must be clearly understood. The following definition from Emmanuel Mesthene (1970) comes close.

> *We have found it more useful to define technology as tools in a general sense, including machines but also including such intellectual tools as computer languages and contemporary analytic and mathematical techniques. That is, we define technology as the organization of knowledge for the achievement of practical purposes. (emphasis added) (p. 25)*

By interpreting "organized knowledge" to include the behavioral, social, administrative, economic, and policy sciences, we would have a definition for "technology" that should serve our purposes well. In other words, the scope of this book includes not only hardware and analytic technologies but "softer" technologies such as psychological tests, therapeutic procedures and advertising, as well as social programs and public policies.

Now we can attempt a definition of "a humanistic technology." Rickover offers the beginnings of one when he argues that technology should be used to serve humanity in general, not just some humans; future generations and not just those interested in their own immediate advantage; and the human "in the totality of his humanity, encompassing all of his manifold interests and needs" (p. 24).

As used throughout this book, humanistic technology also means that those individuals who are most likely to experience the negative consequences of a particular technology should be able to have some influence over the decisions concerning its implementation. In more general terms, technological change should be subject to human control and not inevitably structure our values, purposes, and behavior to conform to its requirements and function; it should be used as an instrument to increase our influence over our lives and not as a means to dominate them.

A humanistic technology refers, then, to the ends and goals of society and its organizations, and of the techniques and disciplines, I/O psychology included, that serve these ends. To be more specific, it means that *technology should be subject to human control and used to increase individual autonomy and create opportunities for fulfilling all human needs, material and nonmaterial, for as many people as is reasonably possible both in the present and in the future.* Admittedly, much of this may be somewhat vague right now, but in the discussion throughout this book, the intent, meaning, and scope of a humanistic technology should begin to take shape.

Alternative Futures and the Idea of a System

Alternative futures: Few people think of the future as a single, completely determined, inevitable set of conditions. Neither is the opposite view widely held, that there are no constraints on future possibilities and that people can create whatever future they so desire. Between these two extremes, there remain diverse opinions concerning the degree of control that can be exercised over the future. Nonetheless, the range of views reflect the common assumption that there is a finite set of attainable futures, some more desirable than others. Which outcome actually occurs is to a certain extent a function of the programs and decisions implemented today and in the years to come. Society's task is to choose among the alternatives and to try to turn them into reality by taking appropriate action.

The differences of opinion arise when we examine the possibilities and preferences expressed or implied and the means prescribed for achieving particular ends. With regard to possibilities, there are those who believe that the major outlines and conditions of the future are relatively immutable and the best we can do is find ways of adapting to or, when necessary, attenuating the adverse impact of these conditions. On the other hand, a more optimistic view argues that with the proper resolve and resources we can significantly alter the future course of society.

Preferences also vary widely and frequently cut across differences in perceived possibilities. Besides the obvious diversity in views that arise regarding specific goals, there is some variability in the degree to which present preferences are seen as either enduring or changing in the future. While some people would argue that even if it were possible to agree on what constitutes a desired future today, we might not express the same preferences several years hence. Conversely, others might claim that some values and preferences are inherent to human nature and can be used to guide present action to shape future reality.

Finally, even when it is possible to arrive at a reasonable consensus on possibilities and preferences, the particular plans for achieving them may also reflect wide differences of opinion.

The perspective of this book generally falls somewhere between these extremes. Specifically, some conditions are perceived as relatively fixed, especially in the short term, while others are seen as amenable to profound alteration, particularly if we look far enough into the future. Some of the proposals are offered as short-range ameliorative actions to buy time to create the opportunity for affecting more significant long-term change. Furthermore, the goals advocated here are broad enough to include a wide range of preferences. Indeed, the overall goal expressed or implied in the chapters to follow is to create more options, opportunities, and mechanisms by which individuals can pursue their own personally defined ends, and the purpose of the book is to describe some of the steps necessary for achieving this alternative future.

The idea of a system: Understanding the range of future possibilities and the means and consequences of trying to achieve desired ends requires an appreciation of the complex interconnections of events, policies, and elements that comprise the total societal system. The "idea of a system" is central to this appreciation, an idea conveyed by Garrett Hardin in the following example:

> *The argument is simple: old maids keep cats, cats eat rats, rats destroy bumblebee nests, bumblebees fertilize red clover, and red clover is needed for horses, which are the backbone of English character training. Ergo the strength of England depends on a bountiful supply of old maids. (1968, p. 455)*

Hardin's example whimsically demonstrates that natural systems are connected in ways so complex that it becomes extremely difficult to predict what will happen when a new element is introduced into the system. Related to this are the mistaken notions we have about specific agents "which will do only one thing" (p. 457). Wishing to do one thing, we usually end up doing many.

> *Wishing to kill insects, we may put an end to the singing of birds. Wishing to "get there" faster, we insult our lungs with smog. Wishing to know what is happening everywhere in the world at once, we create an in-*

formation overload against which the mind rebels, responding by a new and dangerous apathy. (p. 457)

Despite Hardin's emphasis on biological systems we can see that his examples are applicable to systems of all kinds, including socioeconomic, political, and industrial systems, to name just a few. It should also be clear that what is true of a single system is also true of the complex interaction of several systems. In other words, even when we are able to anticipate the consequences of an action within the system of interest, there may be unintended, indirect effects on systems not even under consideration.

To borrow another example from Hardin, consider the effects of the "Pasteurian revolution," the application of bacteriology and sanitation to the control of disease. The ultimate price of this revolution, according to Hardin, was an increase in the amount of starvation in the world resulting from the removal of disease as an effective natural mechanism for population control.

Environmentalists, who, almost by definition, adhere to a systems point of view, have also at times been lax in applying this point of view to systems that are essentially nonbiological in nature. For instance, consider some of the undesirable consequences that may result when an industry or business is forced to close down because of its genuine inability to conform to pollution standards. *

Of course, we do not suggest that the effort to control disease which marked the Pasteurian revolution should never have been initiated; nor do we suggest that companies should be allowed to continue polluting the environment to excess. What is being suggested is that some "other thing" should have also been initiated to compensate for some of the undesirable side-effects of these measures. In the case of disease control, for instance, the most obvious "other thing" would have been the promotion of birth control for population stabilization. With regard to the other example, compensatory actions could include the development of relatively nonpolluting industries to employ those people displaced by closing down the polluting industries. To carry this point a step further, it is important to recognize that these compensatory actions might require similiar moves to counteract their own unintended consequences as well (e.g., job training programs to develop the skills needed by the new, nonpolluting industries).

To summarize, Hardin notes that:

A systems analyst need not, when confronted with a new invention, reject it out of hand simply because "we can never do merely one thing."

---

* A particularly noteworthy example of the efforts some environmentalists have made to deal with the *economic consequences of environmental policy* can be found in Grossman and Daneker (1977).

11

Rather, if he has the least spark of creativity in him, he says, "We can never do merely one thing, <u>therefore we must do several</u> in order that we may bring into being a new stable system." (1968, p. 457)

And, to relate this to the preceding discussion of alternative futures, we might add that it is the interplay of human actions, their consequences, and the circumstances that precipitate them, and other, essentially unforeseen exogenous factors that will ultimately shape our future.

In conclusion, considering alternative futures and understanding the idea of a system means that work organizations must be dealt with as important parts of such larger systems as communities, cities, nations, and the global society—depending on which level of concern is reasonable and appropriate for a particular set of circumstances at a given time. The direct and indirect influences the organization has on these larger systems, and vice-versa, must be considered as thoroughly and as systematically as possible, not only in terms of their immediate and short-term consequences but for the long term as well.

Conclusion: In spite of the apparent good sense of the notion that we should consider the important long- and short-term consequences of our actions and be prepared to deal with them appropriately, the "technocratic world view" and the various techniques generally used to manage complex systems have been severely criticized in recent years (e.g., see Ellul, 1964; Marcuse, 1964; Mumford, 1970; Roszak, 1969). Basically, the complaint is that instead of technology being a means to an end it has become an end in itself by replacing traditional human values with its own self-serving values, of which "efficiency" is the most important. This is a point well taken for it does appear that, as Roszak, Ellul, Marcuse, Mumford, and others have claimed, we have consistently ignored or overlooked certain humanistic considerations in our uses of technology and tended to focus our efforts on those ends most easily served by the technologies of the industrial age. Indeed, all too often the "technological imperatives" of efficiency and rationality have supplanted what should have been our primary goals all along, the improvement of the quality of human life. As we will see in later chapters, this is not a particularly surprising result in light of the complexities of most contemporary systems and the difficulties encountered in trying to make them more responsive to human needs.

But technology does not have a life of its own. It is the result of human endeavor and thus can and should be subject to human desires and decisions and the social and political institutions we create to control and implement the products of our endeavors. The way we as a society design these institutions and the systems they comprise is crucial. If we are going to employ technology to our advantage while avoiding the problems heretofore associated with its use,

12

we will have to temper our systems designs with a humanistic perspective and an eye to the future.

Some Comments Concerning Style, Content, and Organization

By integrating the themes dealing with humanistic values, alternative futures, and the systems idea we have come full circle in the discussion of the perspective of this book. Since the general subject area of the book has also been described, all that remains is to offer a few comments concerning its style, content, and organization.

Subjectivity

No doubt many readers will notice and possibly even be put off by the subjective nature of much of the material to follow. There are several reasons for this subjectivity. First of all, since part of the perspective of this book is futuristic in nature, a certain amount of subjectivity is unavoidable. Looking into the future requires more interpretation, evaluation, and judgment than does looking into the past. Even the process of looking into the past often involves subjective interpretation, and we are now becoming aware that the supposedly objective body of knowledge known as "science" is also subject to interpretation, distortion, and value judgments (see Kuhn, 1970). Speculation on the future, one of this book's primary aims, tends to be even more subjective because the number of unknowns is greater.

The "problem" of subjectivity becomes even more complicated when we start talking about what is or is not desirable for the individual and society, especially in the future. My choice of a humanistic perspective—or at least my particular interpretation of this perspective—is a personal one, based on my own feelings about what is desirable. The dilemma of subjectivity is part of a larger one concerning choices between differing sets of *values,* which, by their very nature, cannot be made objectively. Arguments can be made for the efficacy of a humanistic perspective, especially as it pertains to the use and application of technology; just such an argument was made earlier with the quote from Rickover. The purpose of this book is not to argue this point of view as such, and no attempt will be made to do so in any detail. Instead, the purpose is to take this point of view as given and see how it can be and has been applied. If the applications seem reasonable and desirable, that will be all of the justification needed here. No doubt, discussion of the issues arising from a humanistic perspective and its application within I/O psychology will not end with this book—just as it did not begin with it, as the following chapters will demonstrate.

An Interdisciplinary Emphasis

Because of the interactions and relationships that exist between systems of all kinds—for example, social, political, economic, technological, and biological—it is not enough to approach contemporary problems from the limited perspective of a single discipline. In our increasingly complex and interdependent world it has become necessary to cut across disciplines in order to bring all kinds of relevant techniques, knowledge, and expertise to bear on particular problems. We must be able to transcend academic and disciplinary specialties and look at the "big picture," the relationships that exist between artificially delineated units. Consistent with this view, a primary purpose of this book is to examine the problems that can and have emerged in a post-industrial society from a combined humanistic/futures/systems perspective and to deal with them in an interdisciplinary fashion.

Organization and Content

Chapters 2 and 3 focus on several of the subdisciplines and topics of I/O psychology—personnel selection and training, job satisfaction, work motivation, and job design, as well as the organizational context of these topics—and the existing and anticipated societal problems that may emerge from or cannot be effectively dealt with using traditional approaches to these issues. Alternative approaches that conform more closely to the perspective of this book are also discussed and examined as potential strategies for dealing with these societal problems.

Chapter 4 differs from the two preceding by focusing on an issue, the "problem" of leisure, that is rarely considered within the traditional domain of I/O psychology. The argument made here is that the subject of leisure is intimately related to the more familiar focus of I/O psychology, the world of work, and that a post-industrial perspective on both implies that they can best be dealt with as integrated and interdependent aspects of the lives of individuals and the affairs of society.

In addition, the subjects addressed in the chapters to follow are closely connected with other topics not usually discussed within the context of I/O psychology—for example, education, societal values, technological change, the problems of the cities, and the availability of natural resources. As a result, many of these issues appear several times throughout all three chapters, reflecting the interrelationship between them as well as their relevance to the more traditional concerns of I/O psychology. The final chapter will attempt to tie all these threads together by placing them in the context of issues with a somewhat broader societal concern.

There is one other way in which to view the connections between the material discussed in the chapters to follow, a view that might help to define emerging roles for I/O psychologists in the design of a humane future. The action programs that are described can be categorized into two levels, the organizational and societal. The first level includes activities that are somewhat consistent with the traditional responsibilities and job settings for I/O psychology; that is, activities that take place within the boundaries of particular organizations. The difference is that these activities are guided by concerns that might transcend organizational boundaries and more closely reflect a broader societal perspective. As the following chapters indicate, I/O psychologists have already begun to adopt this perspective on an ever larger scale.

The societal level actions reflect contributions I/O psychologists can and have made to public interest groups, as employees in government agencies, through their professional societies, as expert witnesses, and even within their employing organizations to help establish social policy and programs. I/O psychologists can also work at the organization-society interface by helping to coordinate organizational programs with social policy and vice versa, and examine the implications of one for the other. These potential contributions, and others, are summarized in the following statement from the Committee on Public Policy and Social Issues of the I/O Psychology Division of APA:

The Committee on Public Policy and Social Issues shall encourage and facilitate the participation of Division members in studies, research and service on problems associated with social welfare: (a) by identifying and publicizing to Division members social issues which are germane to their interests and skills; (b) by initiating working relationships with governmental agencies and public-issue-oriented groups and organizations, such that the Division can inform these agencies of the resources available from its members, respond to legitimate requests for assistance from these agencies for services of its members and disseminate to these agencies the results of investigations by its members bearing on the advancement of knowledge in the area of social problems; and (c) by promoting research and other activities of members toward the solution of important national social problems. (American Psychological Association, 1977, p. 9)

In conclusion, it is important to keep in mind that the aim throughout this book is to suggest a modest beginning for an important but often neglected approach to I/O psychology, describe some of its manifestations, offer some ideas and possible new directions, and open up avenues of inquiry. It may very well cause more argument than it settles and raise more questions than it answers.

Summary

At least two paradigms have characterized the discipline of I/O psychology throughout its history: a scientific management emphasis and a focus on social relationships within the organization. Present societal conditions and recent developments in the discipline suggest that a change toward a new paradigm is needed and, perhaps, may already be underway. As seen from the point of view of this book, this new, post-industrial paradigm should reflect three themes: the humanistic application of technology, the consideration of alternative futures, and the understanding of the idea of a system. By adopting the perspectives associated with these themes, I/O psychologists will be better able to deal with the complex and unique issues of the emerging post-industrial age and may also act as agents of social change by contributing to the creation of a more humane and fulfilling future.

Notes and Suggestions for Further Reading

A review of two contrasting usages of the phrase *"post-industrial society"* can be found in Marien (1977). A view of the post-industrial society as an "information economy" is described by Porat (1976).

For a more thorough general treatment of the *history of I/O psychology* see Blum and Naylor (1968), Gilmer (1971), and Korman (1971). Specific aspects of the history appear in a number of sources. For example, Peter Drucker has a considerably more positive view concerning F.W. Taylor's intent and the consequences of scientific management (1968, pp. 271–272). A first-person account of the Hawthorne studies is available in the classic work by Roethlisberger and Dickson (1939) while more contemporary perspectives on these studies can be found in Cass and Zimmer (1975), Parsons (1974), and

Wickert (1975). The relationship between the older, more traditional personnel activities of industrial psychology and the issues generally subsumed under organizational psychology is examined by Bass (1968).

Many of the concerns underlying the "intermediate" and "appropriate" technology movement which was spurred by E.F. Schumacher's book, *Small is Beautiful* (1973), are consistent with the intent of the *humanistic application of technology* perspective as interpreted in this book—with one important exception. As Livingston (1976) notes, an intermediate technology—one which is more sophisticated than the primitive technologies of earlier periods and less expensive and complex than most contemporary "super-technologies"—is not always an appropriate technology. The technology for the storing, retrieving, processing, and transmitting of information is a good case in point. While it is not an intermediate technology in any reasonable use of the expression, it has, in this writer's opinion, tremendous potential for increasing individual autonomy and opportunity and may, therefore, be an appropriate and humanistic technology: the ways in which it can be used in this fashion is one of the central themes of the forthcoming chapters. For more discussion of the appropriate technology concept see "Special Focus: Appropriate Technology" (1977).

For an overview of the rapidly developing field of *futures studies* see Fowles (1978). A shorter, highly readable but overly simplified presentation of the concept of alternative futures can be found in the epilogue to the novel by Theobold and Scott (1972).

There is much, much more to *systems* science than what was presented in the very elementary discussions in this chapter. The author strongly recommends that interested readers pursue this subject in more detail by referring to any of the many books on the subject. To mention just a few, see Buckley (1968), Churchman (1968), De Greene (1973), and Emery (1969).

One need not look far for *evidence of the emerging post-industrial paradigm* in I/O psychology. Perhaps the best indication is the formation of the Public Policy and Social Issues Committee within Division 14 (Industrial and Organizational Psychology) of the American Psychological Association in 1970. To find out more about this committee and its activities the reader can write to the APA offices, 1200 Seventeenth Street, N.W., Washington, D.C., 20036 for the name and address of the present chairperson (also see Porter, 1971). Other examples of the broader societal concern among I/O psychologists can be found in Bass and Bass (1976) and Purcell (1974), as well as the many references cited in the forthcoming chapters.

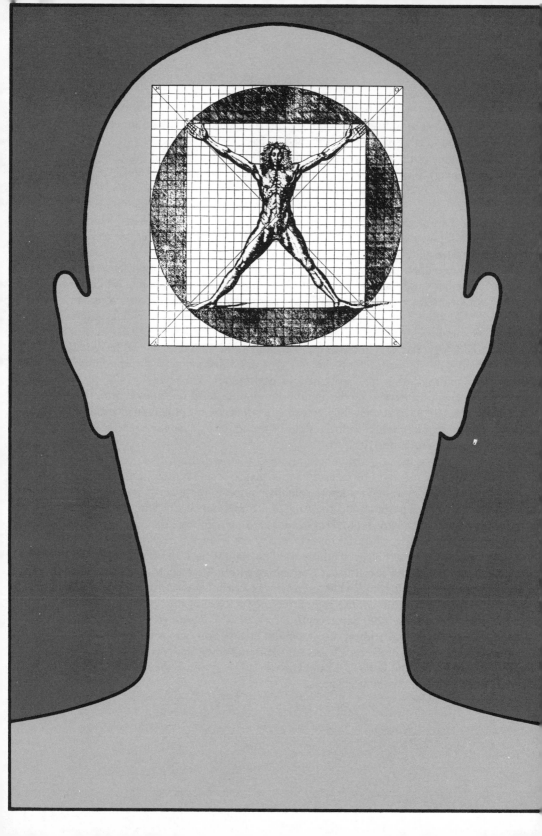

chap. 2

Fitting the Worker to the Job:
Personnel Selection, Placement, and Training

The task of choosing individuals from a larger group of applicants for a job, promotion, or training program has been one of the principal activities of I/O psychology since its earliest days. Personnel selection was also one of the first activities in the field to attract widespread public, judicial, and legislative scrutiny, with much of the concern focusing on the potential social inequities and personal hardships suffered by some people in their frequently unsuccessful pursuit of meaningful and rewarding employment. This attention has, in the last decade, precipitated a considerable amount of effort to identify, evaluate, and alleviate these problems. Much of the following discussion is devoted to reviewing some of these efforts, but first we briefly examine the basic assumptions and procedures underlying the selection process to better understand the source and nature of these problems.

Assumptions Underlying the Selection Process

The first and perhaps most important assumption is that the overriding goal of the selection process is to choose personnel who will perform satisfactorily on the job. As straightforward as this objective might seem, the actual process of measuring job-related behaviors and establishing criteria for success relevant to these behaviors is one of the most difficult problems I/O psychologists often face. For example, if we were trying to develop job-success criteria for a salesperson an obvious measure is sales record. For a machinist involved in a production process we could keep a record of items produced. But, what simple, direct criteria for satisfactory job behavior can be used for an engineer, a cab driver, a secretary, or a manager? Even in the case of the salesperson and the machinist, the performance measures of sales record and number of items produced are not completely adequate. What if the salesperson did not remain on the job long enough to justify the cost of hiring and training? What if the quality of the machinist's work was not particularly good or if he or she were not able to get along with co-workers and supervisors? Indeed, there are probably few jobs for which a single, obvious measure of success is available. Criteria such as number of items produced, job tenure, absenteeism, quality of work, peer ratings, and supervisor's ratings can all be appropriate measures depending on the job and other related circumstances. Since satisfactory job behavior has also been the dominant goal of many other activities within the domain of I/O psychology over the years, developing adequate methods for assessing job proficiency is probably the first and one of the most important issues of concern for many I/O psychologists, regardless of their particular interests and specialties.

The second assumption underlying the processes of selection and placement is that jobs vary, a fact richly illustrated by the more than 21,000 different occupations described by the *Dictionary of Occupational Titles* (U. S. Department of Labor, 1965). As a result, many of the activities related to the selection and placement of personnel—and to the development of training programs, setting of wage rates, and the design of production systems as well—are concerned with analyzing the job for the purpose of defining and describing requirements and tasks. This information can then be used to suggest individual characteristics and behaviors that might be most appropriate for a given job.

The next two assumptions concern the nature of these individual characteristics and behavior and their relationship to performance on the job. The third assumption is that the variations in job characteristics are at least matched by the diversity in the skills, work experiences, personalities, needs, values, abilities, and personal histories of those applying for jobs. It is this diversity that makes the selection process meaningful. If everyone were the same, there would be no need to select among them, except at random, for placement in particular jobs. The problem is; *in what ways* do individuals differ, how can we *assess* these differences in a valid and reliable fashion, and can we *predict* on the basis of these differences which of the applicants will perform most satisfactorily in a given job?

Since the means for assessing individual characteristics and for predicting future job behavior from these assessments are at the core of the controversy surrounding the processes of selection and placement and their societal consequences, a bit of elaboration on this last point is necessary. Ideally, the best selection strategy would be to hire everyone, try them out on the job for a reasonable period of time, and retain those who performed most satisfactorily during the trial period. Clearly, this procedure would be prohibitively expensive for most organizations. A more convenient and less expensive approach is to administer paper-and-pencil tests, solicit references, conduct personal interviews, or use biographical data and previous job histories to predict the relative degree of success of prospective employees on particular jobs. The fourth assumption, therefore, is that there exists a *demonstrable or logical relationship* between these predictors and job performance; for example, an applicant who attains a high score on a test of manual dexterity is more likely to be a better mechanic, everything else being equal, than one who does not.

Shortly, we will have more to say about what constitutes a "demonstrable relationship" and briefly describe recent attempts to develop measures and procedures for improving the predictability of future job performance. Until then, we will conclude the present discussion by tying the four assumptions into a straightforward description of the personnel selection and placement process:

Sound selection and placement procedures involve the use of individual difference measures that are demonstrably or logically related to future job behavior to predict the relative degree of success of prospective employees on a particular job.

Or, to provide a concrete example, given the IQs, previous job histories, and scores on a test of manual dexterity for a group of job applicants, can we select those who will perform most satisfactorily as electronics technicians for a particular organization?

Conclusion

Clearly, if there are more applicants than there are jobs or advancement opportunities (e.g., via promotions or training programs for upgrading skills), some applicants will not be selected. In most cases, they have little choice other than to remain in their present circumstances, that is, unemployed or in an existing and possibly less satisfying job, at least until another opportunity presents itself. The *personal* consequences for those not selected often include financial hardship, loss of self-esteem, depression, anxiety, and a variety of other conditions that frequently result from being unemployed or stuck in a poorly paid, low-level job with little chance for advancement. There are also consequences that affect society in general, such as the high costs of welfare and unemployment compensation, the waste associated with the failure to fully employ human capacities and skills, and the antisocial behavior and attitudes often associated with the personal consequences described above (e.g., the ghetto riots of the 1960s; see *Report of the National Advisory Commission on Civil Disorders,* 1968; also see Brenner, 1976).

That the problems and consequences of unemployment and underemployment are borne disproportionately by women, some minority groups, elderly workers, and teenagers has been the source of considerable concern since the early 1960s. In the ensuing years and continuing today, this concern, especially that aspect reflected in judicial and legislative process, has resulted in an extensive effort to analyze the reasons for this condition and to develop appropriate solutions. Some of these efforts are briefly reviewed in the following section.

Equal Employment Opportunity and Personnel Selection

In the early years of concern for equal employment opportunity, it was clear that part of the problem derived from pervasive stereotypes about the abilities of minority groups, women, elderly, and the young. In particular, the institutionalization of these beliefs in the job recruiting, screening, performance evaluation, and promotion practices of organizations was often the principal source of the problem. For example, many employers were reluctant to expend much effort to recruit from women's colleges or schools with a large nonwhite population, or to consider minorities and women for anything other than relatively low-level jobs. A more subtle form of discrimination was the use of sex-biased wording in job advertisements as illustrated by an ad for telephone "lineman"—in itself a sex-biased expression—with the heading, "We're Looking for Outdoor Men" (from Bem and Bem, 1973). The now illegal practice of labeling help-wanted columns as "Male" or "Female" and classifying job advertisements in these terms is yet another example of sexist language that reflects underlying sexual stereotypes.

Although such abuses have not completely disappeared, they are somewhat less of an issue today and have been considerably overshadowed by far more complex and ambiguous problems. In recent years, the tendency has been to define the source of the discrimination in terms of the nature of the instruments and selection procedures themselves instead of in terms of intentional, if covert, racial, sexual, and ageist stereotypes and prejudices. As a result, the solutions sought have focused on the development of modified or alternative instruments and procedures.

Job-Related Validity

One of the first manifestations of the trend to modify selection procedures was the job-relatedness and validity requirements prescribed by the 1964 Civil Rights Act and later reinforced by the landmark decision of the U.S. Supreme Court in 1971 in the case, *Griggs vs. Duke Power Co.* The plaintiff in this case argued that the Duke Power Co. was in violation of Title VII of the 1964 Civil Rights Act, which requires employment tests and standards to be job-related. The power company's requirements for transfer or promotion—a high school education, its equivalent, or the passing of two aptitude tests—were discriminatory, it was argued, because many blacks were being kept out of higher paying jobs on the basis of nonvalidated requirements. The Court ruled unanimously that selection and promotion criteria that have not been linked to job performance by empirical evidence are in violation of the law. In effect, the Supreme Court decision made it illegal *not* to follow what should have been a standard personnel procedure and part of good professional practice all along; that is, the demonstration of the job-relatedness of all predictors used in selection. In addition to reducing the possibility of discrimination resulting from arbitrary and unfounded job requirements, the use of job-related predictors improves upon the accuracy of prediction which increases the usefulness (''utility'') of the selection procedure for the organization as well.

It might be interesting to note at this point that arbitrary job requirements, such as a high school diploma for a job that does not actually use the skills associated with a diploma, also reflect stereotypes and prejudices. In this case, however, they are subjective and frequently inaccurate judgments of the *characteristics of the job* and not the *characteristics of people* in particular age, ethnic, racial, and sexual categories. The ultimate effect of the 1964 Civil Rights Act and the thrust of all the recent personnel trends and practices described so far in this section have been to make selection procedures more objective and remove them from the realm of guesswork and prejudice.

Differential Validity

Title VII of the 1964 Civil Rights Act drew attention to another issue, an issue that overlaps considerably the concern for job-related validity. Some I/O psychologists felt that even when job-related validity had been established for one group, such as white males, the same predictors and selection procedures might have little or no validity for other groups, blacks and women, for example (see Lopez, 1966).

The primary impetus for the interest in differential validity, the expression generally used to denote this issue, is the well-documented fact that some minority groups consistently score lower on paper-and-pencil tests, particularly those measuring cognitive abilities, than the white middle-class majority. A few writers have attempted to attribute these differences to genetic influences (e.g., Jensen, 1969), but the role of differential cultural experience, cognitive style, language habits, and long-term, preexisting racial discrimination is unmistakable, especially as reflected in the quality of early education, the lack of minority group familiarity with the testing situation and its social context, and even in the poorer nutrition of minority groups. The concern was that because

23

of the effects of discrimination and differential cultural experience, scores on most of the standardized paper-and-pencil tests in use would *not* provide fair predictions of the job performance of many black applicants in spite of their success with white applicants. The interest in differential validity reflected the expectation that the effects of discrimination and cultural experience on selection could be compensated for by developing alternative selection procedures for disadvantaged minorities.

From the late 1960s to the present there have been many attempts to demonstrate the phenomenon of differential validity, examine its legal and professional implications, and develop methodological and statistical mechanisms for dealing with it (see e.g., Boehm, 1972; Crooks, 1972; Farr, O'Leary, and Bartlett, 1971; Fincher, 1975; Fox and Lefkowitz, 1974; Kirchner, 1975; Kirkpatrick, Ewen, Barrett, and Katzell, 1968; Lefkowitz and Fox, 1975; Lopez, 1966; Schmidt, Berner, and Hunter, 1973; Toole, Gavin, Murdy, and Sells, 1972). After years of research and heated argument, a consensus concerning the issue began to emerge. This consensus was perhaps best expressed by Robert M. Guion, one of the first I/O psychologists to draw attention to the problems of unfair discrimination (Guion, 1966 and 1967). He concludes that:

> *Employers should be required, where technically feasible, of course, to study the possibility of differential validity . . . [but] as a general rule, the validity of a test against a specified criterion is likely to be about the same for all comers. There are exceptions to the rule, and there are enough exceptions that they must be taken seriously; they are, nevertheless, exceptions. (1972, pp. 134–135)*

This conclusion is apparently representative of prevailing opinion in the profession today, but a more recent study suggests that this issue may yet be far from settled (Katzell and Dyer, 1977).

Work Samples

The failure to demonstrate the frequent occurrence of differential validity and a growing awareness that paper-and-pencil tests are generally poor predictors of job performance for *any* group (Ghiselli, 1966) has shifted attention to the development of other means for predicting job performance. In recent years most of this attention has focused on the use of samples or simulations of existing job tasks that employ actual tools, materials, and processes in place of abstracted paper-and-pencil tests. These work samples, as they are frequently called, approximate the kind of work a potential employee would be required to perform on the job. They range in complexity from simple, structured mechanical or clerical operations to more difficult activities that include symbolic reasoning and abstract conceptualization all the way to simulations of management tasks for the assessment of executive potential.

Because work samples are nonverbal, relatively culture-free tests, it has been suggested that they would lead to less unfair discrimination than paper-and-pencil tests (Wernimont and Campbell, 1968; O'Leary, 1973). In addition, since the relationship between many predictors and job performance is tenuous at best, the work sample as a "real job task" closely simulating the actual job situation should be a more effective and fairer predictor of future work behavior than tests measuring abstractly defined traits, abilities, and skills that may have only an indirect relationship to the requirements of the job.

Although some evidence suggests that work samples are less biased than paper-and-pencil tests (Schmidt, Greenthal, Berner, Hunter, and Seaton, 1975), one should not assume that they can compensate for the effects of discrimination. For example, Milton Blood notes that since the work experiences of disadvantaged persons are likely to be even more restricted than their educational experiences, such persons might be as unfamiliar with work sample tasks as they are with the content of paper-and-pencil tests (Blood, 1974). Similarly, women who lack appropriate work experience because of previous underemployment or exclusions from the work force might not perform well on work sample tests and could continue to be underemployed or excluded. As a result, the use of work samples for personnel selection alone is not likely to significantly improve upon a disadvantaged person's employment opportunities. However, they can be used to diagnose individuals' skill deficiencies, and, therefore, direct them to appropriate remedial training and generally facilitate the counseling and placement of disadvantaged workers (Jewish Employment and Vocational Service, 1968; Spergel and Leshner, 1968). Moreover, the fact that well-devised work samples would be closely similar to the behavior being predicted suggests that adding them to the repertoire of job-related predictors can help to improve selection decision accuracy and reduce the unfair discrimination resulting from nonvalidated procedures.

Conclusion

Although all of the activity described in the past several pages* has contributed to the development of fairer, more effective selection instruments, procedures,

*This by no means exhausts all of the recent attempts to provide equal employment opportunity. See the "Notes" section at the end of this chapter (pp.53–54) for comments and references on a somewhat different and considerably more controversial approach to this issue that focuses on special hiring preferences and quotas for minority groups and women.

and practices, it still has not, by itself, significantly improved on our ability to utilize fully our most important and potentially abundant natural resource, human capacities and skills. Part of the problem arises from the limitations of the traditional personnel selection model itself. As Stone and Ruch (1974) point out, this model is inherently wasteful since many applicants are rejected when they could be considered for other jobs. Similarly, Owens and Jewell argue that:

> The strength of this classic model lies in its provision for probabilistic demonstration that applicant A is more likely to succeed in a specific job than applicant B. The model fails, however, to provide information about the skills and abilities of either the selected or rejected applicants as they relate to jobs with different requirements. (1969, p. 419)

Another part of the problem has to do with the broad socioeconomic context within which this model has traditionally operated. Since most selection procedures primarily reflect the limited objectives of individual organizations, they cannot by themselves redress job seekers' deficiencies in education and experience and the problems of local, regional, and national economies. These problems originate within society and transcend organizational boundaries. It may therefore be unreasonable to expect to find the ultimate solution to these problems in the modification of the selection procedures of individual organizations.

Clearly then, an alternative approach is needed to enable us to place all individuals who are willing and able to work in jobs that are compatible with their needs and fully utilize their skills and abilities. Fortunately, a broad outline of just such an alternative has begun to emerge in recent years in I/O psychology and in the related concerns of human resource planning and education.* The following section discusses some of the elements of these developments to delineate the basic characteristics of a systematic and comprehensive approach to the maximum utilization of human resources.

A Systems Approach to the Maximum Utilization of Human Resources

Programs and Initiatives by Organizations

Counseling and placement: The first aspect of this approach is the development of a counseling/placement alternative to the traditional selection/re-

---

*Throughout this book the words "human resource" will be used in place of "manpower" where the latter has been traditionally used (e.g., manpower planning, development, forecasting, etc.).

jection model for organizational personnel decisions. As with the selection/rejection model, a set of assumptions underlie the counseling/placement model and several kinds of activity are implied by these assumptions. By comparing these assumptions and activities with their selection/rejection model counterparts, we can begin to see the important differences between the two.

The first assumption of the selection/rejection model is that the overriding goal of the personnel process is *satisfactory job performance.* Alternatively, the counseling/placement model places comparatively more emphasis on the degree of *satisfaction* a prospective employee may derive from his or her job. This does not mean, of course, that performance is of no concern in the counseling/placement model. Indeed, as Guion (1965) points out,

> *The interests of society, as well as of the organization, are served best when the new members are qualified for their jobs. The interests of society are compromised when a fully qualified person is denied a place given to one less qualified. If many serious errors of selection are made, moreover, the organization may fail—with resulting human and economic waste. (p. 5)*

We might add that the interests of individuals are also not served when they are placed in jobs for which they are not qualified.

It would also be incorrect to assume that employee satisfaction is overlooked in the selection/rejection model since a good match between job requirements and personal abilities, skills, and interests will generally lead to employee satisfaction as well as effective performance.

The difference between the two models is in the degree of emphasis they place on the two goals with the counseling/placement model balancing job performance with a greater concern for employee satisfaction whenever these two goals are incompatible. Ideally, the personnel decision can benefit both the organization and the individual even if it is not optimal for either.

The second assumption is that *jobs vary* and that the analysis of how they vary is essential for describing the duties and tasks required for the performance of the job. This analysis is then used to suggest possible predictors and job performance criteria. While this assumption is consistent with the counseling/placement model as well, the latter approach places more emphasis on the use of this information *by the applicant* for the purposes of self-selection. As argued by Fine (1975):

> *While applicants may well apply for jobs when all they have to go on is a job title and a general description, they are far more likely to think twice and self-select when they have accurate information concerning the specific requirements of the job, the performance standards by which their*

work will be measured, and what they will need to know to meet these standards. (p. 61)

According to Fine, this information should also include "the working conditions to which the applicants must adapt" as well as "the opportunity system within which they can aspire and grow" (p. 61). In addition, the counseling/placement model requires that rather than restricting attention to the match between an individual and a single job, his or her compatability with several different jobs or job "families"—that is, classes of jobs with similar characteristics (see Schoenfeldt, 1974)—within the organization must be considered at the same time. Furthermore, to be truly effective, changes in job content and working conditions over time due to such external factors as the economy, the availability of scarce resources (e.g., petroleum-based fuels), and technological developments should also be considered (this will be discussed in more detail in Chapter 3). Finally, the counseling/placement emphasis on the relationship between jobs in a potential career progression, or "ladder," is yet another way in which the two models differ in their use and interpretation of the second assumption.

The third assumption is that people vary and that their job-related variability is the basis upon which selection/rejection decisions are made. The first part of this assumption still holds for the counseling/placement model, of course, but the goal of job satisfaction changes the nature and intent of the activities that follow from this variability and its assessment. In her 1973 APA presidential address which dealt in part with the changing role of psychological testing, Leona Tyler described this difference:

Instead of assuming that someone is going to use the test we are designing to select the person most likely to succeed in a particular situation, such as college, a job training program, or a managerial position, it is possible to begin with an assumption that the purpose of the test is to analyze what each person who takes it has to offer, so that a suitable place can be found for him. Another way of putting it is to say that tests are being designed for the benefit of the test takers rather than for the benefit of employers or admissions officers. (Tyler, 1973, p. 1023)

As in the case of the second assumption, the importance of the information provided by tests, work samples, or job histories derives as much from its use in diagnosing applicants' job-related strengths and weaknesses and counseling them concerning their compatibility with various jobs as from its utility to the organization for selection decisions. In effect, the increased emphasis on

28

providing the applicant with more detailed information on available jobs, working conditions, opportunity systems, and their own individual work-related needs and capabilities enables them to take a more active role in the job selection process. Even more important is the use of this information to help individuals choose careers and recognize the role of the jobs under immediate consideration in their long-term career development.

Regarding the fourth assumption that a demonstrable or logical relationship exists between predictors and job performance, there is little difference between the two models except that in the counseling/placement model the individual is considered for more than one job within the organization at a time.

Training: The systems approach to the maximum utilization of human resources involves more than just an alternative model for matching individuals to jobs. If this matching is done strictly on the basis of an individual's present skills without considering how these skills might be upgraded, we would still be doing far less than what is either possible or desirable. As pointed out earlier, selection procedures by themselves cannot redress prior deficiencies in education and experience. Clearly, increased access to training programs and education is necessary to any systematic attempt to provide equal employment opportunity for individuals currently lacking job skills and experience.

People who have been victimized by job discrimination and stereotypes that unfairly restrict them to certain work roles (homemakers, secretaries, teachers, etc.) and educational opportunities are not the only ones who need increased access to programs for the upgrading of job skills. Most new employees, regardless of their previous training, cultural experience, and employment history, are faced with a job and work setting that is novel enough to require time and opportunity for adjustment and training.

Training is often necessary for employees already on the job as well. New technologies or innovative applications of existing technologies, for example, can lead to significant modifications in the content of the work itself and its organizational context, modifications that frequently put more complex demands on the worker. Increasingly, many experienced, highly trained workers are discovering that their particular skills are inadequate preparation for the changing requirements of their present jobs or the jobs that technology may create anew or in place of existing ones. Therefore, access to education and training to upgrade present skills is as important for the experienced and skilled worker as it is for the inexperienced and disadvantaged. In summary, an organization's personnel procedures must do more than match an individual's existing skills and behaviors to the requirements of the jobs to be filled. They should also indicate the ways in which these skills and behaviors can be modified by training to improve the job-person match.

29

Although the importance of training has long been recognized, especially as an essential complement to selection, new perspectives on the subject have recently emerged from the years of experience with training programs for the disadvantaged. We now know that more lenient entry-level requirements, remedial education, and job skill training are often not enough. The success of these programs also depends on the extent to which they are tailored to the trainees' individual needs (Quinn, Staines, and McCullough, 1974). In addition, some programs focus on developing the disadvantaged workers' "adaptive skills" including their confidence, self-esteem, and ability to respond appropriately to authority, interact effectively with co-workers, and conform to organizational rules for dress, on-the-job behavior, and punctuality (Dunnette, Hough, Rosett, Mumford, and Fine, 1973; Goodale, 1973). As discussed in the next section, training success is also a function of the employer's flexibility and supportiveness. Finally, and perhaps most important, is that good jobs are available to trainees on completion of the program, since the potential mismatch between the realities of the marketplace and the expectations created by the training programs could have severe psychological consequences (TEAM, 1976). The availability of jobs, an additional element of the systems approach to human resource utilization, will be discussed shortly.

Support services and organizational accommodation: One of the problems with some training programs, particularly those that emphasize the development of "adaptive" skills, is that they tend to imply, perhaps unintentionally, that individuals are responsible for their employment difficulties and must, therefore, bear the burden of change themselves. On the other hand, by acknowledging the responsibility of society and its institutions for creating the problem, at least part of the burden of change is placed on the organization. In fact, the evidence clearly indicates that the success of training programs for the disadvantaged is very much dependent on the willingness and ability of the employing organization to provide a supportive environment for the trainee (Conference Board, 1972; Friedlander and Greenberg, 1971; Goodman and Salipante, 1976; Goodman, Salipante, and Paransky, 1973; Koch, 1974). For example, many organizations can be and have been more lenient in their handling of company rules and discipline. It is logically inconsistent to acknowledge that years of conditioning may have lead to traditionally inappropriate work habits and then to insist on strict adherence to organizational rules and norms for appearance, lateness, absenteeism, language habits, and so forth. In addition, more flexible working hours can alleviate some of the problems disadvantaged workers may have in commuting between their homes and their jobs and would enable more women (or men) to pursue a career while raising a family. Companies can also provide commuting information and directions and might even consider establishing their own transportation facilities where feasible (e.g., van pooling; see Patrick, 1976). Medical care, individual counseling, and day care facilities are other examples of the kind of support that can and has been offered by companies seeking to employ more disadvantaged workers and women. Such services might even be related to work behaviors (e.g., reduced turnover and absenteeism) beneficial to the company (see Milkovich and Gomez, 1976). Moreover, many companies have found it necessary to deal with the hostility and insensitivity of supervisors and fellow employees to the unique needs, problems, and life styles of disadvantaged workers and women—not to mention the resentment and insecurity they may feel in response to the special treatment afforded these new employees.

Carrying this a step further, recent evidence indicates that it may be *the most highly skilled of the disadvantaged who have the most difficulty in adjusting to conventional training programs and work environments.* In his theory of "competing competencies," Caplan (1973) argues that the high incidence of vocational failure among inner city youths results not so much from a lack of motivation and skill as from the incompatibility of their particular motivations and skills with the conventional work situation. Many of these youths, Caplan argues, have developed highly effective "street skills" for getting along in the ghetto community, for example, "hustling," gang leadership, fighting, or athletics. The problem is that these skills are inappropriate and often antithetical to the behaviors generally required on the job. Because of this incompatibility, the most competent inner city youths must often sacrifice their sense of self-worth and positive self-image gained in their mastery of necessary street skills when they "step down" to "straight" jobs. Failure in the work situation because their skills are inappropriate can lead them to leave the world of work so that they can reestablish their competence in the street subculture. This not only restores their sense of self-worth but also enables them to do the things they do best and, consequently, the things from which they derive the most satisfaction. If organizations are genuinely interested in increasing employment opportunities for the disadvantaged, they will have to consider ways in which the organization itself and the jobs within it can be changed to capitalize on their skills and produce similar feelings of competence and self-esteem.

Conclusion: In the last several paragraphs, a new theme has begun to emerge that shifts the emphasis of this book from an almost exclusive concern with "fitting the worker to the job" to a concern that is just as important, "fitting the job to the worker." This theme will be dealt with in some detail in the next chapter, so for the time being it will be sufficient to conclude that selection, counseling, placement, training, *and* the redesign of organizations and jobs are all elements of a systematic approach to the maximum utilization of human resources.

If it is not already apparent, the human resources we are talking about include *all* workers and not just those who have been the victims of discrimination over the years. Increased opportunity and organizational flexibility are as important to workers who are not disadvantaged as they are to those who are disadvantaged. Overlooking the needs of one group to address the needs of the other can only breed hostility and conflict, a situation that does neither group any good.

It is also important to recognize that the matching of individuals to jobs is a dynamic process. People's expectations, self-concept, self-knowledge, values, and skills change over time especially in response to life and work experience. Similarly, social, economic and technological changes will alter the nature of existing jobs, eliminate some and create others. Therefore, a successful match between a person and a job at one time is no guarantee that the match will continue to be successful in the future. The matching process must be an ongoing one in which employees' characteristics, needs, and skills are continually reassessed and considered in light of possible future work requirements and rewards and used to guide their long-term career development.

Public Programs, Services, and Policy

Computerized job-person matching: The discussion so far has focused primarily on organizational programs and initiatives for the maximum utilization of human resources, but readers must realize that organizational programs are often not enough. Many of today's most pressing human resource problems transcend the boundaries of individual organizations and will require the implementation of complementary and comprehensive social programs and public policies at the local, regional, and national levels.

The limitations of the counseling/placement model implemented solely at the level of individual organizations illustrate this point well. Few companies have enough jobs available at any given time to be able to consider job applicants for more than one opening, especially during periods of high unemployment. Consequently, the organization must frequently make a selection/rejection decision rather than a placement decision. Although companies may have information about openings in other companies and be able to refer rejected job applicants to these companies, their information is likely to be incomplete and informal. It is unlikely that this information and the subsequent referrals will ever evolve into a more systematic and comprehensive arrangement given the limited resources, traditional self-interest, and competitive nature of organizations in the private sector of our economy.

Fortunately, a supplementary system that transcends the boundaries of individual organizations and is not subject to their limitations does exist. For years, local and regional public employment offices have maintained files on job seekers and available openings throughout the areas they serve for the purpose of matching individuals to jobs. Initially, the matches were performed manually using card files of available jobs and applicants. In later years, many of the job files were replaced by computerized job banks containing listings and descriptions of openings available in the area served by the office. An applicant could then search among these listings for a job opening that corresponded to his or her needs, situation, experience, and skills.

More recently, the United States Employment Service initiated a plan for automating the procedure by developing a computerized system that would automatically match people to jobs. In this system, trained employment service personnel use a standardized coding procedure to describe both an applicant's qualifications and an employer's job requirements in similiar terms (U.S. Department of Labor, 1975). Once this information is entered into the computer a search can be conducted for either the jobs that match an applicant's qualifications (job-centered search) or the applicants that match an employer's requirements (person-centered search).

The advantages of this system are clear: it is faster than manual search procedures with information on potential job-person matches being provided almost instantaneously or within 24 hours depending on the type of computer system used; it is bidirectional, that is, a search can be person-centered or job-centered; there is less likelihood that possible matches will be overlooked; and openings and applicants can be automatically considered as new applicants and jobs are added to existing listings. It can also provide a continual source of information that may be used to evaluate the effectiveness of the system, update files, supply daily feedback on the outcome of job referrals, characterize in both general and specialized terms the present job and labor markets, forecast future job/labor market imbalances, and inventory skills immediately available for use in emergencies. Additional advantages include the possibility of placing computer terminals in shopping centers, schools, rural areas and places of business to increase accessibility to potential employment information. Such a system would also eliminate a considerable amount of paperwork and thus enable employment personnel to give more personalized attention to clients. Furthermore, the eventual linking of all local and regional systems into a national network would provide information on opportunities available in other parts of the country for applicants who are able and willing to relocate. Finally, a system of this sort could serve an important pedagogical service by indicating when an applicant's or employer's expectations are unrealistic. For instance, the system could inform an employer that there are no applicants presently listed who meet all of the job requirements but that there would be several if the salary offered were to be increased by a particular amount (see Astin, 1972).

By complementing intraorganizational programs for counseling, placement, training, and job restructuring with a more efficient, comprehensive, and computerized public employment service we would be taking a significant step along the road toward the goal of maximum human resource utilization. Even this would leave us far short of the goal, however, if there still were not enough jobs available for those who want to work. Recognition of this fact has over the years led to continuing interest in proposals, programs, and mechanisms for providing previously unavailable job opportunities for those unable to find work through existing channels and sources. Some of these proposals are described in the following section.

Creating jobs: Much of the interest in job creation has focused on the problem of youth unemployment because of its typically high incidence and possible short- and long-range personal and social consequences. One of the most frequently proposed solutions to this problem is to create voluntary and transitional (generally, one to two years) national service opportunities for youth to provide important community and environmental services, paid work experience for unemployed youth that might eventually lead to a career, and the opportunity for them to learn work and social skills and a sense of pride and self-worth (Eberly, 1977). These federally supported service opportunities can be developed and administered at the local and regional levels and, in combination with existing opportunities in the military, VISTA, and Peace Corps, offer unemployed youth a variety of work and learning options that could ease their transition into a long-term adult career.

In addition to meeting important social and environmental needs by working as teachers aides, paramedics, and assistants in social agencies, and helping to improve parks and rehabilitate the inner city, youth would receive career counseling, job training, and information on other educational and service opportunities while earning a salary. Local colleges, unions, and industry would play significant roles by providing technical assistance, contributing to education and training programs, offering career counseling and information, and sponsoring community service projects that would utilize participating youth. Besides the obvious benefits to the youths enrolled in the programs and to the communities that would be the recipients of previously unavailable services, the long-term societal gains could be considerable. For example, decreases in crime and the costs associated with welfare and the administration of the criminal justice system might accompany increases in national productivity and quality of life. Moreover, as sociologist Amitai Etzioni points out, a national youth service program could serve as a "sociological mixer" that might facilitate a broader consensus on fundamental national values.

34

A year of national service, especially if designed to enable people from different geographical and sociological backgrounds to work and live together, could be an effective way for people—from parochial and public schools, from North and South, boys and girls, big city and country persons, whites and nonwhites—to get to know each other on an equal footing while working together at a joint task. (Etzioni, 1976a, p. 13)

In recent years people at the opposite end of the age spectrum have also been identified as a possible target population for programs aimed at creating new, socially useful jobs. This group includes individuals forced into retirement who would still like to work at least part-time in jobs that use their skills and experience; the growing group of "young-old" workers (Neugarten, 1975) who retire earlier, live and retain their health longer, and would like to remain active in a new career; and those older workers "whose occupational achievements do not equal their original aspirations [and who] come to look upon their jobs as something which must be performed but not necessarily enjoyed" (Sheppard, 1971, p. 73).

Work that capitalizes on the skills and attitudes that develop with age, namely the accumulation of work and life experience and the increased interest of elderly workers in people-oriented tasks (Fine, 1970), would be particularly appropriate for these individuals. Day care; career counseling of students and younger workers; assisting their less active peers and those a few years older in nursing homes, hospitals, and residences; acting as aides in schools, community agencies, and nonprofit organizations; advising small businesses; and helping to organize self-help groups are just a few of the valuable and rewarding services older workers could offer. To make this possible, local, state, and federal agencies would have to create full- and part-time jobs, set up training programs, and provide facilities, expense budgets, and other kinds of support for volunteer activities.

Besides serving important community needs, new career opportunities may also induce many older workers and retirees to switch into these careers and thus open advancement possibilities for younger workers whose careers have been stymied by the decreased availability of, and increased competition for, higher level jobs. Furthermore, finding productive, paying employment for older workers may become an economic necessity in the future as increased longevity and the aging of those born during the post-World War II "baby boom" add substantially to the number of retirees collecting social security benefits and place an increasingly heavy tax burden on a work force diminished over the years by a lower birth rate. Traditional cultures consider the accumulated experience of the elderly to be an unsurpassed source of wisdom and judgment. It would be a shame to waste this important human resource because we lack the will and imagination to develop the opportunities for its utilization.

Youth, retirees, and older workers are by no means the only groups who might profit by the creation of new career opportunities. Homemakers, workers displaced by technological change, frustrated employees in dead-end jobs, and the disadvantaged—the target of most of the "new career" programs of the '1960s—could all help to meet emerging community needs for public transportation, antipollution enforcement, energy conservation, police protection, social and health services, recreation, and urban renewal. Many of them could be productively employed as "paraprofessionals," a rapidly growing occupational group that is made up of

persons who are selected, trained, and given responsibility for performing functions generally performed by professionals. They do not possess the requisite education or credentials to be considered professionals in the field in which they are working, but they do perform tasks central to the function of the agency. (Delworth, 1974, p. 250)

As suggested above, paraprofessional positions are most frequently found in social service agencies in the public sector and are typically created to assist in their functions (e.g., see "Special Issue: Paras, Peers, and Pros," 1974). Increasingly, however, they are also finding private sector employment, for instance as "paralegals" in law firms and companies (see Revzin, 1975).

Yet another target group for new career programs could be the numerous college graduates who, as recent projections indicate, will have an increasingly difficult time finding jobs commensurate with their educational attainments (Carey, 1976; Levine, 1976). We can ill afford to waste their talents—capabilities that would be very valuable in easing the transition to a post-industrial era—and risk the alienation and discouragement that might accompany their underutilization. The jobs created for this group could be professional level counterparts to the positions mentioned above. Specifically, as Berger (1974) notes, they could be used "to serve the more subtle—but nonetheless real—interpersonal and psychological needs of groups and individuals" (p. 62) by working in highly specialized urban task forces, in newly created agencies for community development, intergroup conflict resolution and for encouraging political participation by the citizenry, as well as by working in superagencies created to coordinate programs and mediate disputes between these agencies, to mention just a few possibilities. Another possibility is the loan of underutilized college graduates to less developed countries in an expanded version of the Peace Corps.

These proposals for creating jobs in the public sector are not above criticism. Essentially, the opposition to these proposals centers around three basic criticisms; fear that these would be "make-work" jobs with little social utility, concern for the costs associated with the programs, and objections to the direct creation of these jobs in and by the public sector rather than governmental policy to produce the conditions under which these jobs would "naturally" develop in the private sector.

In response to the first criticism, it is clear that there are many needed services that are not presently provided in our society. With appropriate guidelines and programs designed to capitalize on existing skills and offer opportunities for developing new skills, there is no inherent reason why these jobs cannot be useful. In response to the second criticism, the costs of these programs could be at least partially offset by reductions in unemployment compensation and welfare payments, increases in tax revenues from salaries earned by workers who would be otherwise unemployed, reduction in the social costs of unemployment (e.g., crime, poor mental health; see Brenner, 1976), long-term gains in productivity resulting from improved work skills and attitudes, especially if these programs include a training component, and increased availability of useful public goods and services produced by people employed in these programs. Finally, across-the-board public spending, tax cuts, and other indirect spurs to growth in the private sector take a longer time to affect employment, have less of an impact per dollar expended, and are not as easily directed at the neediest individuals and groups than direct job creation in the public sector (U.S. Congress, 1975).

In any case, public sector employment should be viewed as only part of a total mix of strategies that could also include indirect job creation in the private sector (e.g., via incentives to business, wage subsidies, tax cuts, or government contracts to private industry) and ongoing evaluation of the costs, effectiveness, and conditional suitability of various approaches to public employment. When the economy is in a downturn, the National Manpower Policy Task Force argues, "the need . . . is to act quickly and vigorously on all appropriate fronts, adopting each strategy as conditions require" (1975, p. 9). Furthermore, with the addition of training programs to facilitate the eventual transfer of employees into private industry, many public jobs could be phased out as employment opportunities in the private sector improve, to be implemented once again at a time of further economic deterioration.

Conclusion

The various programs and proposals that have been reviewed in the last several pages were presented as elements necessary to an integrated system for the max-

37

imum utilization of human resources. These proposals and programs were classified into two categories: actions that individual organizations can take essentially on their own, and social services and policies that are probably most appropriately undertaken by local, regional, and national governments. The two categories were viewed not only as complementary approaches to the problem but as indispensable systemic supplements, a view that characterizes the relationships between the individual elements within each category as well. In fact, one can even detect an approximate parallel and complementarity between the various activities discussed in each category. That is, computerized job-person matching services provided by government agencies correspond roughly with and supplement counseling and placement at the organizational level, while the creation of jobs in and by the public sector corresponds, even more roughly, with corporate efforts to accommodate individual needs, personalities, and circumstances.

Following this line of reasoning suggests the need for a societal level program that will supplement—or, perhaps, incorporate—organizational programs for the development of job-related skills and abilities. Publicly supported job training opportunities have been around in one form or other for some time (e.g., see Mangum and Walsh, 1973). Frequently, these opportunities were part of or associated with programs for public service employment for the disadvantaged and, as we saw earlier, most of the more recent proposals for creating jobs in or via the public sector also provide for job training. The limited success of previous efforts, however, indicates that a more comprehensive approach is needed. This approach should deal not only with the work problems of special groups but offer more training options to a wider spectrum of individuals, not just those who have been society's most visible victims. In addition, the antecedants of the problems must also be addressed by examining the inadequacies of the means by which we first acquire work-related skills. The essence of the problem is part and parcel of the broader issue of education. In other words, can we design an educational system that will meet not only the work needs of individuals and societies but prepare them for the changing and increasingly complex demands of life in an uncertain and challenging future? A suggestion for just such a design is the focus of the next section of this chapter.

An Educational System for the Post-Industrial Society

Educational Goals for the Future

The first step in designing any system is to ask, "What goal should the system be designed to achieve?" With regard to education, as well for the other important societal subsystems, the goal might be the opportunity for all individuals to find fulfillment in all aspects of their lives, as long as the pursuit of this goal is not incompatible with other societal ends. Ideally, achieving personal fulfillment would facilitate the overall well-being of society, and some people would want to make this a supplementary or even the dominant goal. Since one of the implicit purposes of this book is to advocate personal and societal goals that are more likely to be compatible and mutually supportive given the emerging conditions of the post-industrial era, this latter position is consistent with the themes being argued here.

A look at the future of work: Removing this goal statement from the realm of platitude requires a projection of future possibilities to determine what may be needed and reasonably attainable. Although they are not necessarily immutable, several trends are likely to continue into the foreseeable future and to have significant educational impact.

First, professional, technical, and administrative jobs are among the fastest growing occupational categories in our economy and will continue to grow for some time. However, in the future the number of individuals who aspire to attain these jobs and pursue college degrees to meet their educational prerequisites will exceed the number of available jobs (Carey, 1976; Levine, 1976). As a result, there will be increased competition for the most attractive jobs, and many college graduates will have to accept work that provides less challenge, freedom, opportunity for promotion, status, and pay than they may have expected or desired. Even those individuals who do acquire jobs commensurate with their expectations and skills will find it difficult to advance up the career ladder traditionally associated with these jobs because of growing competition with their peers for the meager "room at the top," made even smaller by reduced organizational growth and the elimination of mandatory retirement.

Prospects at the other end of the occupational scale are just as discouraging. Many of the jobs at this end—e.g., hospital orderly, janitor, or restaurant employee—are also among the fastest growing occupational categories in our economy, but are typically less attractive and satisfying than their professional/administrative/technical counterparts. In addition, opportunities for advancement and career progression, regardless of the level of competition for these positions, are even more limited. As O'Toole (1975) notes, hospital orderlies do not progress up a career ladder to become nurses, and hotel chambermaids seldom advance to desk clerk.

Jobs at the intermediate levels of the occupational scale, including emerging paraprofessional positions such as teacher's aides and X-ray technicians, as well as many jobs in the delivery of health services, also offer little opportunity for career advancement. Taking another example from O'Toole, "X-ray technicians do not progress up a ladder and become radiologists" (1975, p. 32). In the few cases where advancement into professional positions is theoretically possible, increased competition with more highly educated workers would push these traditionally available opportunities out of the reach of a growing number of ambitious and talented individuals.

In conclusion, the overall picture suggested by these projections indicates severely restricted opportunity for upward career mobility, thwarted expectations, mounting job dissatisfaction, and the social and personal costs that might develop as a result (more on this in Chapter 3), not to mention the increased waste of human potential at a time of unprecedented need for its utilization. All of this could lead to a particularly difficult situation for women and minorities whose previously modest career expectations have been heightened in recent years by equal employment legislation, liberation movements, and media coverage of their newly raised consciousness.

Before discussing the possible educational implications of these developments there are three other trends that deserve mention. The first is the evolution and proliferation of new models for the design of organizations. Traditionally, most organizations have been characterized by rigid, "top-down" bureaucratic structures, authoritarian leadership styles, and well-defined functional specialization. Lately, some organizations have begun to increase employee participation in the decisions that directly affect their work and in decisions about company policy. Accompanying this has been a growing interest in the use of work groups in the place of assembly lines and temporary problem-oriented task forces in the place of functionally differentiated divisions and units; in other words, the "ad-hocracies" referred to by Toffler (1971) and the "organic-adaptive" organizations described by Bennis (1966).

The second trend is the impact of technological change on the nature of work and work organizations. Further applications of new and existing technologies in the design of work processes will alter the skill requirements and the social and organizational context of many jobs. In addition, some jobs will no doubt be eliminated and new ones created. Although the short-term nature of these changes can often be reasonably projected, more detailed, longer range estimations of such variables as future supply of particular occupations and their *specific* skill requirements is dependent upon so many other frequently unknown or poorly defined factors as to represent little more than an exercise in futility (e.g., see Pascal, Bell, Dougharty, Dunn, and Thompson, 1975).

The possibility of future resource shortages is yet another trend that must be considered. Resource shortages would restrict the production of material goods which, in turn, could have a significant impact on the design of manufacturing processes. For example, it would most likely be necessary to produce fewer but longer lasting goods, and production systems designed to maximize quantity, such as the assembly line, may not be the same systems that would maximize durability. Therefore, resource shortages might require alternative approaches to work system design, perhaps a modern version of the "craft" trades that existed before the industrial revolution. Replacing the assembly line with groups of workers responsible for assembling entire automobiles or their main subsystems, as is being done in Sweden, is one example that comes immediately to mind.

Resource shortages could affect the world of work in several other ways, including the replacement of machine labor with human labor in some industries, reduced employment opportunities in manufacturing and increased opportunities in service industries, and reductions in the length of the work week, to mention just a few. Since several of these outcomes are mutually exclusive— e.g., replacing machines with humans would tend to create *more* manufacturing jobs—the ultimate implications of resource shortages would depend largely on the complex political, economic, and social policy decisions that would have to be made in anticipation of, concommitant with, and following the onset of these shortages. The specific impact of resource shortages on the nature of work and its skill requirements and organizational context is, therefore, exceedingly difficult if not impossible to predict, a conclusion similar to the one reached about the impact of technological change.

Implications for educational goals: The conclusion with which the preceding section closed, the difficulty of predicting how resource shortages and technological change will affect jobs specifically, suggests that educational goals should reflect less concern for the development of specific work skills in the early years, skills that may very well be obsolete and nontransferable in later life, and be more concerned with laying down a basic foundation upon which successive layers of specialization can be built as needed. The basic foundation should of course include the "3 R's," although the need for fluency with new media, communication modes, and information processes might require the modification or addition of further dimensions to these skills.

This basic foundation should also include the development of interpersonal competencies for getting along in the increasingly team-oriented and participative workplace as well as include the acquisition of theoretical and applied knowledge in the physical and human sciences.

Concerning this last point, Peter Drucker (1968) argues that knowledge is increasingly becoming the foundation for skill, enabling people to acquire advanced skills rapidly and successfully.

> *The man or woman who has once acquired a skill on a knowledge foundation has <u>learned to learn</u>. He can acquire rapidly new and different skills.*

41

> *Unlike apprenticeship, which prepares for one specific craft and teaches the use of one specific set of tools for one specific purpose, a knowledge foundation enables people to un-learn and to re-learn. It enables them, in other words, to become "technologists" who can put knowledge, skills, and tools to work, rather than "craftsman" who know how to do one specific task one specific way [emphasis added]. (1968, p. 268)*

In Drucker's use of the expression, "knowledge" is information that is applied "to doing something," and what is relevant is "the imagination and skill of whoever applies it" (p. 269). When viewed in this manner, it becomes apparent that the content of the knowledge is less important than the *processes* by which an individual seeks out information, organizes it, and applies it to a variety of tasks and problems. Learning how to acquire and organize knowledge and then to be able to apply this knowledge to learn new skills, solve problems, formulate plans of action, discover new knowledge, and create opportunities, images, and products is the key; to use a somewhat overused expression, "learning-to-learn," but also, going beyond that, *learning how to apply what has already been learned.*

With these skills, individuals would have the tools to prepare themselves for an uncertain and changing world of work. They would have the capacity to adapt to and influence change, and they would be better able to identify real-world possibilities and limits and examine their own needs and abilities in relation to these conditions. In terms more immediately relevant to the world of work, individuals with this foundation would be able to acquire the specific skills needed on a job in a relatively short period of time if the facilities, programs, and resources necessary to develop them are provided by their employers. They would also have the ability to envision the alternative sequences of jobs and experiences that make up a career and act appropriately.

To facilitate further their ability to adapt to a changing world of work it would also be necessary that they have access to avenues by which they could redirect their careers. Learning-to-learn and learning how to apply what is learned would be almost useless if there were no means by which an individual could use these skills to acquire and apply new ones. This is particularly important in light of the first trend that many of the fastest growing occupational categories in our economy have either limited career ladders or will experience increased competition for the advancement opportunities that are available. Therefore it is imperative that educational institutions and work organizations develop enabling mechanisms and resources for "horizontal" career redirection so that individuals can explore alternative career paths and pick up new skills as needed.

Educating for leisure and citizenship: Preparing people for leisure and citizenship are two additional educational goals that are frequently overlooked or given short shrift by many educators in their headlong rush to develop training programs for work-related skills. The growing role of leisure in contemporary society cannot easily be ignored, and even if the amount of free time does not increase dramatically in the forseeable future, it is a good bet that the importance we attribute to it will. For reasons that will be discussed in Chapter 4, the citizen of the future may not be able to rely so heavily on commercial entertainments and diversions and may have to play a more active role in creating his or her own leisure; for example, by using imagination, curiosity, resourcefulness, and the desire to experience and learn to transform many everyday activities into stimulating and informative events. The problem is, this ability to "play" is frequently lost as people learn to meet the demands of school and work. As a result, we may have to look to the same institutions for its renewal and reinforcement.

Our personal futures and the future of our society depend as much on how satisfied and effective we are as citizens as it does on how satisfied and effective we are in our work and leisure. In a democratic society all citizens have the responsibility to participate in, and even express disagreement with, the decisions that influence the future direction of their society. This responsibility is even more important today, the issues more complex, and the processes involved more difficult than ever before because of the continuing development of potentially dangerous technologies and the serious social and environmental problems they can create or extend.

Enlightened and effective citizenship requires an understanding of and respect for the basic and enduring human values that underlie the "images of the future" toward which we strive and their implicit priorities, goals, and structures. Clearly, the changing nature of work and the extension of the meaning of work to include many more activities than it has in times past may profoundly alter our traditional values and images. The value connotations associated with the concept of "productivity" is a particularly important case in point. It is very difficult to measure or even define what constitutes individual productivity in much of the service-oriented work that increasingly characterizes the post-industrial age. How can we meaningfully assess the productivity of workers in service areas such as health care, education, recreation and counseling? How about artists, waiters, and musicians? Or homemakers, students and athletes? If there continues to be a proliferation of the kind of anti-growth sentiment inspired in part by the highly publicized and controversial "Limits to Growth" study (see Meadows, Meadows, Randers, and Behrens,

1972) the social value interpretation of productivity that emphasizes "more, more, and more" will become inappropriate in the future. Our ability to develop alternate values and life styles for living in a world based on something other than growth in material standard of living is a challenge that educators can ill afford to overlook.

Yet another emerging educational need is the ability to appreciate and understand the complexity of the systems interactions and constraints that will shape our society in the years to come. Individuals will also have to learn to examine the implications of these societal forces for the inventing of their *own* futures while accepting the inherent uncertainty of the outcome.

At first glance, it might seem that this "laundry list" of learning objectives must surely exceed the capacity of even the most utopian design for education. Admittedly, the goals are ambitious, but the continuity and underlying communality to most, if not all, of these work, citizenship, and leisure skills suggests that the task is possible. They all involve adaptability, curiosity, resourcefulness, imagination, the ability to communicate and cooperate, a sense of responsibility and self-discipline, awareness of one's ability to influence his or her own destiny and the future of society, and an acceptance of life's uncertainties. People with these skills, functioning in a society that allows and encourages their use, should be able to integrate, perform effectively in, and derive satisfaction from their work, their leisure, and in their role as citizens.

Suggestions for Design

The question remains, "What educational policies, designs, structures, and resources would help to meet these learning needs?" As argued earlier, to keep options open and maintain flexibility, students should *not* be pressured to commit themselves to a single career and to begin acquiring specific job-related skills at an early age. The primary and secondary school years should focus, instead, on developing a base on which specialized job skills can later be superimposed, and offer the first formal opportunities for self-directed learning.

Clearly, this would involve profound modification of traditional educational formats, structures and procedures. Several of the more obvious possibilities include providing opportunities at the secondary level for flexible, self-determined scheduling of school hours and calendars to accommodate those students who wish or need to work; offering a variety of options and allowing more student choice from among these options; encouraging independent exploration, self-discovery, "learning-by-doing," and the active involvement of the student in creating the learning experience; and partially breaking down

44

the formal distinctions that separate work from play and teacher from student. An additional suggestion is offered by child psychologist M. J. Ellis in the following:

> *Many of the activities in a classroom should not have consequences tied to specific ends. What is needed are reinforcements attached to the attributes of responses rather than the responses themselves. Thus in a setting or activity where children are dealing with problems that are relevant to their own experiences and capacities, praise should be attached to the way in which the problem was solved and the characteristics of the solution. Creativity, novelty, elegance, or simplicity of both process and outcome in terms of the individual child should be the prime concern. . . . What was elegant or novel or creative for them must be rewarded. To add adult or culturally oriented constraints to solutions is to circumscribe the possible responses and over time place limits on the potential creativity of the child. (1973, p. 127)*

In light of the relative lack of research linking early educational experiences, structures and processes with later attitudes, behaviors, and skills, these suggestions are more appropriately viewed as working hypotheses than as facts. Nonetheless, since they would reduce constraints on the learner's goals and the ways in which they were pursued and provide more opportunity for the student to experience autonomy, self-discipline, and flexibility, it is reasonable to expect them to contribute to the development of these skills for use in later life.

Existing primary and secondary school curricula might also be revised to include more opportunity for students to participate in group projects that introduce them to the interpersonal skills needed in much of the service and team-oriented jobs of the future, and experiences aimed at familiarizing them with the expanding technology for the processing of information.

Furthermore, the schools could begin to acquaint students with the world of work by providing better career counseling and inviting representatives of the business community into the school to advise and assist them in the exploration of career opportunities. Part-time work outside the school, cooperative arrangements with local businesses, and work-study options would be valuable for general information, skill learning, and work experience. Although most of these activities are already commonplace in many schools, recent studies suggest that more systematic, thorough, and effective approaches are needed (e.g., *The First National Assessment of Career and Occupational Development: An Overview*, 1976; Gottlieb, 1975).

45

With this solid foundation established in the early years, specialized job training, work experience, and counseling could then be made available to older students and adults through business, industry, and private vocational schools, and union and government training programs. Every effort would have to be made to ensure the continued, lifelong availability and easy accessibility of these programs so that individual learners have as few obstacles in their paths as possible and can select among a wide range of options at their discretion.

Working on community projects, serving in the military, VISTA, or the Peace Corps, and initiating informal student-directed experiences would also contribute to an individual's career planning and work skill development, especially if they included the opportunity for further training and learning. The proposals for a national youth service that were made earlier could be the principal vehicle for many of these experiences.

In addition, as many writers, educators, and others have recommended in recent years, ''community education and work councils''—made up of representatives from education, business, labor, government and the community—could be established to provide career counseling and guidance to students and parents to help find jobs and training opportunities for students, to initiate and coordinate cooperative educational arrangements between schools, businesses, unions and the community, and advise schools and training programs about emerging work needs (Ferrin and Arbeiter, 1975; Wirtz, 1975).

The role of colleges and universities would be to produce and provide access to more advanced and theoretical educational material and to identify, coordinate, and certify similiar resources available in the private sector, the community, and elsewhere. Among the many proposals and projects for accomplishing these objectives, probably the most exciting and promising are those that incorporate the rapidly developing technology for processing and transmitting information. In light of the growing interest in this topic, we will examine in some detail one of the most extensive, ambitious and, in the opinion of many, utopian proposals that have recently been made to gain a better understanding of the promise and shortcomings of this powerful post-industrial technology.

Information technology in education: The title of this section might lead the reader to expect an inventory of specific present and future devices, gadgets, and techniques along with glowing descriptions of their educational potential. The use of computers for tutorial-type, individualized instruction; videotape to free teachers from the drudgery of continually repeated lectures and demonstrations; behavioral technologies to improve the educational process; and so on are *not* the primary topics to be covered in the next several pages. Aspects of these issues will be touched on, to be sure, but the purpose of this section is not to discuss specific applications of specific technologies to improve the educational process itself—a topic about which we know very little as yet, in any case. It will deal, however, with the primary theme of a 1972 report by the Carnegie Commission on Higher Education proposing the use of information technology in the design and delivery of an educational system to meet the objectives outlined earlier.

In their proposal the Carnegie Commission called for the establishment of a system of regionally organized "cooperative learning-technology centers" composed of several college and university level institutions within the area defined by the region. One of their functions would be to act as a clearinghouse for member institutions for information about the availability and use of new instructional materials and to provide professional expertise in the development of these materials for dissemination by computers, television, film, and audio and video cassettes. These centers would also affiliate with "extramural" systems that might include the business, labor, youth service, and community-based training opportunities described earlier.

The role of the computer would be central in a system of this sort both as an instructional tool and control unit. As an example of the first use, computer-aided instruction (CAI) offers unique possibilities for creating highly sophisticated, interactive learning environments. In this system, the student usually interacts with a computer by means of a remote terminal. The computer controls the presentation of the instructional materials, the student responds, and based on an analysis of that response, the computer presents further material. Several approaches have been tried, ranging from basic question and answer situations to complex formats taking into consideration the initial characteristics of the student and his or her pattern of responses during learning.

Another approach to CAI involves simulation and gaming, a training technique used extensively in industry, colleges, and the military for developing complex decision-making skills. In this approach the student inputs decisions to a computer model, which simulates several relevant real-world processes. The consequences of each decision are fed back to the student in the form of computer output. Ideally, students should be able to use this information in subsequent decisions fed into the computer model and eventually, it is hoped, in the decisions they will be called upon to make in the real-world.

Among the advantages simulations offer in this respect is the active student involvement in the learning process and the relatively immediate knowledge of results of their decisions. Concerning the latter, in real life there is often a long delay before the effects of a particular decision are known. As a

47

result, decision makers can lose track of some of the variables that originally influenced their decision, making it difficult for them to see where they went wrong if the decision outcome is less than ideal. In addition, because of the time problem and the real-life consequences of a decision, decision makers are not able to conduct the appropriate "experiments," if they can perform any at all, that would enable them to sharpen their decision-making powers. In theory at least, a simulation provides a nonpunitive, experimental setting where time is sufficiently collapsed for the student to learn how to interpret and use data about complex operations, coordinate the various parts making up a system, and deal effectively with risk.

Perhaps the most important educational application of the computer would be its use in coordinating and controlling the various instructional subsystems that would make up the "cooperative learning-technology centers." As pointed out by the Carnegie Commission:

> If it were desired, computers could operate fully automated, multimedia classrooms, combining taped lectures, films, audio presentations, slides, and other materials according to a preset agenda. We have already observed the use of computers as control units for remote-access learning systems that provide random availability of audio- and video-tape programs on commands transmitted by a telephone dial. (1972, p. 24)

All learning materials, including library holdings miniaturized and stored in video cassettes, could be transmitted on demand to combined television, hard-copy reproduction, and computer terminals located in classrooms, study carrels, and even in the home. This material could also be transmitted to local centers staffed by teachers, advisors, and resource personnel who would be available to provide individual counseling and tutoring. The role of faculty members in a system such as this would be to prepare the learning materials to be disseminated and to provide much of the individualized counseling and tutoring. In effect, using information technology in this way would enable us to return to more personalized modes of instruction including the classical ideal of the one-to-one teacher-student relationship.

Although he does not deal specifically with the educational use of information technology, O'Toole (1977) offers an additional role for schools that could easily be integrated into the system proposed here. Since "few employers are competent to teach the theoretical information that underlies work, and even fewer are in the position to examine or meaningfully credential their workers" (p. 173), he suggests that educators could work with employers to improve the quality of on-the-job training.

Educators could offer theoretical instruction on the job, and they could develop supporting courses in the classroom, perhaps team-taught with supervisors from the company. In addition, educators could serve as expert consultants—developing sound curricula, helping to overcome the learning problems of older and disadvantaged workers, and, most singularly, offering a system of recognition and transferable credits for what workers learn. (p. 173)

I/O psychologists would have much to contribute to these efforts as well as function in their more traditional roles in the development of training and counseling programs, performance criteria, and related organizational policy.

Summarizing the relative advantages: Clearly, many problems would have to be resolved before this concept could become an operational system. Even from this sketchy outline, however, one can see that it represents a substantial improvement over many of our present educational procedures, structures, and institutions. One of the problems with the present system is that it tends to limit accessibility to formal education to a prescribed period of our lives and to geographical locations in which abundant learning resources are readily available. Removing education from the constraints of time and place can provide many people with the opportunity to integrate a broader range of educational experiences into their daily lives; for example, to study American history, learn how to type, program a computer, make pottery, *and* acquire highly specialized job skills required by a specific work organization or profession or needed to pursue a new career. Integrating and coordinating the facilities, resources, and programs of academic institutions, businesses, community service agencies, trade unions, private vocational schools, government training programs, youth service options, and individual apprenticeships and tutorials would create an unprecedented ability to adapt educational resources to changing needs. With this system it would also be possible to put people who want to learn in touch with appropriate facilities and resources, involving them as active participants in the setting up of learning experiences tailored to their specific needs, situations, learning styles, and the skills and material to be learned.

Among the other advantages of the proposed system are the following:

1. It could result in a citizenry more familiar and comfortable with two of the most important aspects of the post-industrial society, that is, an extensive and sophisticated information technology and , as noted by Alvin Toffler in *Future Shock* (1971), the problems of change itself.

2. Regional job banks could be tied into this system to enable educational

49

resources to adjust more effectively to fluctuating local needs for particular kinds of work skills.

3. It could be adapted to serve as a combined information source, planning aid, and leisure outlet for personal, family, and community use.

4. Because diverse educational opportunities are created by such a system, the present emphasis on high school diplomas and college degrees could be reduced. As a result, an individual's suitability for a particular job could be based more on his or her specific accomplishments, experiences, and achieved competencies than on the often irrelevant credentials that degrees and diplomas supposedly represent.

5. The use of information technology to process, coordinate, store, and transmit educational materials to more learners could increase the productivity of the educational enterprise, a particularly important consideration in this era of rising costs and tight budgets.

One last advantage that this system might offer is its potential for eliminating, or at least reducing the segmentation that our present educational system produces in the lives of individuals. We spend the earliest years of our lives in play, the next 10 to 20 years in school, then about 40 years working, and if we are fortunate enough to still be alive, in reasonable mental and physical health, and financially secure, we can return once more to play, or at least to its adult counterpart. There are exceptions to the above, and some overlap between the various stages does exist, but the picture of relatively extended periods in our lives dominated by different kinds of activities is essentially accurate. Of course, much of this segmentation is necessitated by the different stages of human growth and development, stages for which some activities seem to be more appropriate than others, but one might easily wonder whether the situation is unnaturally exaggerated by the structures and institutions of our present society, including those related to the processes of education. The segmentation of our lives into education, work, and leisure often leads to abrupt transitions and the concomitant problems of adjustment as people move from one role to another. It also serves, in effect, to segregate generations from each other, for example, school-age youth are essentially separated from the older worker and the retired person is frequently cut off from both. By making education a continuing process rather than one which generally only occurs for an extended, well-defined period of our lives, much of this segmentation could be reduced, and an individual's life and work experience could serve as a foundation and impetus for the pursuit of learning in the later years.

Conclusion

We still have a long way to go before we know enough about our budding information technology to be able to use it to its best advantage. We will gain little by using videotape cassettes to store educational "modules" such as lectures, discussions, demonstrations, and job training materials if the content of these modules has little instructional value. Information technology can make education more accessible and flexible and enable material to be presented in forms never before possible, but it cannot on its own improve significantly on the content of the materials themselves. We have to develop a broad-based instructional technology drawing upon the knowledge, techniques, and expertise of many fields and disciplines to go along with our rapidly expanding technological capability. I/O psychologists could work with educators, systems engineers, telecommunications specialists, and human resource planners to define present and future learning needs, develop training techniques, educational packages, and delivery systems, and devise appropriate means for evaluating and credentialing learning experiences. That a system of the sort proposed here can be done is at least suggested by the success of the several information technology-based educational systems already in operation (e.g., see Abt Associates, 1974; Alpert and Bitzer, 1970; Hammond, 1972; Hartnett, Clark, Feldmesser, Gieber, and Soss, 1974; Molnar, 1975; Morgan, 1976; Perry, 1977).

However, as Robert Hutchins warns in his widely acclaimed book, *The Learning Society* (1968), we must also be aware of the potential dangers of applying technology to education in this fashion. Depersonalization of the learning process and exclusion from education of those who have difficulty in adjusting to new technologies (e.g., see Michael, 1972) are just two of the problems that can emerge if we are not careful in the planning and design of technology-based educational systems. An additional problem is the possibility that the technology, structures, and processes developed to create educational options among which individuals can choose may instead be converted into a system for control and indoctrination to serve the ends of a technocratic power elite. All the more reason why we must realize, as educational technology expert Anthony Oettinger argues, that the nature and extent of the impact of technology on education will depend on institutional change and the design of the social, political, and economic systems with which the educational system must interact (Oettinger, 1971).

Nonetheless, these concerns must be treated as cautions to guide action not as deterrents to block it. The need and opportunity for change and conscious design of the future is upon us. We can ill afford to ignore the challenge.

51

Summary

The goal of providing equal employment opportunities for all workers has challenged many I/O psychologists, employers, legislators, and the courts since the mid-1960s. The frequently heroic attempts to fulfill this goal by modifying the procedures used to select workers for jobs, training programs, and promotions have fallen short, so a more comprehensive and systematic approach is clearly needed.

One element to this approach is to place more emphasis on the counseling and placement of job applicants and less emphasis on selection/rejection decisions. The ways in which organizations can upgrade applicants' job skills and accommodate themselves to individual needs and situations should be considered as well.

Extraorganizational policies and programs are also needed to help provide equal access to jobs. A computerized job-person matching system implemented on a regional or national level would complement the counseling and placement activities of individual firms. A more flexible and accessible system for continuing education, made possible by the judicious use of information technology, would play a particularly important role in meeting emerging work, citizenship, and leisure objectives. All of these initiatives would still be inadequate, however, if there were not enough jobs to go around. Direct and indirect efforts by the public sector to create jobs should, therefore, also be included in any systematic attempt to achieve the vexing and elusive goal of equal employment opportunity for all.

Notes and Suggestions for Further Reading

Lest the reader get the impression that I/O psychologists are to blame for the employment problems of minorities, women, youth, and the elderly, it is important to note that the procedures they developed for the selection of job applicants have reflected their own job requirements and the constraints placed on their activities by the goals of the organizations for which they worked; or, if employed in academic settings, by the needs of the principal consumers (industry and the students who expect to be employed in industry) of their products and services (research, teaching, consulting). For example, since it generally "costs" the organization more to employ someone who ultimately does not perform up to expectation than it does to reject someone who would, I/O psychologists have been called upon to develop stringent and relatively inexpensive screening mechanisms that would minimize the first kind of error and, as a consequence, increase the possibilities of the second. Although the societal costs of the latter can be considerable (see Brenner, 1976), they generally affect individual organizations only indirectly. It should come as no surprise, then, that these costs are rarely considered in the economic calculus of individual firms. Another example of the influence of organizational cost considerations on the activities of I/O psychologists can be found in the nature of the selection strategy they generally follow. As pointed out early in this chapter, the best strategy would be to hire everyone, try them out on the job for a reasonable period of time, and retain those who performed most satisfactorily during the trial period. Needless to say, this procedure is costly for the organization, if ultimately cheaper in the long run to society. In light of these considerations and constraints, one can readily see why I/O psychologists have relied on the selection instruments, procedures, and models they do—that is, until required to do otherwise by government regulation and judicial edict. Although they do not deal explicitly or extensively with the issue of societal costs, Blum and Naylor (1968, pp. 44–56) and Dunnette (1966, pp. 174–183) do discuss the related concept of *personnel decision utility (costs and accuracy)*. From their discussions the traditional role of I/O psychologists with respect to this issue can be inferred.

In counterpoint to the above and to illustrate how *equal employment opportunity can benefit organizations,* Cavanagh (1976) argues that the employment of more women and minorities can lead to a greater emphasis on good interpersonal relations with supervisors and co-workers and the flexibility and creativity frequently associated with increased diversity of attitudes and information.

The *Uniform Guidelines on Employee Selection Procedures* (1977), jointly published by the United States Civil Service Commission, Equal Employment Opportunity Commission, Department of Justice, and Department of Labor, is an indispensable reference for anyone interested in the specific personal selection procedures one should follow to comply with federal standards.

A strategy for equal employment opportunity that has received substantial attention and been the subject of considerable controversy over the last several years is *"affirmative action."* The difference between this strategy and those described on pp. 22–25 seems to be that the latter focus on methodological approaches for removing barriers to equal employment opportunity while affirmative action programs, in effect, require organizations to make an "extra effort" to overcome the effects of past discrimination. To accomplish this, most affirmative action programs emphasize special hiring and admissions preferences and, in some cases, quotas for women and disadvantaged minority groups. The legal, methodological, and ethical implications of the affirmative action strategy are still being debated in the courts and elsewhere, particularly within the context of the recent Supreme Court case, *Allen Bakke* v. *Regents of the University of California.* This case, which had not yet been decided when this book went to press, will no doubt have an impact on personnel selection procedures, but it is possible that the underlying issues will not be resolved for some time. See Sharf (1977) for comments on this particular case, Holt (1977) and Robertson (1977) for a discussion of the implications of other recent judicial decisions, Glazer (1975) for a critical perspective, and Robison (1977) for a cogent overview of affirmative action, and "Equal Employment Opportunity and Other Legal Issues in Industrial Psychology on Bias in Selection" (1976) for several articles proposing alternative theoretical and methodological models for dealing with test bias and discussion of other issues relevant to affirmative action. Novick and Ellis (1977) propose an alternative approach to affirmative action that replaces "group-parity" (compensatory treatment based on race, sex, or ethnic origin) with procedures for identifying and compensating disadvantaged individuals, regardless of their race, sex, or ethnic origin.

As pointed out in the chapter, *work samples* can be used for purposes other than personnel selection. For example, they have been used in vocational counseling and the diagnosis of the special training needs of *disadvantaged and physically and emotionally handicapped persons* (see Jewish Employment and Vocational Service, 1968; Spergel and Leshner, 1968). This application has also been expanded into the *"sheltered workshop"* concept for the training and employment of persons previously considered to be unemployable (Neff, 1968; Levitan and Taggart, 1977; U.S. Department of Labor, 1977).

Another application of the general principles underlying the work sample is the *assessment center.* This application is quite different than the one just described in that it is used to assess the supervisory and administrative potential of candidates for managerial positions (Howard, 1974; MacKinnon, 1975; Moses and Byham, 1977). This technique has also been the focus of the pilot project initiated by the APA Industrial and Organizational Psychology Division's Committee on Public Policy and Social Issues to demonstrate the uses of I/O psychology in nontraditional settings; in this case, to enhance the organizational effectiveness of an agency in the public sector (see Moses, 1976 and pages 24 to 32 in *The Industrial-Organizational Psychologist,* 1977, *15(1)*).

The *problems of individuals in the middle years of their careers* has drawn a considerable amount of attention in recent years and is being addressed by I/O psychologists from a variety of perspectives, including the use of assessment centers to understand midcareer processes and changes (*Symposium: An*

Assessment Center for Mid-Career and Middle Life, 1977). For an overview of midcareer issues and problems see "Paper Session: Career Trends, Personality, and Life Satisfaction" (1976), "Special Issue: Mid-Life Career Change" (1977), and *Symposium: Work as an Aspect of Human Development in Mid-Life Years* (1976). Descriptions of counseling programs for persons undergoing midcareer crises can be found in Entine (1976) and Ryterband (1976).

General references on the related topics of *vocational psychology and career counseling and development* include Crites (1976), Hall (1976), Holland (1973), Super and Bohn (1970) and Van Maanen and Schein (1977).

For a review of the *processes that occur as new members enter organizations* see Wanous (1977). Wanous distinguishes between the organizational perspective, which is primarily concerned with the new employee's ability to perform satisfactorily, and the individual's perspective, which focuses on their interest in satisfying their personal needs by taking a job with a particular organization. This distinction parallels our discussion of the differences between the selection/rejection and counseling/placement models respectively. Since Wanous mainly deals with the individual's perspective (how they choose a particular organization and the role of information and job previews on this choice), the review is highly relevant to several of the issues covered in this chapter.

For more information on the U.S. Employment Service's plans and projects for a *computerized job-person matching system* see Stevenson (1976). Although there are no formal plans as of this writing to convert this into a nationwide network, job applicants in one region can find out via the present system about jobs and demand for specific skills in other locations across the country (see Baxter, 1976). Programs to provide *financial assistance for workers interested in relocating to areas where their job opportunities are greater,* would be an important element in a comprehensive nationwide system. For a description of a program in operation in Sweden see "Fact Sheets on Sweden" (1976) and Zanker (1977).

The general concept of *computerized data banks,* which would include the job-person matching system described here, has been subject to considerable criticism in recent years because of the potential threat they pose to personal privacy. Because of the limited nature of the data that would be contained in a job bank it should provide less of a danger to privacy than would a general purpose national data center. Nonetheless, adequate safeguards would have to be established before any national computerized job person-matching system was put into operation (see Sawyer and Schechter, 1968).

For more detailed discussion of *public service employment* see Gartner, Nixon, and Riessman (1973), Lekachman (1974), National Manpower Policy

Task Force (1975), and National Commission for Manpower Policy (1975 and 1976). Existing *programs for the elderly* are described by Batten and Kestenbaum (1976) and Bowles (1976).

For a *review and history of government policy and programs for the development and utilization of human resources* see Clague and Kramer (1976), Jakubauskas and Palomba (1973, pp. 218–224), Mangum and Walsh (1973), Mirengoff and Rindler (1976), Patten (1971, Chapter 13), and Levitan, Mangum, and Marshall (1976, Part 3).

The *relationship between education and work* has been one of the most discussed topics in recent years. The voluminous material dealing with various aspects of this issue is overwhelming. Among the most noteworthy general references, particularly concerning their comprehensive recommendations for social and educational policy, are the books by O'Toole (1977) and Willard Wirtz (1975). A book that has sparked much controversy is Berg (1971). The concept of *career education* is especially central to this controversy. See Hoyt, Evans, Mackin, and Mangum (1972) for a description of the concept and supporting arguments, Grubb and Lazerson (1975) and O'Toole (1977) for criticisms, and Kemble (1976) for a concise distillation of the principal issues in this controversy. An important assumption underlying the educational system proposed in this book is that individuals would avail themselves of increased educational opportunities if they were available, inexpensive, and convenient. Evidence supporting this assumption can be found in the research by Coolican (1974) and Hiemstra (1975) on *adult education and self-planned learning.* Best and Stern (1977) discuss the limitations associated with a linear distribution of education, work, and leisure throughout a person's life (i.e., an extended period of education followed by work followed by retirement). They present an alternative, the *cyclic life plan,* and review several means by which these more flexible life plans could be realized. Two recent books offer sharply contrasting views of the present *value of a college education;* Freeman (1976) argues that the lifetime income advantage of a college degree relative to a high school diploma has all but disappeared while Bowen (1977) argues that the monetary return of a college education is still significant and has several important nonmonetary returns as well.

The concept of the *"learning society"* where individuals have access to a wide variety of educational programs throughout their lives is covered in more detail in Carnegie Commission on Higher Education (1973). There is considerable overlap between their proposals and the discussion in the text.

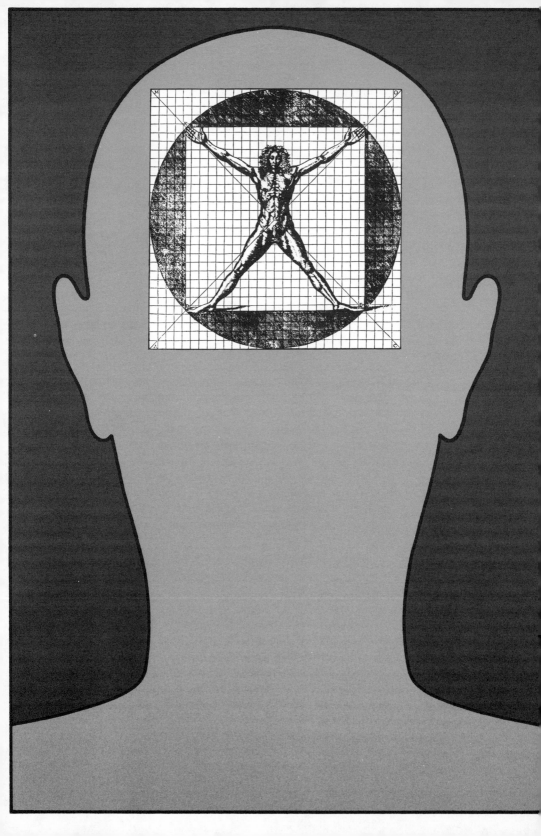

chap. 3

Fitting the Job to the Worker:
Job Satisfaction and
the Design of Work Systems

Job satisfaction—its nature, causes, and consequences—has attracted the
attention and concern of I/O psychologists, as well as managers, social critics,
and, of course, workers since the earliest days of the field. Much of this interest,
especially on the part of work organizations and their managers and owners,
derived from the belief that satisfied workers are more productive than
dissatisfied ones. However, the now-classic review of the research by Brayfield
and Crockett (1955) and the more recent review by Vroom (1964) have lead to
the conclusion that a strong, pervasive, and direct relationship between job
satisfaction and performance had not been demonstrated after years of
research. As a result, other reasons have been sought to justify concern for this
issue.

From the standpoint of the organization alone there are several
justifications. First, there is some evidence that job satisfaction may be
associated with lower rates of absenteeism and turnover (Locke, 1976a; Porter
and Steers, 1973; Vroom, 1964). In addition, McCormick and Tiffin suggest
that having dissatisfied employees may lead to various kinds of "hidden"
costs for the organization and have other "unmeasurable (but
nonetheless real) effects on the total organizational efficiency" (1974, p. 330).
Some examples of these "hidden costs and unmeasurable effects" are that
dissatisfied workers may require more supervision, generate more grievances
and complaints, and be more likely to create an unfavorable corporate image
than satisfied ones, making it difficult to recruit other workers and leading to
poor community relations. Evidence of yet another possible consequence of job
dissatisfaction, industrial sabotage and theft, has been recently reported by a
research team from the University of Michigan's Institute for Social Research
(Quinn, Mangione, and Baldi de Mandilovich, 1973). Using workers'
anonymous responses to a questionnaire, they found that among male workers
over 30, those who were dissatisfied with their jobs had more often

spread rumors or gossip to cause trouble at work; done work badly or incorrectly on purpose; stolen merchandise or equipment from their employers; damaged their employer's property, equipment, or product accidentally, but not reported it; or damaged their employer's property, equipment, or product on purpose. (pp. 39-40)

One last reason why organizations should be concerned about job dissatisfaction is that although there may not be a *direct* cause and effect relationship from job satisfaction to job performance, there certainly is a relationship of some sort between them, and by learning more about one we are bound to learn more about the other.

Job Dissatisfaction and Quality of Life

All of the reasons outlined above for being concerned about job dissatisfaction are similiar in nature to the rationale underlying the concern for increased job performance; that is, they all derive from the traditional goals of work organizations related to productivity, effectiveness, and efficiency. However, there is another rationale for being concerned about job satisfaction that is considerably less pragmatic and, as a result, more consistent with the overall perspective of this book. This rationale focuses on the responsibility of the organization for providing a satisfactory quality of life for those who spend a substantial portion of their lives within them—their employees. Therefore, workers can no longer be treated strictly as means for fulfilling traditional corporate goals. The way they experience their everyday work lives and the satisfaction they derive from their jobs is increasingly being dealt with as an end in itself, an end that is just as important as organizational productivity, profit, and growth. Serving both ends, whenever possible, or striking an equitable balance between the two, when not, is the emerging challenge for work organizations in the post-industrial society.

Much of the interest in the early 1970s in worker dissatisfaction, "blue-collar blues," "white collar woes," and the "humanization of the workplace"—as illustrated by the extensive media coverage, scientific research, professional conferences, congressional hearings, government task force reports (e.g., *Work in America,* 1973) and the popularity of the best-selling book *Working* by Studs Terkel (1974)—reflected this concern. Another factor spurring this interest was the feeling that job dissatisfaction may have potentially serious societal consequences. Consider, for example, the various claims explicitly contained in or implied by the following quotes:

If . . . a bored and angry blue-collar worker on a repetitive job develops traits of violence, anger, sadism, slight depression, and indifference . . . he will sometimes be a bad citizen in the sense that he will be easy prey for demagogues who appeal to his resentment and his desire for revenge. [*]

Maybe more of our contemporary malaise is due to introjection of non-prideful, robotized, broken-down-into-easy-bits kind of work than I had thought. (Maslow, 1965, p. 13)

<u>What happens when you get home?</u> Oh, I argue with my wife a little bit. That's natural. Turn on T.V. get mad at the news. . . . I don't even watch the news that much, . . . I look for any alternative to the ten o'clock news. . . .

When I come home, know what I do for the first 20 minutes? Fake it. I put on a smile. I don't feel like it. I got a kid three and a half years old. . . . What's work to a three-year-old kid? If I feel bad, I can't take it out on the kid. . . . You don't take it out on your wife either. This is why you go to the tavern. You want to release it there rather than do it at home. What does an actor do when he's got a bad movie? I got a bad movie every day. (excerpted from an interview with a steel-worker as reported by Terkel, 1972, p. 14)

"It's a downer day, man—let's lift it up!" Tommy passes a joint to Yanagan who draws the smoke deep, then hands it to me. For a moment I hesitate till Little Joe pats me on the shoulder and says: "What are you waiting for? When you're feeling bad you take medicine, right? Well, this place makes you feel sick, and you got the medicine right in your hand!"

The smoke striking into my lungs sends my blood leaping. And soon the flying sparks, the hot steel, the raging, exploding furnaces above us seem like frivolities on a carnival night. (Kremen, 1972, p. 26)

To sum up, we can see that job satisfaction is important for organizations, for individuals, and perhaps even for the well being of society as a whole. The considerable amount of attention this issue has received in recent years also suggests that job dissatisfaction is widespread and, as such, represents a serious problem for both organizations and society. *If* this is indeed the case, then consideration of the ways in which this problem might be alleviated is necessary.

[*]From a letter by Erich Fromm quoted in U.S. Dept. of Labor (1968).

It is important, however, that recommendations for large-scale organizational programs and social policy be based on something other than speculation, anecdotes, single case examples, media reports, and subjective, potentially biased impressions of actual situations and conditions. If they are not, we risk spending large amounts of money, time, and effort on unnecessary and unproductive programs while other, more pressing problems are neglected. Fortunately, better evidence is available to give us a more objective picture of the extent, nature, and societal consequences of job dissatisfaction and to help us determine whether or not a problem even exists at present or is likely to exist in the future.

Before examining this evidence it would help to review some of the theoretical and normative underpinnings of this issue so that we may better understand the conditions that can lead to job satisfaction and the extent to which the organization of work in modern industrialized societies creates or precludes these conditions. As was mentioned in Chapter 1, I/O psychology has changed and developed in many ways since its beginnings. Nowhere have these changes been more profound than in the way I/O psychologists over the years have viewed job satisfaction and its determinants.

Human Needs and Contemporary Work

The dominant view of the worker during the first 20 to 30 years of this century was the one commonly, if mistakenly, inferred from Taylorism and the principles of scientific management. This view emphasized the role of such *physical* factors as monetary incentives and the reduction of fatigue in worker satisfaction and productivity, stressed the importance of close supervision, and led to job designs that minimized worker autonomy, responsibility, and skill.

One of the most important results of the Hawthorne studies was the demonstrated inadequacy of this narrow view of human nature in the work place. In the spirit of scientific management, the Hawthorne studies were undertaken to study the effects of various physical factors on job performance. According to most interpretations of the results of these studies, they demonstrated instead the influence of such interpersonal factors as peer-group approval, leadership style, and other *social* influences on productivity and satisfaction. This marked the beginning of a new era in I/O psychology. No longer could industry assume that the physical aspects of work were the only factors to be considered in attempts to motivate and satisfy employees. Workers had to be viewed now as social beings, as organisms having more complex needs than was previously believed. This emphasis prevailed throughout World War II and developed further into the "human relations" movement of the 1950s with important contributions by Homans (1950), Whyte (1955), and Likert (1961), among others.

In the latter part of the 1950s another school of thought emerged from the work of Maslow (1954), Herzberg (Herzberg, Mausner, and Snyderman, 1959; Herzberg, 1966), Argyris (1964) and McGregor (1960). The cornerstone of this school was the notion of *"self-actualization"* or psychological "growth" and the role of the nature of the *work itself* in setting the conditions for the satisfaction of these needs. According to Maslow, when an individual's "lower order" needs (physiological, security, social) were met, "higher order" needs for self-esteem, self-fulfillment, self-expression, and the realization of one's potentials would emerge as predominant. Specifically, individuals would strive to achieve their full potential, to grow and develop in accordance with their own, personally defined goals. Maslow viewed the process as self-perpetuating, in that the individual would continually find and strive to achieve new goals and means of self-expression. Satisfaction was not only to be derived from the achievement of goals but from the challenge of exercising and acquiring valued skills and competencies. Herzberg later translated these needs into more specific work-related characteristics including opportunity and recognition for task achievement, responsibility, opportunity for advancement and growth, and challenge. These "motivator" factors, which are intrinsic to the work itself, were viewed as being of more enduring importance in job satisfaction and work motivation than such extrinsic, contextual variables as pay, physical comfort, and social relationships on the job (the factors emphasized by the scientific management and human relations "schools").

Reserving comment on the validity of the self-actualization theories and acknowledging that all three "schools" are represented to some degree in contemporary views of job satisfaction, one can safely conclude that it is the latter view that provides at least the implicit *raison d'etre* for the recent focus on job dissatisfaction as a potentially serious societal problem. In this context, what is essentially a psychological construct and object of psychological theory and research dovetails with the long-term concern of social and political philosophers for "work alienation," as this problem is frequently called. From Alexis deTocqueville and Karl Marx to Erich Fromm and Herbert Marcuse, social critics and philosophers have argued that industrialization and technological change and their impact on the organization of work have alienated large numbers of workers and have had profoundly negative personal and societal consequences. There are some differences of opinion as to what specific aspect of industrial work is the cause of this widespread alienation—the separation of workers from the product of their labors, the ownership of the means of pro-

63

duction by persons other than the workers themselves, the monotony of most industrial work, the inability of the workers to control the pace of their work, and so on—but the overall tone of the various theories is quite similar. Representative of many contemporary views are those of the controversial philosopher, Herbert Marcuse. He contends that although the immediate "survival" needs of most workers have been largely taken care of, those essential for their development as self-actualizing individuals (needs that might otherwise be met by challenging and meaningful work), have been deliberately withheld by the technology-based industrial system and the elite (e.g., factory owners) who run it. Instead, these higher order needs are sublimated, repressed, and manipulated by advertising and the easy availability of empty and meaningless consumer goods. Workers are further "enslaved" and their passivity reinforced by their increased need to work so that they can afford to purchase more and more of these goods (Marcuse, 1964).

Most of the attention paid to job dissatisfaction, historically as well as recently, has centered on assembly-line work. The highly standardized, subdivided, and repetitious operations; the machine-determined pace and the separation of the worker from the final product; the lack of intrinsic interest and challenge in the content of the work itself; the underutilization of skills, education, and abilities; the lack of autonomy, responsibility, and the opportunity for individuality and creativity: all of these factors and more have been cited at one time or other as having negative psychological effects on the average assembly-line worker.

Considering that less than 2 percent of the work force are on assembly lines, it would appear that the problem of job dissatisfaction is, at worst, limited to a very small percentage of workers. However, as several writers have pointed out, the assembly-line principle—which is, in effect, a logical if unintended extension of Taylor's principles of scientific management—has been applied as a general model to work of all kinds (Blauner, 1964; Friedmann, 1961). Along this line, Drucker argues that:

> *Without assembly-line or conveyor belt, clerical operations in large-scale business enterprises are today increasingly organized the same way in which Henry Ford organized the production of the Model T. The typists' pool of a large insurance company, check-sorting and check-clearing operations in a big bank, the sorting and filling of orders in a mail-order house, and thousands of other operations in business and government offices do not differ in substance from the automobile assembly-line, however much they may differ in appearance. (1962, p. 3)*

64

Others have extended this idea even further. For example, French Marxist Serge Mallet claims that engineers and technicians are part of a new working class because

> *their skills are inevitably broken down, compartmentalized, and routinized, and they are unable to realize the professional skills for which they were educated. Thus they are "reduced" to the role of a highly trained working class. (as presented by Bell, 1972, p. 180)*

According to philosopher Andre Gorz, this is becoming increasingly true of other segments of the professional class as well.

> *The industry of the second half of the twentieth century increasingly tends to take men from the universities and colleges, men who have been able to acquire the ability to do creative or independent work; who have curiosity, the ability to synthesize, to analyze, to invent, and to assimilate, an ability which spins in a vacuum and runs the risk of perishing for lack of an opportunity to be usefully put to work. (Gorz, 1967, pp. 105–106)*

The important point common to all of these views is that because of the way work is organized in modern industrialized societies there is little opportunity for most workers, regardless of the level of their jobs, to utilize their particular skills and abilities. As a result, the argument goes, they are not able to satisfy their higher order (i.e., self-actualization) needs through their work.

How accurate are these theories, opinions, and views? Is there widespread alienation among the work force at all levels of our society? What do workers themselves cite as major sources of dissatisfaction in their jobs? These and related questions are the next issues to be considered.

Reviewing the Evidence

Extent, trends, and causes: Until recently, the scientific assessment of job satisfaction largely reflected the limited organizational and academic concerns of managers and scholars for organizational effectiveness and theoretical understanding of its psychological processes. In the last several years, however, measures of job satisfaction have increasingly been used, along with other "social indicators" (see notes for Chapter 5), to assess "quality of life," to monitor

65

societal change and warn of emerging problems, and to formulate and evaluate the effectiveness of social policy and programs (Seashore and Taber, 1976).

Because of the recency of this latter perspective and the inherent difficulties in measuring such an elusive, poorly defined and subjective parameter, job satisfaction has not been monitored as systematically or repeatedly as wages, work hours, or levels of employment. In addition, as Quinn, Staines, and McCullough (1974) point out, "earlier measurements of job satisfaction have been circumscribed by their application to very unique populations of workers or by the tendency of most investigators to develop their own job satisfaction measures" (p. 3). This is at least partly due to the limited organizational and academic objectives referred to above. As a consequence of all of this, the available data on job satisfaction are frequently incomplete, ambiguous, not easily compared with other relevant measures, and not of sufficient scope to serve as effective social indicators. Nevertheless, some important if occasionally equivocal conclusions can be drawn from the existing studies.

In what is probably the most thoughtful and thorough paper to date on the subject, a team of researchers from the University of Michigan's prestigious Survey Research Center (SRC) analyzed and compared the results of seven national surveys of workers conducted by the National Opinion Research Center (NORC) and the Survey Research Centers of the Universities of Michigan and California (Quinn et al., 1974). The percentage of "satisfied" workers in the years covered by these surveys (1958–1973) ranges from a low of 81% in 1958 to a high of 92% in 1964. The most recent survey covered in the SRC paper (1973) indicated that 90% of all workers surveyed expressed at least some degree of satisfaction with their jobs.

Clearly, these results do not indicate the problem is as serious or pervasive as the opinions, theories, and public speculation described in the preceding two sections suggest. The SRC research team points out, however, the possibility that the survey figures may actually *underestimate* the degree of dissatisfaction among the workforce. One reason is that job satisfaction questions may elicit a form of defensiveness on the part of survey respondents which can bias their answers by making them appear to be more satisfied with their jobs than they really are. The source of this defensiveness could be their feelings that being dissatisfied is their own fault for having chosen the wrong job in the first place and not doing anything about getting a different one. Another reason why survey responses may underestimate actual job dissatisfaction is that these responses could be an attempt on the part of the worker to rationalize unpleasant work situations. When workers begin to feel dissatisfied on the job and do not perceive a reasonable chance for improving the situation or getting a different job, they may lower their expectations and demand less of their job

66

rather than suffer chronic dissatisfaction. The possibility that job dissatisfaction may actually be underestimated by these surveys is reinforced by the fact that more subtle, indirect measures of job satisfaction usually give higher estimates of the percentage of "dissatisfied" workers (see Table 2).

Table 2. Levels of Job Dissatisfaction as a Function of the Question Asked

Percentage of "dissatisfied" workers	Question
14	A. All in all, how satisfied would you say you are with your job?
22	B. How often do you leave work with a good feeling that you've done some things particularly well?
36	C. Knowing what you know now, if you had to decide all over again whether to take the job you now have, what would you decide?
37	D. If a good friend of yours told you (he/she) was interested in working in a job like yours for your employer, what would you tell (him/her)?
43	E. How often do you get so wrapped up in your work that you lose track of time?
51	F. If you were free to go into any type of job you wanted, what would be your choice?

Source: Quinn et al., 1974, p. 51.

Additional evidence concerning this issue is offered by Kahn (1972). From the results of two other studies, he concludes that for most workers

> *it is a choice between no work connection (usually with severe attendant economic penalties and a conspicuous lack of meaningful alternative activities) and a work connection burdened with negative qualities (routine, compulsory scheduling, dependency, etc.). In the circumstances, the individual has no difficulty with the choice; he chooses work, pronounces himself moderately satisfied and tells us more only if the questions become more searching. Then we learn that he can order jobs clearly in terms of their status or desirability, wants his son to be employed differently from himself, and if given a choice, would seek a different occupation. (p. 179)*

On the other hand, there is always the possibility that some workers may actually understate their level of job satisfaction for fear that this information may get back to their company or co-workers and have a negative effect on future salary negotiations and on their relationships with their less satisfied peers.

In light of these difficulties, *absolute* measures of job satisfaction at a given time must be viewed with skepticism. Even if they could be taken as gospel, these measures are less useful for guiding social and organizational policy than *relative* measures which compare, for example, satisfaction in different occupational and demographic groups or at different times. Furthermore, unless there are indications to the contrary, one can reasonably assume that whatever biases reflected in the measures for one group or time are probably reflected in those for the other. As a result, any nontrivial differences in measured job satisfaction are likely to be valid as well as socially significant.

For most purposes, then, the absolute amount of job satisfaction at any given time is not as informative as trends in job satisfaction over time. In other words, is dissatisfaction on the increase? Not according to the SRC researchers.

In spite of public speculation to the contrary, there is no conclusive evidence of a widespread, dramatic decline in job satisfaction. Reanalysis of 15 national surveys since 1958 [several Gallup surveys plus the NORC and U. of Cal. and U. of Mich. surveys described earlier] indicates that there has not been any significant decrease in overall levels of job satisfaction over the last decade. (Quinn et al., 1974, p. 1)

It is important to note that various nationwide demographic and economic indicators which might reflect job dissatisfaction—turnover, absenteeism, labor unrest, productivity—also provide no conclusive evidence of significant trends (Flanagan, Strauss, and Ulman, 1974; Henle, 1974; Wool, 1973).

While the data presented so far indicate no severe existing or developing job dissatisfaction problems for American workers as a whole, other comparisons do reveal problems for certain economic, demographic and occupational groups. In particular, most studies consistently indicate more dissatisfaction among younger workers (a difference that has existed for over 15 years, according to the SRC researchers), nonwhites, and workers with some college education but no degree (Altimus and Tersine, 1973; Glenn, Taylor, and Weaver, 1977; Quinn et al., 1974; Schwab and Heneman, 1977; Sheppard and Herrick, 1972). Although the data also indicate that the so-called "blue-collar blues" can occur at all levels of the work force (Seashore and Barnowe, 1972) including managers (DeMaria, Tarnowieski, and Gurman, 1972) and engineers (Ritti, 1971), it does appear to be more prevalent at the lower levels, particularly among operatives, nonfarm laborers, and nondomestic service and clerical workers (Quinn et al., 1974).

The evidence concerning *causal factors in job satisfaction* is particularly important for our purposes and helps to explain many of the results described in the last few pages. Generally, the data indicate that such intrinsic characteristics as interesting and challenging work, opportunity to use one's valued skills and abilities, responsibility, autonomy (i.e., control over work methods and pace), and the availability of the resources needed to perform effectively are more important for *most* workers than extrinsic factors (financial rewards, comfortable working conditions, satisfactory relations with co-workers) although aspects of the latter, particularly good pay and job security, were of considerable importance as well (e.g., see Lawler, 1973b; Quinn et al., 1974; Srivastva, Salipante, Cummings, Notz, Bigelow, and Waters, 1975; Weaver, 1975).

There are, however, some very important occupational, demographic and personality differences among workers in the relative importance they assign to these factors. For example, blue-collar workers tend to be more interested in financial rewards than in having challenging and interesting work (Fein, 1973; Quinn et al., 1974; White, 1977). Other factors that apparently influence the relative importance of various job characteristics are the level of attained education and age, with better educated and younger workers being more interested in intrinsic factors (Andrisani and Miljus, 1977; Quinn et al., 1974; Quinn and Baldi de Mandilovitch, 1975).

Before proceeding let us try to summarize what has been presented so far and, keeping in mind the various qualifications made here and elsewhere, draw some tentative conclusions. First, challenge, responsibility, autonomy, and opportunity for growth on the job appear to be almost as important as the self-actualization theorists have claimed, although the paramount importance of these characteristics is, perhaps, not as universal as their theories would suggest. It also seems that these theorists may have underestimated the enduring significance of such extrinsic characteristics as pay and job security. Furthermore, there are as yet few indications of the intense, widespread job dissatisfaction predicted by the work alienation theorists or suggested by the many journalistic accounts that have appeared in the past several years, and no clear evidence that present levels are significantly increasing. In other words, a substantial majority of American workers express at least a reasonable degree of satisfaction with the characteristics of their jobs, but there are identifiable groups of workers with jobs that do not sufficiently meet either their intrinsic or extrinsic needs.

Personal and Societal Consequences

Earlier in this chapter several quotes were presented to illustrate some of the speculations that have been made concerning the personal and societal consequences of job dissatisfaction. If, as these quotes suggest, job dissatisfaction does cause apathy, violence, drug abuse, family problems, antisocial attitudes and behavior, racial and ethnic prejudice, poor mental health, and so on, even a relatively small amount of dissatisfaction represents a serious problem and warrants immediate concern. How serious and valid are these hypothesized consequences?

Mental and physical health: In one of the first systematic studies of the relationship between job dissatisfaction and mental health, Kornhauser (1965) reported consistent relationships between dissatisfaction and a measure of mental health that included feelings of inadequacy, low self-esteem, anxiety and tension, hostility, life dissatisfaction, and low personal morale. Because of the nature of Kornhauser's research, others have argued that it is impossible to determine whether the job dissatisfaction was a cause of the poor mental health or whether some other factor such as a characteristic of the work itself was the source of both the dissatisfaction and the poor mental health (see Locke, 1976; Quinn et al., 1974).

More recent evidence, however, has shed light on this relationship. Based on a study of over 2,000 men in 23 occupations ranging from factory worker to university administrator, a team of researchers from the University of Michigan's Institute for Social Research concluded that the anxiety, irritation, depression and somatic complaints (e.g., difficulty in sleeping, loss of appetite, sweaty palms) reported by their subjects *"appear* to be influenced by dissatisfaction with the work rather than by the actual characteristics of the work itself" (Caplan, Cobb, French, Van Harrison, and Pinneau, 1975, p. 197). They also found that this dissatisfaction was affected, in turn, by the "goodness of fit" between several perceived job characteristics and the worker's desires for these characteristics (work complexity, work load, responsibility for others, and overtime hours). Other evidence, however, does suggest that characteristics of the work itself and its organizational context may have a moderating effect on this relationship; that is, *symptoms of poor mental health may be less likely to occur when a person has the resources and freedom of action needed to cope effectively with otherwise unsatisfactory job situations* (see Karasek, 1976 and Zaleznik, Kets de Vries, and Howard, 1977). As we will see shortly, this result is consistent with other recent research which suggests an important role for autonomy on the job in a variety of highly desirable work-related outcomes.

The impact of job dissatisfaction on physical health and longevity has also begun to attract attention in recent years, partly due to the growing interest in psychosomatic medicine and occupational health. There is even some evidence linking physical health with the psychological consequences described above (Caplan et al., 1975) and a considerable body of research implicating occupational stress in a variety of diseases (see House, 1974 for a review of this research). Unfortunately, the problem of defining "stress," methodological limitations of some of the most frequently cited studies of the relationship between satisfaction and disease, and at least one major study indicating no relationship, make it difficult to rule out other possible causes or delineate the specific connection between the two (Locke, 1976; McClean, 1976; Weintraub and Smith, 1973). Nonetheless, the bulk of this evidence—particularly the longitudinal study by Palmore (1969) identifying job satisfaction as the best predictor of longevity of all the factors examined in his study (including tobacco use and overall physical functioning)—suggests that the negative impact of job dissatisfaction on health is a possibility that should not be overlooked.

Drug use: In spite of the claims, speculation, and anecdotal reports linking drug use on the job and work dissatisfaction, empirical evidence concerning this issue is almost nonexistent. While research results suggest that the use of drugs on the job is pervasive (e.g., Jennings, 1977; Levy, 1972; Rush and Brown, 1971), there is little data at present, other than clinical observations (see *Work in America,* 1973), specifically tying drug use to job dissatisfaction, working conditions, and job characteristics. The one notable exception is provided by the national survey of workers, described earlier, conducted by the Survey Research Center at the University of Michigan (Quinn et al., 1974). Using a self-administered questionnaire to collect data on how often workers had used drugs or chemicals, other than vitamins or aspirins, to help them get through the workday (the question included prescribed medicines and tranquilizers as well as illegal drugs), they found a significant relationship between job dissatisfaction and drug use for men who were 30 years old or older.

Nonwork attitudes and behavior: The extent to which on-the-job behaviors and attitudes influence individuals' nonwork lives has been the object of a considerable body of psychological and sociological theory and research over the last two decades. We will discuss this work in more detail in the next chapter, so the next few pages will focus on only a limited but particularly important set of attitudes and behavior.

The connection between work-related variables and *sociopolitical attitudes and behavior* has attracted a good deal of attention (see Allardt, 1976). Kornhauser also examined this relationship in his study, discussed previously, and concluded that the same variables that were related to low personal morale and poor mental health were also related to various "antidemocratic political feelings" (1965, p. 267). Similarly, in their study of 370 white, male, blue-collar union members, Sheppard and Herrick (1972) concluded that the dissatisfied workers in their sample were more likely to have little trust in others, to be convinced that the lot of the average worker was getting worse, to be pessimistic about the future, and to be less confident about their impact on the political process and the degree of governmental concern for them than satisfied workers. They also found a relationship between job satisfaction and voting choices, those who were most dissatisfied were more likely to have voted for George Wallace in the 1968 presidential election. Other findings included a relationship between job satisfaction and attitudes toward racial minorities with the dissatisfied tending *not* to believe that blacks wanted to get ahead by using the same methods as other Americans. They also felt that unions and management had favored minority groups in providing good training and jobs.

Other studies have added some specificity to these findings by indicating that it is not the dissatisfaction *per se* but the objective conditions of the job that may be exerting an influence on sociopolitical attitudes and behavior. In particular, such intrinsic work characteristics as autonomy and challenge seem to be associated with more active, self-directed, and participatory political, social, and leisure orientations and behavior (Elden, 1977; Emery and Phillips, 1976; Karasek, 1976; Kohn, 1969; Kohn and Schooler, 1969 and 1973; Meissner, 1971; Torbert, 1973). Explanations for this relationship typically focus on the "educative effect" of autonomous, challenging work on the acquisition of nonwork skills and attitudes—that is, self-directed work develops the skills necessary for more active and autonomous functioning in nonwork (e.g., see Pateman, 1970). We will return to this issue again so the important point for our purposes at this time is that the objective conditions of work, particularly job autonomy, rather than the subjective response of dissatisfaction/satisfaction seem to be the influencing factor in the development of various sociopolitical attitudes and behavior.

Another factor that is sometimes linked to job dissatisfaction, at least via anecdote and speculation, is *violent behavior*. The Kerner Commission report on civil disorders (see *Report of the National Advisory Commission on Civil Disorders,* 1968) which was undertaken to study the reasons behind the wave of urban ghetto riots in the mid-1960s, consistently found high rates of unemployment and underemployment in riot cities and concluded that these factors were a close second to police practices as a source of grievances among inner city residents. The profile and characteristics of the "average self-reported rioter" indicated that, if employed, he or she was more likely to be in a menial or low-status job than their noninvolved neighbors and was also more likely to be intermittently employed. When asked about their attitudes concerning employment, the self-reported rioters were more likely to feel dissatisfied with their present jobs than were the noninvolved.

The problem with interpreting these findings within the context of job satisfaction is that it is impossible in this data to separate out the effects of the work itself from the confounding variables of living standard and socioeconomic class. Most explanations of crimes of violence tend to emphasize the latter variables. The suggestion is there, however, that job dissatisfaction *could be* an important factor in violent behavior, and until there are more systematic investigations that separate out the effects of socioeconomic class, objective work characteristics, and job satisfaction, we must keep this possibility in mind.

The last nonwork behavior and attitude to be discussed here is the notion of *"alienated consumption,"* a cornerstone of many of the work alienation theories referred to earlier. Andre Gorz describes it as follows:

> *It is because the worker is not "at home" in "his" work, because this work, negated as a creative activity, is a calamity, a pure* means *of satisfying needs, that the individual's active and creative needs are amputated, and he no longer finds his sphere of sovereignty except in non-work, that is to say in the satisfaction of passive needs, in consumption, and in domestic life. (1967, p. 71)*

It may not be clear why this could be an undesirable state of affairs. The alienation theorists would argue that by focusing on material consumption and the needs this consumption fulfills, we may be overlooking or even denying an essential aspect of our psychological makeup, the need for growth and the actualization of our potentials. According to their view, this behavior ignores what is essentially human in us and can turn us into apathetic, unfeeling, isolated, and passive automatons making us more subject to manipulation by authoritarian and repressive influences.

The problem with this argument is that it is highly pejorative and value-laden. For other theorists and researchers, a principal focus on the consumption of material goods is reasonable, even desirable behavior for workers whose jobs, prior experience, and values have led them to develop primary interests and involvements outside of work (Faunce and Dubin, 1975).

There are other reasons, less subjective and value-laden, than those offered by the alienation theorists for being concerned with ever increasing rates of material consumption. Following the publication of the controversial "Limits to Growth" study in 1972 (Meadows et al., 1972) many people began to fear that continued growth in the production of material goods would eventually produce severe shortages in our natural resources—e.g., oil, natural gas, minerals—and unacceptable increases in environmental deterioration. *If* these fears ultimately prove to be well-founded, and *if* it really is the case that workers who are dissatisfied with their jobs are more likely to compensate for this dissatisfaction by increasing their consumption of nonessential material goods, then we

73

have another highly compelling reason for being concerned with job satisfaction and its possible consequences.

A recent series of studies conducted on a group of British blue-collar workers suggested that there may indeed be substantial numbers of workers who have rejected many of the values traditionally associated with work and adopted an "instrumental" orientation in its place (Goldthorpe, Lockwood, Bechhofer, and Platt, 1969). These workers viewed their jobs as a means to an end and were willing to tolerate unpleasant work in order to obtain a higher standard of living contingent upon the financial rewards often associated wtih this kind of work. In other words they compensated for the lack of intrinsic rewards in their work by seeking satisfaction outside of work, especially through the consumption of material goods. Goldthorpe et al. point out, however, that their nonwork orientation was not a product of the characteristics of their work, but existed prior to their acquiring the job. Such past experiences as former jobs, geographical locations, and family background shaped their expectations and values and "constituted the motivation for these men to take, and to retain, work of a particularly unrewarding kind which offered high pay in compensation for its inherent deprivations" (p. 182).

The significance of this result can be found in its implications for the ways in which the solution to this "problem" (if it is, indeed, a problem) is approached. If there were a direct cause and effect relationship between either the objective characteristics of the work itself or job dissatisfaction and "alienated consumption," then the solution would be to change the job. If the causes are the expectations and values that influence the decisions workers make about what kind of jobs to seek out and accept, then the best solution might be to focus on the experiences, conditions, social context, and so on that created these expectations and values. We will have more to say on this subject shortly.

Conclusion

Before summarizing the evidence concerning the negative consequences of job dissatisfaction and discussing the various strategies for alleviating this condition, it is important to note that not all of its consequences are inevitably undesirable. Several writers have pointed out that some dissatisfaction may be necessary to prevent complacency and the development of reluctance or inability on the part of individuals to change themselves (e.g., by acquiring new skills), their jobs, or job environments when necessary (Quinn et al., 1974; Seashore and Taber, 1976). In addition, organizations can benefit when dissatisfied workers leave to seek employment elsewhere, since it gives them the opportunity to inject "fresh blood" via new employees with different skills, ideas, and values, not to mention the greater enthusiasm they often bring to their new jobs. For many organizations faced with increasing limits on further growth (e.g., universities and colleges) the attrition of dissatisfied employees may be the only way to prevent eventual stagnation.

Nonetheless, the evidence does indicate some potentially serious societal and personal costs associated with job dissatisfaction. Although the relationships are generally not strong, reflecting the moderating influence of such other factors as individual differences, the overall picture does suggest that even the relatively small amount of dissatisfaction indicated at present is a situation we can ill afford to ignore. If we underestimate the problem and do nothing, we could be in far more trouble than if we overestimate and do something. In any case, statistics are small consolation to the many workers who experience their day-to-day work life as dull, demeaning, and insignificant. Furthermore, there are various indications, which will be discussed shortly, that the problem could get worse in the future. How to design jobs and organizations to increase satisfaction is, therefore, an issue that deserves serious and immediate attention.

The apparent relationship between the objective characteristics of the work itself and sociopolitical attitudes and behavior could be an additional impetus to action. In an increasingly complex, interdependent, and pluralistic society, tolerance for divergent points of view and a willingness and ability to participate in the sociopolitical processes of the society are the only ways to preserve democratic principles. If our work systems can be designed to help affect these principles, can we risk not taking advantage of the opportunity?

Whether it be to serve the frequently overlapping objectives of organizational effectiveness, individual quality of life, or societal change, strategies for changing jobs, organizations, and their social, cultural, political, and economic context should have a high priority in the research and policy agenda for the post-industrial society. Indeed, the nature of these strategies and their implications has been the focus of considerable interest and argument over the last several years, so we will now turn our attention to this important and frequently controversial topic.

Strategies for Increasing Job Satisfaction

In the last several years, managers, I/O psychologists and others have begun to move away from the early scientific management emphasis on job specialization, the breaking down of jobs into their simplest forms so that they would not tax worker's abilities, to the diametrically opposed idea of "enlarging" a job to utilize more fully a worker's skills and capacities. The idea of job enlargement, or job enrichment as it is increasingly called today (see Herzberg, 1968), is not as new as the recent attention and publicity would suggest. In fact, one of the first job enlargement programs was conducted at IBM in the late 1940s (see Walker, 1950 for a description of this program). The primary rationale for the early programs was based on the mistaken assumption that the job satisfaction resulting from more challenging and varied work would automatically increase worker productivity. Much of the new interest in job enlargement, on the other hand, has grown out of the recent focus on job satisfaction as a determiner of an individual's quality of life and of society's overall well-being (e.g., *Work in America*, 1973).

What job enlargement entails has been an issue of considerable controversy over the years. Originally, it meant the combining of several related tasks or activities, requiring approximately the same level and kind of skill, into a single job with the idea that an enlarged job would offer greater variety and would, therefore, be intrinsically more interesting and challenging than one that was highly specialized. Unfortunately, this was often interpreted as merely adding routine, fragmented tasks to other routine, fragmented tasks to create a "larger" job just as routine and not significantly less fragmented.

In response to the limitations of "horizontal" enlargement, as the process described above was frequently called, the aim of the more contemporary approaches is to enlarge jobs along the "vertical" dimension by adding tasks that cut across hierarchical levels to give workers more autonomy, responsibility, and control over their own work. This can be accomplished in a number of ways: by allowing workers to exercise more control over the pacing of their work; by giving them more discretion as to how the tasks may be performed; by permitting them to carry the work through more stages (inspection, maintenance, etc.) rather than having them do the same thing over and over; and by generally bringing the worker into the decision-making process in matters concerning their own work. It is worth noting that jobs enlarged in this way can also meet the objective of "horizontal" enlargement for increased task variety; that is, a worker who can plan, control, and carry his or her work through more stages has more varied tasks to perform.

One of the more widely heralded of the recent approaches to job enlargement, the autonomous work group or team, incorporates the "vertical" emphasis on increased control and discretion (for the group, at least, and, it is hoped, for the individual as well) while creating the potential for more variety and challenge. The basic idea underlying this concept is that groups of workers should be given responsibility for sufficiently large (i.e., "whole") tasks and allowed to exercise a fair degree of control over how the work is to be accomplished. In practice, this usually means that the workers as a group determine the distribution of the work among the group members and the layout and design of the individual jobs. In addition, the group is often responsible for checking the quality and quantity of the work performed by the members and by the group as a whole. In some cases the group may even be responsible for solving production problems involving the group, and make decisions concerning the promotion, disciplining, and hiring and firing of its members. The group members often elect their own leader from among themselves to serve as their spokesperson and act as a liason with supervisors and management personnel. Managers, supervisors, and support personnel (e.g., industrial engineers) act primarily as consultants and advisors, although management, in most cases, retains responsibility for making organizational decisions and determining the overall objectives and standards for the group.

In theory at least, the work group offers several advantages as a strategy for enlarging jobs. First, it provides workers with the opportunity to experience more variety in their jobs by allowing them to trade tasks with other group members whenever possible and desired. Second, because work groups generally have the responsibility for producing whole products or "meaningfully" large portions of products, the individual worker within the group may be less likely to feel that his or her work is fragmented and unconnected to an identifiable product. Furthermore, allowing workers to exercise some control over their immediate work situation enables them to design their work in a way that is more satisfying to them. Finally, since the people who perform the tasks often have the most insight into the best way of doing them, work groups (and any other approach that encourages and allows workers to exercise control over their jobs) can make good use of their knowledge concerning their work, a subject about which they should be particularly expert.

Another approach to the redesign of work systems that has also received a great deal of attention in recent years differs from the work group concept both at the level at which workers exercise control and the nature of the issues with which they deal. The *sine qua non* of this approach is the inclusion of workers into decisions affecting basic organizational policy. The expressions "industrial democracy," "workers' councils," and "participative management," among others, have all been used to describe widely differing degrees and manifestations of this approach. The systems employed may range from the use of employee suggestions to the actual management and ownership of the organization by the workers themselves, while the issues with which they deal can include everything from matters immediately related to their work to important policy decisions concerning wages, products, prices, or capital investment. The particular form these strategies take frequently reflect the political climates and ideologies of the countries in which they are implemented with the more radical end of the continuum (workers' management of industry) appearing most frequently in Yugoslavia and the Scandinavian countries where the rationale tends to focus on issues related to social equity and power sharing (Hunnius, Garson, and Case, 1973). In the United States, these approaches have generally been implemented on a smaller scale (both in terms of their incidence and the scope of the workers' involvement) and typically reflect the more pragmatic concerns for productivity and profit (see Jenkins, 1973).

The last strategy for the redesign of work systems to be described here— often used as part of a training program as well as an alternative to horizontal enlargement—is job rotation, a procedure in which an employee regularly changes jobs within a single organization. With this procedure it is possible to introduce variety into an employee's work experience if not in the particular job tasks themselves. In addition, if the rotation is from one job to a related job in a progressive series of movements, the worker may be better able to get a feeling for the total process involved in producing the good or service of which he or she is a part, acquire work experience with different but related job tasks, and develop a broader, more flexible repertoire of job skills as a result.

Frequently, more than one or all of the approaches described in the last few pages are used in combination to alter work and its organizational context on a more extensive scale. These approaches may also be supplemented with a variety of coordinated changes in other related aspects of the organization including the pay and benefits system, leadership styles, organizational rules and policies, production technology, interpersonal relations between co-workers, subordinates and supervisors, work schedules, information flow and communications, recruitment and selection, and training. The assumption underlying these broader, "systemic" change strategies is that the organization is a complex, interdependent "sociotechnical" system and that changes made in one aspect of the system will necessitate compensatory changes in others. For example, moving from assembly-line production to work groups puts greater demands on the interpersonal skills of the workers involved and can alter the nature of the relationships between supervisors and subordinates, and incorporating new technologies into production processes may require workers to exercise more responsibility and flexibility which, in turn, could necessitate changes in recruitment, selection, and training as well as in leadership styles, organizational policy, and rules concerning behavior, dress, and discipline. As Porter, Lawler, and Hackman (1975) note, the reverse is also true; existing conditions in one aspect of the organization can impose limits on the changes one can reasonably make in other aspects. They illustrate this by pointing out that organizations with most of the power and authority centralized at the top of the hierarchy and with relatively fixed and well-defined rules and procedures ("mechanistic" organizations) can not "enlarge jobs in what has been called a 'vertical' direction without disrupting the rational coordination of the organization" (p. 308). The reader may recognize the correspondence between this systemic approach to organizational change and the systems perspective described in Chapter 1.

In conclusion, from this brief review of strategies for the redesign of work systems one can see the wide variety of approaches that have been tried. The question is, of course, how successful have these experiments and programs been? Do they increase job satisfaction? What other effects do they have? Are some strategies better than others for achieving particular objectives? Do other factors moderate the impact of these strategies? Have general principles, guidelines, and prescriptions emerged from the many experiments and programs that have been implemented over the last several years? In the next section we summarize some of the relevant research and assessments of the impact of actual programs to begin to provide answers to these questions.

Conclusions from the Research

Evaluating the effectiveness of the many work redesign projects and experiments that have been conducted over the years and extracting general principles and guidelines from these efforts is an especially difficult task. For one thing, much of the evidence is anecdotal in nature and frequently consists of little more than company reports and journalistic accounts. For another, this evidence is typically based on case studies of actual programs where the opportunity for experimental manipulation and scientific observation is limited by the more immediate pragmatic concerns of the organizations in which they have been implemented. As a result, the kind of experimental control, systematic evaluation, and specification of goals needed to verify the subjective impression of those describing and evaluating the various programs rarely exists. In spite of these difficulties, however, comprehensive objective assessments of some of these programs have been supplemented with careful laboratory-based research to begin to provide answers to several of the questions posed above.

In general, the work redesign strategies described in the preceding section can lead to increased job satisfaction and improved work quality (Ford, 1969; Hackman and Lawler, 1971; Katzell and Yankelovich, 1975; Lawler, 1969; Srivastva et al., 1975). The relationship between job enrichment and quantity of production (e.g., number of items produced) is less clear, with the research suggesting that such other factors as performance feedback, collaboration

79

among co-workers, rewards based on performance, clearly defined and challenging goals, and improvement in the technological efficiency of the work flow are at least as important as changes in the work itself (Hackman, 1977; Katzell and Yankelovich, 1975; Srivastva et al., 1975; Umstot, Bell, and Mitchell, 1976).

Probably the most important result from the research on job redesign is the identification of some of the specific factors that appear to be most instrumental in improving work satisfaction and performance. The "core job dimensions" proposed and examined by Hackman and Oldham, listed below, are particularly noteworthy examples of the work content characteristics found to be associated with satisfaction and performance (1975 and 1976; Oldham, Hackman, and Pearce, 1976).

Skill variety. The degree to which a job requires a variety of different activities in carrying out the work, which involve the use of a number of different skills and talents of the employee.

Task identity. The degree to which the job requires completion of a "whole" and identifiable piece of work—that is, doing a job from beginning to end with a visible outcome.

Task significance. The degree to which the job has a substantial impact on the lives or work of other people—whether in the immediate organization or in the external environment.

Autonomy. The degree to which the job provides substantial freedom, independence, and discretion to the employee in scheduling the work and in determining the procedures to be used in carrying it out.

Feedback from the job itself. The degree to which carrying out the work activities required by the job results in the employee obtaining direct and clear information about the effectiveness of his or her performance. (Hackman and Oldham, 1975, pp. 161–162)

The relationships between their "core job dimensions" and work outcomes are illustrated in Figure 1.

These results, in effect, play down the role of specific work redesign strategies in improving satisfaction and performance and focus attention instead on the particular job characteristics these strategies should embody. For example, from these dimensions one would predict that strategies which increase workers' participation in decisions they perceive as having little impact on their jobs—and, therefore, little impact on their experienced *auton-*

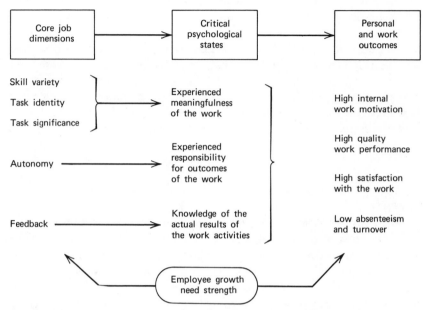

Figure 1. The job characteristics model. (From *Improving Life at Work: Behavioral Science Approaches to Organizational Change*, by J. Richard Hackman and J. Lloyd Suttle (p. 129). Copyright ©1977 by Goodyear Publishing Co. Reprinted by permission.)

omy—should be less effective than strategies that give them more control over their immediate work situation. And, in fact, this is just what the available evidence indicates (e.g., see Kohn, 1976; Lawler, 1969; Obradovic, 1970; Ramsay, 1976). The important point is that the job of the work designer is to select the appropriate mix of strategies, or invent new ones if necessary, which will structure jobs so that employees will experience as much of the core dimensions as possible (within the constraints imposed by the nature of the job, costs associated with alternative strategies, the need to coordinate with other employees, inflexible and expensive production technology, etc.)

Hackman and Oldham's research also indicates that there are at least two factors that moderate the relationship between the five core dimensions and satisfaction and performance. The first is the degree to which the employees are satisfied with the *organizational context of the job*. Specifically, Oldham et al., (1976) find that workers who are relatively satisfied with their pay, job security, and their co-workers and supervisors performed more effectively on jobs high on the core dimensions and derived more satisfaction from their job performance than workers who are not. The reader may recognize that this finding is consistent with the rationale underlying the "systemic" or "sociotechnical" approaches to work redesign described earlier, which emphasize the interdependencies between the work itself and its social and organizational context.

The other factor they identify is the degree to which employees desire personal development and growth in their work. That is, employees whose needs for growth and development are low are not likely to perform as well or derive as much satisfaction from work high on the core dimensions as those for whom these needs are more important. In fact, when low growth needs and dissatisfaction with the work context are both present, enlarged jobs can even lead to a decrement in performance.

The Role of Individual Differences

The last result described above is especially important because it relates to one of the most heated controversies surrounding the implementation of work redesign strategies. The essence of this controversy centers on the general applicability of job enlargement; in other words, do all or almost all employees desire work that is meaningful and provides feedback and autonomy, or are there significant and pervasive individual differences in the way workers respond to certain kinds of jobs?

Over the years, the individual differences hypothesis has been supported by a considerable body of research (Brief and Aldag, 1975; Dubin and Champoux, 1977; Hulin and Blood, 1968; Robey, 1974; Vroom, 1960; Wanous, 1974). This research, along with the previously mentioned studies by Goldthorpe et al. (1969) and Quinn et al. (1974), indicates that some workers do not desire opportunities for growth and personal development in their work but tend, instead, to view their jobs as "a provider of means for pursuing extra-occupational goals" (Blood and Hulin, 1967, p. 285). The primary means, of course, are salary, job security, and fringe benefits.

On the other hand, several studies of more recent origin suggest that these differences may not be as large or as immutable as the evidence cited above indicates (Abdel-Halim and Rowland, 1976; Hackman and Oldham, 1976; Ruble, 1976; Stone, 1976; Susman, 1973). Although employees with strong growth needs seem to be the most receptive to enlarged jobs, in these studies *even those whose needs for work autonomy, meaning, and feedback were weak responded positively to jobs with these characteristics.*

Moreover, it has been suggested that these needs, values, and orientations may be partly a function of the nature of an individual's previous job experience (Hackman and Oldham, 1976; Kohn and Schooler, 1973; Kornhauser, 1965). As a result of these experiences, many workers may have learned that they cannot expect growth opportunities in their jobs and have learned to devalue these opportunities and focus their concerns on its extrinsic rewards. Furthermore, these expectations may be reinforced by their perceptions of the work experiences and orientations of their parents, peers, and others with similar socioeconomic and educational backgrounds (Blood and Hulin, 1967; Goldthorpe et al., 1969; Kohn, 1969; McCall and Lawler, 1976; Payton-Miyazaki and Brayfield, 1976). Given these circumstances it is easy to understand why many workers envision for themselves no alternative to a tightly supervised, repetitive job or cannot identify with the alternatives that do exist, especially if their present jobs offer some degree of monetary and interpersonal satisfaction.

If it is true that "instrumental" expectations, values, and needs are to some degree a result of job experiences and behaviors, then it seems reasonable to assume that work orientations can be altered in the opposite direction as well, that is, toward more emphasis on growth satisfaction, by redesigning jobs in an appropriate fashion. To use Hackman and Oldham's words:

> It may be that individuals' needs _change_ or adjust to meet the demands of the situation in which they find themselves. Thus, the needs of an individual may actually become more "growth oriented" when he is confronted with a complex job which seems to demand that the individual develop himself and exercise independent thought and action in his work. (1976, p. 275)

If correct, the implications of this conclusion are far-reaching. First, the relatively low levels of job dissatisfaction reported by the national surveys reviewed earlier could be explained by the possibility that workers who have had little previous experience with growth-oriented jobs may have learned _not_ to expect these opportunities in their work and adjusted their values accordingly.

More importantly, it also suggests a strategy for breaking up the vicious cycle in which workers are socialized by their work experiences and their perceptions of the experiences, values, and norms of their parents, peers, and social class to expect and seek the kinds of jobs and life styles that reinforce their "alienated" and consumption-oriented expectations and values. That strategy, of course, would be to redesign their jobs to facilitate the development of stronger growth-related attitudes and behaviors.

The author feels some uneasiness over this last point. On the one hand, it appears to reflect a moral and ideological judgment of what workers _should_ want from their jobs and the way they _should_ live their lives. If these judgments

83

were the only rationale for redesigning jobs, the author would be far less inclined to suggest and support this strategy. However, the desire for materially affluent life styles would be incompatible with a resource-limited world and a possible source of destructive societal conflict and tension. In addition, as noted earlier there may be a relationship between social and political passivity and restrictive jobs—a passivity that is increasingly inappropriate, even dangerous, in a highly complex and interdependent democratic society where the political participation of as many citizens as possible is necessary to insure the preservation of democratic principles. Under these circumstances, what may appear at first glance to be a moral judgment might eventually turn out to be a societal imperative.

This line of argument is disconcerting because it implies that forcing or coercing employees into accepting enlarged jobs, even when they express satisfaction with their present circumstances, is justified by the potential societal benefits and the possibility that they may eventually like these jobs better than their former ones. Lawler (1976a) offers an important perspective on this particularly thorny issue:

> even if an individual who is coerced to try an enriched job finds that he or she likes it, the whole experience may simply reinforce the person's feelings of dependency. In order for persons to gain increasing feelings of independence and experience psychological success, they must feel personally responsible for their behavior. Individuals who are coerced into trying things rarely feel that they are in control. Quite to the contrary they feel that once again someone has successfully showed them what is best, thereby causing them to experience psychological failure.
>
> In this writer's view, there is also an ethical issue involved here—that psychologists must avoid deciding what is best for people. Otherwise we will end up taking a manipulative role. This suggests that individuals should be given valid data about what kind of job situation exists but that, in the end, they must decide without coercion to try the situation. (p. 204)

Indeed, one could even argue that to be consistent with the intent of job enlargement to give employees more control over their work, it is necessary to accept the possibility that some workers may choose *not* to accept more autonomy and responsibility in their jobs. This noncoercive approach may also remove one of the objections to job enlargement by organized labor, the "unilateral method of imposing new techniques upon the workers" (Wallick, 1973, p. 17) that job enlargement has too often meant.

84

The dilemma posed by all these considerations has no simple solution. Fortunately, the choice is not always, or even frequently, between coercion/imposition and nothing. A more gradual, participatory compromise is often possible. For example, for those workers who express more interest in the extrinsic rewards of their work than in the degree of challenge and autonomy it offers, resolving their existing dissatisfactions with pay, job security, relations with co-workers and supervisors, and other aspects of organizational policy and the work context should probably precede any attempts to enlarge work content (Dyer, 1976; Dunham, 1977; Oldham, 1976; Oldham, Hackman, and Pearce, 1976). Assuaging workers' and their unions' fear of layoffs if the redesign should increase productivity is another consideration that should precede the actual implementation of job changes. Involving the workers who will be affected by the work restructuring in the design, planning, implementation, and evaluation of the change effort is an additional factor that can also reduce resistance, increase motivation, and enable the project to profit from the workers' first-hand knowledge of their jobs (e.g., see Srivastva et al., 1975). And, finally, the gradual introduction of job changes tailored as much as possible to the rate at which an individual develops more confidence, proficiency, and interest in more challenging work might considerably reduce initial opposition to these changes. Some day almost everyone may desire more challenge and responsibility in their jobs. Until then, when necessary and to the extent it is feasible to do so, individual differences in responses to and preferences for various work characteristics should be recognized, respected, and accommodated while keeping open the option for future change.

Toward a Technology for Designing Jobs and Organizations

In effect, the conclusion reached above is consistent with the theme of the last chapter, the achieving of a *correspondence* between employees and jobs for the purpose of maximizing the utilization of human resources to increase both satisfaction and performance. The difference is in the approaches emphasized; in Chapter 2 the focus was on selection, counseling, placement, and training *to fit the worker to the job;* in this chapter the focus is on *changing the job to fit the worker.* These approaches are certainly not incompatible. Indeed, the argument being made here is that they are complementary approaches, capable of being integrated into a practical and systematic strategy where aspects of each are implemented and combined in various degrees and combinations to optimize worker/job correspondence. For example, one can reasonably envision a computerized counseling/placement service, similar to the one described in

Chapter 2 but with an added capability for indicating possible changes in job design, that could provide all job applicants with job-related information about themselves, the nature of the organizations looking for employees, and the kinds of jobs and work situations the various organizations are able to provide or create compatible with the applicants' needs, personalities, and capacities. If, on the basis of this information, a correspondence between the applicant and a particular organization appears to be possible, individualized training and job design—with the worker playing an important role in the design of his or her own work situation—would be the next step.

Some of the essential ingredients of this system already exist or are presently under development, particularly the analysis and description of jobs and human characteristics for a variety of work-related purposes (e.g., Dunnette, 1976; Fine, 1974; Fleishman, 1975; Gough, 1976; Holland, 1976; McCormick, 1976) and the analytical and diagnostic techniques for linking redesign strategies, job characteristics, individual differences, and attitudes and behavior (e.g., Hackman and Oldham, 1975; Hackman, Oldham, Janson and Purdy, 1975; Walters and Associates, 1975). To make this system truly effective, especially in light of the interdependencies between job designs and their organizational context, it would be necessary to add such situational factors as supervisory styles, interpersonal context (e.g., individual vs. group work), production technology, compensation system, organizational climate (employees' perceptions of organizational practices, conditions, etc.), and work schedules (more on this in Chapter 4) to the set of descriptors upon which job/person matches might be made (e.g., Moos and Insel, 1974; Payne and Pugh, 1976).

Much of this might sound hopelessly, even naively utopian if it were not for the fact that approximations to this system—albeit very rough approximations—have been implemented or proposed in a number of situations. For example, a social technology for organizational change, often referred to under the general rubric of "organizational development," has been growing rapidly for several years. The elements of this technology include programs for increasing the interpersonal competence of co-workers and supervisors, modifying hierarchical structures, organizational rules and production processes, as well as for redesigning jobs in the ways described in this chapter. These programs are integrated and implemented in various ways for the purpose of changing organizational values, goals, and policies to improve the effectiveness and adaptability of the organization to the changing environments and demands of the contemporary world. In effect, the successful application of these strategies frequently results in more flexible organizations that can accommodate a wider range of individual needs, attitudes and behaviors (see Bennis, 1969; and Beer, 1976).

86

Other strategies for "individualizing organizations" have been proposed in recent years although this author is not aware of any significantly large scale attempts to implement these proposals. For example, Kahn (1973) proposes the development of "work modules" of two hours or more that could be combined to form a person's job. The number and particular combination of modules would be a function of the worker's preferences and the needs of the employer. Sandler (1974) recommends extending the cafeteria approach, in which employees select among several pay and fringe benefit options, to include such other aspects of the organization as workweeks and job designs. He suggests that employees could switch from one option to another as their needs change, as well as aid in the development of new options, thereby helping the organization evolve.

Similarly, Lawler (1976a) proposes the creation of relatively autonomous subunits within the organization having approximately the same function but varying widely in their climate, leadership styles, job designs, compensation systems, and so on. Matches could then be made between individuals and appropriate subunits within the same organization. Although it would be impractical to create options to represent all possible combinations of job designs, compensation systems, and organizational climates, Lawler points out that several factors would limit the number and kinds of subunits an organization might need. For example, the type of product and market would restrict the kind of subunits that are feasible (e.g., authoritarian management, routine jobs, and rigidly defined, hierarchial bureaucratic structures may not be effective for marketing a technically sophisticated product in a rapidly changing environment). In addition, by studying the labor market to see what types of workers the organization is likely to attract, an organization can determine the kinds of subunits that would be needed to fit the majority of them. Personnel selection procedures could be used to help fit individuals into the appropriate subunits, or organizations could give job applicants information about the nature of the subunits available and allow them to decide where they would most likely fit. A recent study supports the feasibility of this last suggestion (Giles, 1977), and the reader may recognize that it is a reflection of the counseling/placement approach described in Chapter 2.

A final example is provided by Sidney Fine's work on the development and application of an extensive job analysis approach to the design of individualized "new careers" for the disadvantaged (Fine, 1967 and 1969). His work suggests the possibility that a job design technology could be used to put together from "scratch" jobs that would match an individual's unique needs and circumstances as well as fulfill important and productive functions. That this job "invention" technology would be particularly appropriate in the design of the public service jobs proposed in Chapter 2 is further suggested by Fine's application of his technique for essentially this purpose.

Conclusion: For the foreseeable future, the enlargement or individualization of all jobs and organizations must remain a utopian ideal; the complete realization of this ideal, the end state, is ultimately unattainable. But it is not the end state that is important, especially in a dynamic society where conditions, and even ideals, constantly change. What is important are the improvements in the circumstances and experiences of human existence that the pursuit of this ideal can bring about.

In the final section of this chapter we will identify several reasons why work may have to be more responsive to human individuality in the future. We will also see the emergence of opportunities for designing work and organizations that would be more responsive to these human needs. The ability of I/O psychology to anticipate, plan for, and take advantage of these developments and opportunities will play a crucial role in the process of designing a future which at least approximates these utopian ideals.

Alternative Futures for Work

Chapter 2 explored the educational implications of several potential future trends. In this section, we examine these trends once more but from the perspective of their future impact on the nature of work, work organizations, and job satisfaction. Other relevant trends and potential developments will also be discussed in the pages to follow.

It is important to keep in mind that the objective is to *project alternative possibilities and not to predict future certainties.* Alternatives other than those presented here are possible but the focus will be on those that at the present time appear to be most likely. Although "surprises" that would profoundly alter the nature of these forecasts can occur—for example, worldwide economic collapse, nuclear war, widespread natural disasters—the severity of their impact would so threaten civilization as we know it now that the work-related implications would be unimportant by comparison, at least until the more immediate problems of survival are resolved. Nonetheless, the impact of serious although not catastrophic developments—continued resource scarcities, in particular—will be considered when appropriate.

The discussion will be organized into two principal sections: the first dealing with factors that could significantly influence job dissatisfaction in the future and their implications for the design of work, the second exploring factors that could facilitate the redesign of work systems to counteract this potential growth in dissatisfaction.

88

Rising Expectations, Decreasing Opportunities

In Chapter 2 we noted a growing disjunction between the supply of the jobs generally considered to be the most attractive in our economy—the administrative, technical, and professional categories—and the demand for them as indicated by the number of individuals seeking the higher education these jobs typically require. In other words, many college-educated workers may find it necessary to accept jobs that do not enable them to use their education to an appreciable degree and offer less pay, status, and advancement opportunity than they expect or desire. The potential mismatch between expectations and reality and the dissatisfaction it would engender could be accentuated by the heightened expectations typically associated with increased educational levels (Seybolt, 1976) and by a continuation of the recent trends that point to a growing desire among students and younger workers for more meaning, autonomy, career advancement opportunities, and financial rewards in their work (Gottlieb, 1975; Yankelovich, 1974).

As was also noted in Chapter 2, many of the college-educated workers who are not able to find jobs commensurate with their education may offer more competition to less educated workers for the most attractive jobs traditionally available to the latter group. Furthermore, the overabundance of college-educated workers may lead some employers to upgrade their job requirements regardless of the actual skill levels needed for effective job performance, and make it even more difficult for the less educated to acquire the more desirable jobs compatible with their skills. The one hopeful note for less educated workers in this otherwise dismal scenario is the possibility that the trend away from ''credentialism'' and the use of nonvalidated educational standards in personnel selection could tend to restrain this unwarranted inflation of job requirements. In addition, many employers may decide not to hire overqualified employees who might be more dissatisfied with their jobs and require higher salaries, especially when employees with less education would be able to perform as well. Of course, while this possibility would ease the plight of the less educated worker, it would do so at the expense of those with more education, making their already difficult situation even worse. In any case, the prospects are not encouraging.

There are several potential developments that could help to alleviate this problem. For example,

1. As Rosenthal (1973) notes, high school students may ''become aware of the plight of new college graduates who are not able to enter the field of their choice and, thereby, change their aspiration for a college education'' (p. 25).

He adds, however, that because "current society esteems a college degree and recognizes the benefit of a college education to aspects of life other than work, such changed aspirations are not anticipated in great numbers" (p. 25). This conclusion is reinforced by a recent study which indicates that going to college may have a substantially beneficial impact on a person's marital relationship, health, and childrearing, leisure and civic behavior (Bowen, 1977).

2. The threat of unemployment could also lead some students and younger workers to lower their expectations and feel fortunate just to have a job regardless of how underutilized their skills may be. One must wonder, nevertheless, about the psychic costs that may attend such personal compromises, not to mention the waste of human resources it would represent.

3. The increased availability of unemployment insurance and other forms of income maintenance, the improved mobility of the labor force, the rising number of families with two wage earners, and the growing interest in leisure and more flexible life styles could lead some workers to drop out of traditional career paths entirely, especially if the jobs along the way are relatively unsatisfying and the chances of advancing into more desirable positions are increasingly blocked. They might, instead, try to create careers or enterprises of their own, working just long enough in relatively low-skill, unattractive, uninvolving but easy-to-get jobs—particularly, if these jobs begin to offer more opportunity for flexible and part-time work scheduling—to pay off bills, purchase a desired item, set up a "grub-stake" to support more personally important vocational or avocational ends, or establish eligibility for unemployment insurance (e.g., see Feldstein, 1973; Munts and Garfinkel, 1974).

4. The possibility of a financially secure, comfortable, and fulfilling retirement (discussed in Chapter 4) and the increased availability of meaningful new careers and opportunities for voluntary service to the community (Chapter 2) could induce more workers to retire early and, as a result, open up a number of attractive high-level jobs for younger workers. These inducements to early retirement could become even more necessary to compensate for the effects of recent legislation raising the mandatory retirement age and the eventual elimination of all mandatory retirement rules. While the number of workers choosing to remain in their jobs past the traditional retirement age of 65 is not expected to be large enough to severely exacerbate the employment and career advancement problems of younger workers in general, delayed retirement from the most desirable jobs would most likely be more prevalent and could create a problem of a more specific nature.

5. As described in Chapter 2, the large-scale creation of professional-level jobs for the potentially underemployed college graduate and paraprofessional jobs for those with less education would help to alleviate the problem considerably.

If these developments do not occur on a sufficiently large scale, it may become necessary to offset potentially significant gains in worker dissatisfaction and compensate for decreased upward mobility by redesigning many jobs to bring them more in line with the escalating educational levels of the workforce and the greater importance more highly educated workers attach to jobs that challenge and develop their skills (Quinn and Baldi de Mandelovich, 1975). Employers may also find it advantageous to restructure low-skill, low-status jobs to keep job vacancies and turnover down to acceptable levels, especially if the developments and trends described in point 3 above make it difficult to attract and hold workers in these positions (see Wool, 1976). Furthermore, the need to accommodate more diverse individual needs, behaviors, characteristics, and circumstances may receive an additional impetus from the growing number of women, minorities, and other special groups (e.g., the physically and mentally handicapped) seeking to enter the labor force in the next several years. The growth of multinational organizations could further increase this diversity as workers from different countries and cultures continue to cross international boundaries in their pursuit of work.

Societal and Technological Change as a Catalyst for Worklife Improvement

The impact of technology: The work-related effects of technological change, particularly in the form of automation, has been the subject of considerable controversy and concern for many years. Early fears (hopes) that technology would lead to mass unemployment (leisure) now appear somewhat simplistic, particularly in light of the moderating effect of economic variables, societal values, managerial decisions, organizational policy, and specific engineering design considerations (Bowen and Mangum, 1966; Davis and Taylor, 1975 and 1976; Kreps and Spengler, 1966). Nonetheless, since technological change and automation, in combination with these other factors, can have a significant impact on many other aspects of the world of work, assessing the potential effects remains an important if complex task. Despite the difficulties associated with forecasting the work-related implications of technological change (e.g., see Fechter, 1975), certain general trends do appear evident. As De Greene (1975) notes:

91

The consensus of experts is that the long-term effects of automation and technological change will be: (1) the elimination of jobs and occupations based on the lowest abilities and skills (however imprecisely these might be defined and measured); (2) parallel growth of professional, technical, and white-collar work; (3) a need to upgrade higher level skills to continually avoid technological obsolescence; and (4) a continued shift from emphasis on the production of goods to the performance of services. (p. 53)

From their own research and their extensive reviews of the research of others, Louis Davis and James C. Taylor have been able to add considerably more detail to these general conclusions (see Davis and Taylor, 1975 and 1976; Taylor, 1974). They assume that sudden mass unemployment due to technological change is unlikely to occur in the foreseeable future; they argue, therefore, that the most important effects of "post-industrial technology in organizations are on the design of jobs" (1976, p. 387) and their social and organizational context. The nature of these effects, according to Davis and Taylor, derives from the impact of advanced technology on the traditional roles workers have played in production processes. Rather than supply energy, guide tools, and perform routine activities, as have been their principal functions in the past, workers in more advanced production systems are increasingly involved in the control and regulation of the work and the diagnosis and adjustment of malfunctions. Since the conditions of work under these emerging conditions are stochastic and not deterministic (i.e., "important" events are randomly occurring and unpredictable), the worker must be able, in effect, to counteract the unexpected with a minimal degree of supervision. To reduce system downtime, workers may even have to learn how to anticipate faults and develop alternative strategies for corrective action well in advance of systems' malfunctions. As a consequence of these conditions, Davis and Taylor conclude that:

First, the workers must have a large repertoire of response, because the specific intervention that will be required in any one instance is not known. Second, they cannot be dependent on supervision for direction because they must respond immediately to events that occur irregularly and without warning. Third, they must be committed to undertaking the necessary tasks on their own initiative. (1976, pp. 388–389)

Davis and Taylor's review of the research tends to support their hypotheses although some important qualifications are indicated. In general, they find that automated production technology does tend to reduce the need for traditional motor skills and increases the requirement for such perceptual and decision-making skills as the ability to respond rapidly in emergencies and to detect, diagnose, and repair malfunctions. They also find that automated technology is apparently more compatible with autonomous work group functioning than with single jobs. The research, therefore, tentatively indicates that advanced technology is associated with increased responsibility and discretion in individual jobs as well as in the autonomous work groups this technology may engender.

Changes in the supervisory and organizational context also appear to be associated with more technologically sophisticated production systems. As Taylor (1974) notes:

> *The trend with advanced technology is in the direction of supervisors doing less in the way of traditional management—supervising behaviors of others, attending to selection or training functions, and the like—and more in the way of acting as a facilitator, boundary controller, and communications link for the work group, or becoming more technically skilled operators themselves . . . at more sophisticated levels of technology (automation), conventional notions of work and skills no longer apply. Workers, individually or in groups, supervise machines or processes, so that the conventional notion of supervision is no longer applicable. (pp. 4–5)*

Davis and Taylor (1975) conclude further, albeit tentatively, that "modern technologies are associated with flexible, adaptive, more formless organizations . . . or with bureaucracy based on a consensus and sense of industrial community" (p. 408).

In spite of these conclusions, Davis and Taylor carefully reject the role of "technological determinism" in the composition of jobs and organizations, since there appears to be enough flexibility in the design of the technologies and the social and organizational systems in which they are embedded to make possible a wide range of outcomes. The actual impact of technological change is as much a function of management ideology, especially as reflected in the specific design of the technology itself and of the associated work processes and content, as of the general level of sophistication the technology embodies. In other words, the assumptions about human nature held by the designers and managers of the sociotechnical systems that comprise the organization, for example, workers viewed as "cogs in a wheel," will guide these designs, and the observed impact of the technology on individuals and jobs will, in turn, tend to confirm their assumptions.

A recent study by Rousseau (1977) illustrates this point by demonstrating how the particular design of the work process and organizational context may moderate the relationship between the level of technological sophistication and the nature of the job. Among the organizations examined in her study she found autonomy and task identity to be higher in the organizations in the "mediating" category (an intermediate level of technological sophistication) than those in the technologically advanced "intensive" category. Rousseau speculates that this result may have been a function of the structures and policies of the particular organizations she sampled.

In this sample, nurses were the predominant group of employees in the intensive category and the resulting mean job characteristic levels may be due to the authority structure of hospitals. Nurses may experience more routinization in their work due to the concentration of problem-solving behavior in the role of the physician. (p. 40)

Furthermore,

the relatively high Task Identity in mediating organizations, in contrast to intensive technologies, may be a function of the work assignment practices in intensive organizations. For example, nurses in this study reported that the assignment of patients to nurses on the basis of proximity and load regardless of a nurse's past experience with a particular patient was a source of dissatisfaction. (p. 40)

Davis and Taylor's reviews of the research further illustrate the fallacy of "technological determinism" by identifying several studies that are not consistent with the conclusions described earlier, an inconsistency that increases as they move from the relatively specific topic of individual jobs and skills to the more diffuse topic of organizational structure. The reason for this, they suggest, is that it is easier for management to accept changes in individual jobs than it is for them to tolerate modifications of group arrangements and, especially, of organizational control structures, "since such modifications come even closer to touching the organizational life space of managers themselves" (1975, p. 233).

The point of all this is that, as Davis and Taylor note, the flexibility associated with advanced production technologies "presents us with a number of opportunities to develop new, more humane organizational forms and jobs leading to a higher quality of working life" (1975, p. 236). However, if we use industrial age values and assumptions to guide the design and implementation of these post-industrial technologies, the opportunities will be lost. Given the

94

recent forecasts of widespread underemployment and job dissatisfaction described in the preceding section, the importance of taking advantage of and planning for these opportunities has never been greater.

The journey to work: In the pre-industrial era the home was in close proximity to the workplace. However, with the growth of urbanization and, especially, the widespread availability of the automobile, people's residences and places of employment have become separated by greater and greater distances. Today, traffic congestion, air and noise pollution, continued growth in the consumption of limited fuel resources, the use of valuable land for freeways and parking lots, and the inequities suffered by those without access to adequate transportation are among the many problems that have come to be identified with the journey to work.

It is frequently proposed that we solve these problems by developing more efficient, convenient and comfortable public transit systems to lure people away from their dependence on the private automobile. The proposed alternatives have taken many forms: fixed-rail mass and personal rapid transit, the expansion of more flexible bus systems including even more flexible "dial-a-bus" services, the greater use of jitneys and taxicabs, to mention just a few.

In addition to providing attractive alternatives to the private automobile, incentives for using these facilities and disincentives for using private automobiles have also been employed to encourage people to shift to public transportation. Reducing fares on public transit especially during off-peak hours to stimulate non-rush hour use of these facilities, raising automobile tolls on bridges and tunnels, placing a toll charge on freeways, reducing tolls for automobiles carrying more than one passenger, and eliminating or taxing all-day parking in cities are all examples of the kinds of incentives and disincentives that have been tried or considered. Incentives for more efficient use of automobiles by car pooling have also been proposed and implemented, e.g., reserving special freeway and feeder lanes for express buses and cars with a minimum number of passengers. Promotion campaigns advertising the benefits of public transit, and educational programs and the dissemination of information on how to use these facilities are additional methods used to change people's attitudes toward public transportation. Of course, none of the approaches (singly or in combination) will be successful unless the facilities are available to provide the kind of service that would represent an attractive alternative to the one person per vehicle use of the automobile.

A recent analysis of the problems of public transportation indicates that even the thoughtful application of the approaches suggested above may not significantly reduce private automobile use in many situations ("Where Transit Works," 1976). This study argues, instead, that only by changing land-use policies and urban development patterns will public transportation ever be able to reduce the need for highways, increase the mobility of those who cannot drive, reduce pollution, and conserve energy. Specifically, they conclude that people will be more likely to use public transportation:

1.   the higher the density and the larger the size of a downtown or another cluster of nonresidential activity [employment];

2.   the closer their neighborhood is to that nonresidential concentration;

3.   the higher the residential density of their neighborhood;

4.   the better the transit service.

The density . . . of the nonresidential concentration is most important. The distance is second in importance. High residential density by itself will do little for transit if there is no dominant place to go. (p. 7)

In other words, the best strategy for solving the journey-to-work problem might be to reverse the tendency for our cities and suburbs to sprawl out over large areas and concentrate future development in places where people and jobs already exist—in effect, to bring work and home closer together.

Additional advantages of urban "clustering" are that it allows more efficient delivery of social and municipal services (e.g., police and fire protection, sanitation) and would allow us to set aside more land for wildlife conservation, recreation, and agriculture. Furthermore, earlier fears that high population densities cause pathological behavior (e.g., see Galle, Gove, and McPherson, 1972) have not been supported; more recent research indicates the influence of other factors on this relationship (Freedman, 1976; Lawrence, 1974; Stokols, 1976). Indeed, some writers have even argued that higher urban densities can produce diversity and vitality, are able to support a variety of businesses and enterprises, and can lead to positive interpersonal experiences as well (e.g., Jacobs, 1961; Soleri, 1969). Unfortunately, empirical evidence that either supports or refutes these claims is hard to find.

There is another strategy for solving journey-to-work problems that is similar to clustering in that it focuses more on land use planning and development than on transportation systems but differs in the sense that it leads to an almost diametrically opposite result. Instead of encouraging higher employment concentrations in urban centers, this strategy emphasizes the *decentralization* of organizations to bring them closer to where people live.

There are two general approaches to decentralization, approaches that are not necessarily mutually exclusive. The first includes various proposals for the

96

development of relatively self-sufficient communities that contain drastically scaled-down and autonomous work organizations. These organizations would be loosely modeled after pre-industrial craft and cottage industries and use production systems, energy sources, and technologies that are "appropriate" to the size and resources of the enterprise and local community (see Goodman and Goodman, 1960; Schumacher, 1973). In addition, workers would live nearby and be principal consumers of the products of these organizations. Because of the reduced scale of these enterprises and the communities of which they would be part, the production processes would be more labor- and less capital- intensive than those in larger industries, more emphasis would be placed on recycling and the use of renewable resources (e.g., solar and wind energy), and there would be more opportunity for community and worker control.

The overall, perhaps somewhat overidealized picture is of a village marked by a casual pace, social cohesiveness, and clean air. The work and nonwork lives of individuals and the community in general would be highly integrated and, with particular reference to the topic at hand, the distances between workplaces, shops, recreational facilities, and residences would be small enough to be traversed on foot or by bicycle. Of course, all of this could not be achieved without sacrificing some material affluence and the excitement, diversity, and pulse of city life.

"Telecommuting" as an alternative to travel: A problem with the approach outlined above is that most organizations would be unwilling to scale down their operations to the appropriate size or break themselves up into completely independent smaller units with no formal overarching ties. What they will do, and have been doing for some time, is divide their operations into subunits, branch offices, and the like which can then be located in local communities, suburbs, and adjoining towns. Rather than a single monolithic office located in the downtown area of a major city, organizations have begun to open up outlying satellite offices with formal functional ties to the pared down central offices that remain in the urban centers. In effect, this moves jobs to where people live instead of the other way around. This development is limited, however, by the need for people and groups within an organization to be physically present in order to work with other people and groups, operate machinery, transfer materials, and so on.

Increasingly, though, the machinery, materials, and interactions are becoming information-based. That is, information in its various forms comprise the "stuff" upon which much, if not most, post-industrial work systems operate. Insurance, banking, education, government, the media, and many of the clerical and administrative functions of other industries involve the acquisition, processing, and dissemination of information and knowledge. Since the sub-

97

stance of these work processes (information) are abstractions and not physical materials, the processes themselves are less dependent on the inflexible machinery and manufacturing systems that characterize most industrial age organizations. Therefore, as industrial and business operations become more information-based and more widely use the new sophisticated technologies for processing and transmitting information, the design of work systems could have unprecedented flexibility. For example, because new communications systems make it easier to access, process, and transmit data from various remote locations, it would not be necessary for all employees to be physically present in one central location at the same time. The emerging information-based character and technology of the post-industrial economy makes it possible for more organizations to decentralize their operations by placing offices and workshops in the communities where workers live without losing the functional integration needed for effective performance.

This decentralization can take several forms: Neighborhood centers within walking distance or a short commute from workers homes linked via telecommunications with a downtown central office; a network of neighborhood centers offering services to a number of organizations and clients much like the secretarial, legal, and answering services that have begun to appear in recent years; employees of different organizations using the same local centers thereby enabling these organizations to share the costs of the communications hardware; a nationwide network of interrelated organizations, divisions, and individuals linked via telecommunications; and even the possibility that employees could work from their homes using terminals linked to a central office or processing facility. There are other possibilities, of course, but these are among the most frequently mentioned (see Nilles, Carlson, Gray, and Hanneman, 1976).

The following scenarios illustrate some of the potential uses, forms, and activities of telecommunications. They are presented in order of increasing likelihood, in the opinion of their author (Gray, 1973), with the fourth depicting a system already in operation in the United Kingdom.

Scenario I: *You wake up in the morning, wash, shave, and have breakfast. You dress in your casual clothes and head into your den. You turn on your data screen and your video phone. You are at work. You don't travel downtown to your office nor do you travel home in the evening through rush hour. All the information you need is at your fingertips and is available to you on your data screen. You can dictate to a central typing pool. You can insert information into the company files. You can contact any other executive in your company instantly. You can switch into a conference mode. . . .*

Scenario II: *It is the second day of your three-day semi-annual national professional society meeting. You leave your house and go to the Downtown Convention Center. Yours is one of twenty national meetings going on simultaneously in the Center. The meeting room contains thirty other people almost all of whom work within a fifteen mile radius. You are inter-connected with forty other cities where similar groups meet. On the screen in front of you is a picture of the current speaker larger than life. He is five hundred miles away. When he finishes, questions are directed at him from six different locations. Faces of the questioners are shown on a split screen. The next speaker is from two thousand miles away. The one to follow him happens to be in your room. Since you have heard the local man talk before on this subject, you head out into the "Lobby." The "Lobby" is a separate room in which some forty different pictures are being shown simultaneously. Each of these multiple pictures shows the "Lobby" at the other meeting centers. Looking around, you see your former colleague Joe Snyder who is now on the east coast. You send a message to tell him you would like to talk. You walk over to the video phone booth, are connected, and have an informal talk about what he is doing and what you are doing. The booth is provided with blackboard, chalk, viewgraph projector and other technological aids for communication. . . .*

Scenario III: *It is the morning rush hour and throughout the neighborhood mothers are busy preparing their children to go off to school. Then, about 8:15 many of them get into their vehicles or walk to the local shopping center. However, their objective is not to go shopping but to go to work. They enter the local office of Honesty Insurance Company. This office is one of many scattered around the city by this company. Each office performs specific clerical functions related to the five million insurance policies that Honesty maintains in this region. This particular group is concerned with accident claims. They receive many of their data inputs from customers through a local post office lock box. One of their tasks is to convert their input into records that are transmitted to the Company's central computer. They also have to deal with a series of transactions that have been initiated either by other offices or by the computer itself. These are waiting for them when they arrive since they were transmitted on an overnight basis. This office has twelve workers plus a supervisor. The work force in this office is slightly smaller than average, some centers having as few as eight and some as many as twenty-five. Work proceeds through the day. Around 2:30 a number of the clerks leave to return*

99

home to meet their children and at about 3 o'clock a new group, consisting of high schoolers, come in for part time employment. . . .

Scenario IV: *Four executives in London and three in Glasgow head for the local headquarters of the Post Office. They enter the studios of the new "Confravision" service being offered by the Post Office for business meetings between major cities. They sit down at a table in front of microphones. Special overhead cameras are available for displaying charts and graphs. Stereo sound is provided so that participants at each end can easily identify who is speaking. Each participant sees all others. A 30 minute meeting is held and it is agreed that Glasgow would take additional marketing responsibilities in central Scotland. The meeting is adjourned and the executives head back to their offices. . . . (Gray, 1973, pp. 1–2)*

Another possible application with particularly unique characteristics, potential and consequences—the computer conference—is described below by Murray Turoff, one of the pioneers in the development of this concept.

At its simplest level, computer conferencing is a written form of a conference telephone call. Using a computer terminal, a person can talk to a group of people by typing messages and reading, on a display screen or a printout, what the other people are saying. The computer automatically informs the group when someone joins or leaves the discussion. When a person signs off, the computer marks his location in the discussion and picks up at that point when he rejoins the conference. Computer conferencing differs from verbal communication in some very important ways. People engaged in computer conferencing can be both geographically and chronologically dispersed. In computer conferencing, everyone may "talk" or "listen" at the same time. A person can make his contribution to the discussion at his own convenience, rather than having to wait until other speakers have finished. He can work at his own pace, taking as much or as little time as he needs to read, contemplate, or reply. He can "leave" the conference at any time, knowing that the computer will store all of the messages that he has missed and show them to him whenever he is ready. Each message is assigned a number and labeled with author, date, and time for easy identification and retrieval. Computer conferencing is a truly self-activating form of communication. ("The Future of Computer Conferencing," 1975, pp. 182–183)

Using the computer in this manner adds to the already considerable flexibility and potential of the other telecommutation modes. For example, conferences could be coupled with computer models, instructional packages and other computer-based routines; it enables more sophisticated analysis and processing of the content and emergent structure of the conference (examination of interaction patterns, retrieval of discussion by key word themes, dates, and author); and makes it possible for participants to remain anonymous thereby facilitating uninhibited exchanges and removing potential social psychological influences on discussion and decisions (e.g., charismatic and authoritative personalities, status of participants, and sexual, racial, and personal biases).

Because of the complexities, initial expense, and recent origin of the idea of telecommutation, there is not yet a great deal of evidence upon which to evaluate its feasibility, potential, and implications. Nevertheless, much of the data that is available suggest that (1) most of the required technology is already available, (2) telecommuting is economically feasible, (3) most routine clerical and some managerial functions can be effectively performed from remote locations using existing technology, (4) many employees will find this mode to be an acceptable way to work, (5) it can have a positive effect on work conditions and effectiveness, (6) and if instituted on a broad scale, telecommuting can have a significant impact on energy consumption, transportation patterns, and urban development (e.g., see Harkness, 1973; Johansen, Vallee, and Palmer, 1976; Nilles et al., 1976; Tyler, Katsoulis, and Cook, 1976).

One particularly important implication of telecommuting is that it would enable people to work who might not otherwise be able to do so; for example, those without access to transportation, part-time workers who do not have the time to commute to central locations, and the handicapped and elderly with limited mobility. In addition, the easy accessibility and storage capabilities of remote terminals and the subsequent development of such software modes as the asynchronous computer conferencing described earlier add further degrees of freedom to the scheduling of work. These eased restrictions on work time and place, together with the generally increased flexibility associated with information-based work provide unprecedented opportunity for individually designed jobs.

The idea of telecommunications as a partial substitute for travel is relatively new. As a result, there are many unanswered questions and potential problems. To what extent can telecommunications substitute for face-to-face communication and under what circumstances? What is its ultimate impact on recent attempts to revitalize urban centers? What are the implications for management, human resource policy, collective bargaining, equal employment opportunity, and land use and transportation planning? What human factors and social psychological variables could make telecommuting an effective option for the future?

In spite of these uncertainties, "telecommutation" is feasible and its societal implications are legion. The need for I/O psychologists to consider this possibility and its consequences in the design of jobs and organizations, and examine its interactions with other urban development and transportation planning issues is just another manifestation of the broadened systems imperative that is challenging the discipline today and shaping its future.

Resource shortages: A fundamental objective in most, if not all, modern societies is continued growth in the abundance of consumer goods and services. Since most of our work systems are designed to provide a continually expanding supply of these goods and services, scarcities in the resources necessary for producing them could profoundly alter the goals and forms of work and organizations in the future.

Consider, for example, the potential impact of anticipated shortages in raw materials. Because of the limitations resource shortages would place on the manufacture of material goods, consumers would find it increasingly difficult to purchase products with the expectation of replacing them easily and inexpensively as they wear out or become obsolete. As a result, product durability would have to replace quantity as the overriding goal of production systems and their component work processes. Mass production systems, as exemplified by the assembly line, would then not only be unnecessary but might even be inappropriate for achieving quality goals (e.g., durability), especially in light of the incompatability between their repetitive and restricted nature and the emerging values of younger workers (Gottlieb, 1975; Yankelovich, 1974). On the other hand, some evidence suggests that enriched jobs would be more likely to lead to longer lasting, higher quality products (Hackman and Oldham, 1976; Lawler, 1969).

An alternative scenario is also possible. Specifically, if other means can be found to insure improved product durability, it would be possible to retain the more labor-efficient modes of production such as the assembly line and reduce work hours instead. Any further increases in the productivity of labor resulting from innovations in production technology could lead to even further decreases in work hours. These reductions could be distributed among the entire work force in the form of shorter work weeks, longer vacations, employee sabbaticals, earlier retirement, or some combination of these. Of course, some workers might have difficulty in adjusting to significant increases in their nonwork time, a problem that could be compounded by the limits imposed by resource shortages on the production of leisure-related goods (this issue will be discussed in more detail in the next chapter).

Or, instead of reducing the average lifetime work hours for all workers, the number employed in manufacturing industries could be cut back, with some of those displaced by these cutbacks finding jobs in service industries. The mechanisms described in Chapter 2 for increasing accessibility to job training and for facilitating career redirection would be particularly important under these conditions, as would the creation of new public service careers (also described in Chapter 2) for those unable to find employment in the private sector. Furthermore, the relative number of repair and maintenance jobs would increase in response to the need for keeping equipment and consumer goods in working order since the production of replacements could be severely curtailed. All of this would tend to augment the present trend toward a service economy, which according to Daniel Bell (1973) is one of the principal characteristics of the post-industrial society.

The discussion to this point has focused on the work-related impact of shortages in the raw materials from which products are made. Severe shortages in the nonrenewable energy resources needed to run factories and businesses could create somewhat different alternative future possibilities. If energy were the only resource in short supply (i.e., if raw materials remain abundant) it would still be possible to maintain or increase the production of goods—and, therefore, the material standard of living—by replacing these dwindling reserves of energy with human labor. Some of this human energy could be supplied by hiring unemployed workers, retirees, and homemakers on a full- or part-time basis. If this were not enough to meet production quotas, however, many workers would have to work longer hours. Since some of this work might involve the heavy physical labor or repetitious, low-skill information handling tasks (e.g., filing, simple arithmetic computations) that were previously performed by energy-consuming technologies, it is difficult to believe that this state of affairs would be acceptable to very many workers. In effect, these conditions (i.e., energy shortages coupled with a continued commitment to the goal of material affluence) would tend to *expand employment in manufacturing industries,* thereby reversing the trend toward a post-industrial service economy.

Alternatively, we could try to adopt a lower standard of material affluence and alter the goals and designs of our production systems accordingly. This is essentially the same conclusion that was reached with respect to raw material shortages and creates many of the same options—an accelerated shift toward services, reduced work time, and restructured jobs and organizations.

The need to conserve nonrenewable sources of energy could add some new wrinkles to these options, however. For example, economist Lester Thurow (1973) notes that some service industries consume large amounts of energy and illustrates this point by citing the Massachusetts Institute of Technology and the affiliated hospitals of Harvard University as two of the largest users of electricity in the Boston area.

Furthermore, the design of jobs and organizations would have to rely less on nonrenewable sources of energy and the technologies that are dependent on these sources and, as in the case of shortages in raw materials, would also have to reflect increased concern for product durability. Recent interest in the use of such *renewable* sources of energy as the sun and wind, the decentralization of organizations to reduce travel from home to workplace, and the development of technologies that are more "appropriate" to these conditions and are more labor-intensive and require less energy and capital provide some interesting suggestions as to how these jobs and organizations might look. Establishment of the small, nonbureaucratic, decentralized community-based enterprises that were discussed earlier in the context of the "journey to work," enterprises that would use local resources and skills in conjunction with relatively simple, scaled down technology and production processes, is being advocated by many individuals and groups concerned with the problems of rising energy prices and unemployment in both developed and developing nations (e.g., see Livingston, 1976; Schumacher, 1973). Under these conditions there would be less need for highly specialized skills, greater opportunity for worker autonomy and flexibility, and more emphasis on cooperation and participation both within the organization and between the organization and the community than in the current system (Bass, 1976; Livingston, 1976; Michael, 1977). With less pressure to produce large quantities of goods, the increase in physical labor that would result from the decreased availability of labor-saving technology is more likely to fall within acceptable bounds and might even be welcomed by some workers desiring less sedentary work. In addition, the use of telecommunications in place of travel would receive a boost by increased scarcities in nonrenewable sources of energy.

It is also important to consider the impact of resource shortages on societal and personal values and the implications for work. In the short run, limitations on the availability of material goods would probably lead to economic dislocations and uncertainty concerning our ability to achieve the degree of affluence we have learned to expect in our lives. As a result, the values shifts indicated by the research studies mentioned earlier (Gottlieb, 1975; Yankelovich, 1974) would be checked or even reversed. That is, workers would no longer be able to take material affluence for granted, and the acquisition of possessions might once again begin to emerge as the dominant value in our society. This would, in turn, create a serious conflict between the reemergence of these traditional values and the limitations on the availability of consumer goods imposed by the need for material equilibrium.

If so, the development of mechanisms and policies for institutionalizing values more consistent with conditions of material equilibrium will have to be given a particularly high priority in our agenda for the future. In the place of life styles based on anticipated continuing growth in the material standard of living, it would be necessary to put more emphasis on the intrinsic satisfactions one can derive from jobs that require responsibility and the use of valued skills and allow more flexibility in their location and scheduling. The increased availability of low resource-consuming services and high quality, long-lasting goods could also help to compensate for decreases in material affluence, in addition to creating employment situations that offer the chance to make particularly valuable contributions to societal welfare. Furthermore, the increases in nonwork time that might result from resource shortages could create unprecedented opportunities for self-fulfillment, personal growth, and cultural and aesthetic achievement.

Conclusion: Clearly, the future of work is far from certain; it is not an inevitable set of conditions shaped by immutable forces. Indeed, the situation is quite the opposite. Trends and developments that appear irreversible today may not seem so tomorrow. Nor are their specific consequences unambiguous. The future is ultimately determined by many forces, and by focusing on only a small, although significant set of variables, the best we can hope to do is delineate a range of alternatives that at best represent a sample of all the possibilities.

Nonetheless, even the relatively few alternatives that have been examined here indicate a wide variety of possibilities, possibilities that include opportunities to improve the human condition as well as problems that can threaten our most cherished dreams. The future of work can reflect human vision and conscious endeavor if we recognize these possibilities, and the means by which we may guide our way among them.

Summary

The growing awareness of the importance of job satisfaction has created considerable interest in recent years in the causes and consequences of job satisfaction and the ways in which work can be improved. Although there are presently no signs of widespread and mounting dissatisfaction, its potential personal and societal consequences suggest that a problem of some magnitude may nevertheless exist.

Several approaches to the redesign of jobs and organizations to increase worker satisfaction have been tried over the years with varying degrees of success. From this experience and the research that has been conducted on this subject, certain principles, guidelines and issues for further examination have begun to emerge. One of the most controversial of these issues focuses on the

105

origin and role of individual differences in workers' responses to their jobs and their implications for the design of work systems. Should these individual differences be considered in job redesign efforts? Can the possibility that job changes may have important societal benefits and alter workers' needs, orientations, and capacities be used as a justification for imposing enriched jobs on those who are initially resistant to these changes? Is there some middle ground? This issue is far from settled and will no doubt be a subject of research and debate in the years to come, significantly shaping the future of work and organizations in the process.

Several other factors may also play important roles in the future of work and organizations. One such factor is the possibility that the increased educational attainments and career aspirations of younger workers will not be matched by growth in the number of jobs compatible with their educational levels and career objectives. The impact of technological change in the workplace and the use of telecommunications to decentralize work organizations must also be considered. Resource shortages is yet another factor that could significantly influence the future of work.

Although the first factor may increase job dissatisfaction, the other three may provide new opportunities to redesign work systems to offset this increase and accommodate individual needs and situations. Whether or not they are used in this manner is a function of present action, policies, and decisions. Therefore, the future of work can be shaped as much by human endeavor as by developments over which we have little control.

Notes and Suggestions for Further Reading

There are several *books of general readings* available that cover in more detail many of the topics discussed in this chapter as well as several other related issues not included here. The collection by Dubin (1976) provides a sociological perspective on the relationships between work, organizations and society. O'Toole (1974) contains several of the papers commissioned by the special task force to the Secretary of Health, Education and Welfare for the *Work in America* report (1973). Meltzer and Wickert (1976) focus on the topic of organizational behavior, and Biderman and Drury (1976) address issues relevant to the use of job satisfaction as a social indicator for measuring the quality of work. The collection by Davis and Taylor (1972) consists of particularly seminal, previously published papers as well as a very informative geneology of the various influences, forms, and movements in the history of work systems design. Hackman and Suttle (1977) offer the most recent state-of-the-art review of work design principles, as of this writing, and include several articles dealing with the related issues of career development, reward systems, group behavior, managerial practices, strategies for organizational change, and the role of community and political interest groups and the government. Warr (1976) contains overviews of relevant theory and research and discussion of some of the ethical issues in job and organizational change. Davis and Cherns (1975a) is a particularly useful reference for its broad coverage of many of the issues included in the aforementioned books. Many of the individual papers contained in all of these books have been referenced throughout this and the preceding chapters.

The books edited by Best (1973a) and Rosow (1974) are *less technical and research-oriented* than the ones mentioned above and as a result are more accessible to a general readership. Both books are available in paperback.

The novel by Harvey Swados (1957), the best-selling book of interviews with workers by Studs Terkel (1974), the overview of recent and emerging work reforms by Paul Dickson (1975) and Charlie Chaplin's classic movie "Modern Times" offer particularly compelling *literary, journalistic, and cinematic perspectives* on several of the issues covered in this chapter.

The writings of the nineteenth century philosophers de Tocqueville, Marx, Weber, and Durkheim are of special *historical interest.* More recent classics include Blauner (1964), Friedmann (1961), and Walker and Guest (1952), as well as several of the references cited in the text. The early work of the researchers at London's Tavistock Institute for Human Relations on sociotechnical systems laid the foundation for many of the contemporary theories and practice in work design and the use of autonomous work groups (e.g., Emery and Trist, 1960; Herbst, 1962; Rice, 1958; Trist and Bamforth, 1951; Trist, Higgin, Murray, and Pollack, 1963). The previously mentioned report on *Work in America* (1973) has sparked much of the recent interest and controversy surrounding the issue of work as a potential social problem.

As noted in the text, most studies of job satisfaction find that overall satisfaction generally increases with job level. A recent study, however, has come to the opposite conclusion. After accounting for the effect of such factors as money and prestige, Weaver (1977) concludes that *laborers are more satisfied than professionals with the intrinsic aspects of their jobs.*

The interrelationship between *intrinsic and extrinsic motivation* has been the focus of much speculation and research in recent years (Brief and Aldag, 1977; Broedling, 1977; Deci, 1975a and 1975b; Dermer, 1975; Dyer and Parker, 1975; Hamner and Foster, 1975; Notz, 1975; Pinder, 1976; Scott, 1975). One of the central issues is the extent to which extrinsic rewards lower an individual's intrinsic motivation, if at all. Deci's work suggests that the effect may be considerable. If so, the implications for the design of work, compensation systems, and organizations in general would be significant.

Case studies of alternative work systems in action can be found in Davis

FITTING THE JOB TO THE WORKER: JOB SATISFACTION AND THE DESIGN OF WORK SYSTEMS

and Cherns (1975b). Maccoby (1975) provides a first-hand report on one of the more recent and innovative projects in the United States. The monthly newsletter *World of Work Report* is a particularly valuable up-to-date source of information on new developments, experiments, and real-world applications (available from Work in America Institute, Inc., 700 White Plains Road, Scarsdale, N.Y. 10583). The "Resource Package for Job and Organizational Design" (available from the Center for the Quality of Working Life at the University of California, Los Angeles) contains a listing of other information sources as well as an annotated bibliography of general readings, including several cited in this chapter.

Many of these case studies are of projects in other countries and reflect the leading role of these countries in the development of new approaches to workplace reform, particularly in the area of worker participation. References that provide *international perspectives on job satisfaction and work design* include Espinosa and Zimbalist (1978), Foy and Gadon (1976), Hunnius et al. (1973), Jenkins (1973), Qvale (1976), Riskin (1974) and Warner (1976). In addition, Tannenbaum, Kavcic, Rosner, Vianello, and Wieser, (1974) compare worker participation in five countries (Austria, Israel, Italy, United States, Yugoslavia), and Bouvin (1977) and Prendergast (1976) examine the implications of recent Swedish legislation on democracy in the workplace.

Most *labor unions* in the United States have viewed work redesign with mixed feelings. For discussion of their concerns and the implications of work redesign for their future roles see Barbash (1977), Bluestone (1973), Kassalow (1977), Salpukas (1974) and Wallick (1973). European trade unions have been decidedly more sympathetic and have frequently taken the initiative in developing and implementing some of the more innovative approaches. In addition to the references cited in the preceding paragraph, see Davis and Cherns (1975a, Part VII).

The concept of *producers' cooperatives* where worker participation is broadened to include worker ownership has interested labor leaders, political economists and others for some time and is beginning to attract the attention of I/O psychologists as well (see Hammer, 1977 and Stagner, 1977).

As was mentioned earlier in this chapter, several researchers have suggested the intriguing *possibility that employees' personalities, orientations, and values can be altered by job redesign* (Hackman and Oldham, 1975; Hilgendorf and Irving, 1976; Kohn and Schooler, 1973). Although this hypothesis has been supported by the observations of those involved in actual job enrichment projects (e.g., see den Hertog, 1976), systematic longitudinal research examining this issue is almost nonexistent; an exception is the study by Brousseau (1977).

108

For a review of *practical guidelines for implementing work redesigns* and some of the problems and obstacles that may be encountered see Glaser (1976), Hackman (1975), Sirota and Wolfson (1972a and b) and Walters and Associates (1975).

The *technological and societal limits on job redesign* are explored by Levitan and Johnston (1973).

The thorny issue of *government legislation to improve the quality of work life* is discussed by Beer and Driscoll (1977), Lawler (1974 and 1976b), Locke (1976b and 1976c) and Herbert (1977). In several respects, this issue parallels the discussion in the first two paragraphs of the Notes section of Chapter 2. As in the case of equal employment opportunity, most organizations would be reluctant to initiate programs aimed at increasing employee satisfaction unless they feel that the benefits to the organization are not exceeded by the costs of the program. Since social costs carry as little weight in quality of work life decisions as they do in personnel selection, and because a direct causal link from satisfaction to productivity has yet to be demonstrated, many organizations may have little incentive for initiating job enrichment programs on their own. For these reasons, Lawler and Beer and Driscoll argue that the government should begin to consider the development of standards, incentives, and public reporting procedures to improve the quality of work life just as they have for pollution, occupational safety and health, and equal employment opportunity. Locke provides a dissenting opinion.

The implications of job redesign for the distribution of power in the organization (i.e., relatively more for workers and less for supervisors and managers) is discussed in more detail by Nord (1974, 1976, 1977), Pateman (1975), and Zimbalist (1975). These writers also address the implications for the broader political and economic system of which work organizations are part.

Two possible *consequences of the growing disjunction between workers' educational levels and future job requirements* that were not mentioned in the text are "intellectual atrophy" (see Berg and Freedman, 1977) and the increased radicalization of underutilized college graduates (see Blumberg and Murtha, 1977).

The increased entry of women into the labor force at all occupational levels constitutes one of the most significant developments of the last several years and will undoubtedly have a significant impact on the future of work, organizations, and society. This issue has come up at several times throughout this book, and there is far more to the subject than can be dealt with in any detail here. The reader is therefore urged to consult some of the many references on *women and work* that have appeared in recent years (e.g., Agassi, 1975; Blaxall and Reagan, 1976; Frank, 1977; Hennig and Jardim, 1977; Howe, 1977; Huber, 1976; Kanter, 1977a and b; Katzell and Byham, 1972; Kreps, 1976; Kreps and Clark, 1975; Nieva and Gutek, 1976; Sawhill, 1974; Terborg, 1977).

The *use of technology to improve the productivity of service industries* is discussed by Jeffery (1975) and Levitt (1975 and 1976).

The interplay between *land use, urban planning, social inequities, transportation, the economy, and work* is a particularly complex and important issue that may increasingly influence the kinds of issues with which I/O psychologists have dealt in the past and to which they may contribute in the future. Some examples are the transportation and employment problems of the urban disadvantaged (see Goering and Kalachek, 1973; Marando, 1974; Piovia, Hill and Leigh, 1973), the relationships between the economy, worker characteristics, and residential patterns (e.g., see Ganz, 1974; Guest, 1976; Wolforth, 1965) and alternative transportation systems and employment (see Bezdek and Hannon, 1974). Other examples can be found in Ginzberg (1974) as well as in the text.

For more information on *telecommuting* see Johansen (1977); Overby, Hutchison and Wiercinski (1974); Short, Williams, and Christie (1976); and Valle, Johansen and Spangler (1975) as well as the references cited in the text.

Despite its importance, very little has been written about the potential *impact of resource shortages on work and organizations.* The implications for the overall economy and its general structure have received considerable attention (e.g., see Weintraub, Schwartz, and Aronson, 1973; Grossman and Daneker, 1977), but little of this attention seems to have filtered down to the level of individual organizations and the shop floor. Some of these issues are discussed in Day (1973), O'Toole (1976), and Tichy and Devanna (1977) and in several of the references cited in the text (particularly Bass, 1976 and Michael, 1977), but it is clear that the subject has not attracted the concern it deserves.

Although this chapter does not specifically address the *future of organizations and management,* much of the discussion did deal with various aspects of this broad topic. Nonetheless, there is much more to the topic than has been included here and the reader may want to consult the rapidly growing body of literature on the topic. Some general references are Argyris (1973); Bennis (1966); Conference Board (1973); Kahn (1974); Leavitt, Pinfield, and Webb (1974); Roeber, (1973); Schmidt (1970) and Trist (1976). In brief, the general consensus appears to be that if organizations are to adapt to change they will have to become less dependent on formal hierarchies of authority, well-defined functional specialization and differentiation, and rigidly fixed policies and rules. In place of this traditional bureaucratic model, there will be an increased emphasis on participation of employees in organizational decisions, more tolerance for diversity, a greater use of temporary problem-solving groups in place of formally differentiated departments and divisions, an increased need for interpersonal effectiveness, and a continuing commitment to experimentation and organizational change. Furthermore, as Michael (1973) and Nanus (1975) note, organizations may undertake more long-range planning which will, in turn, put new stresses on organizations and the people within them. The nature of these stresses and the strategies for dealing with them are examined in some detail by Michael. (Michael's book is strongly recommended to anyone interested in the interactions between long-range planning and organizational change and behavior).

The growing importance of such *voluntary organizations* as public interest, political action, and religious groups, professional associations, and labor unions (see Smith, 1973) could add new dimensions to the study of organizations and the people of which they are composed (e.g., Walker, 1975).

Cross-cultural issues and perspectives in I/O psychology, particularly important concerns in the increasingly interdependent "global society," are reviewed by Barrett and Bass (1976) and Triandis (1973).

The development of the space shuttle and recent interest in the creation of *space colonies* for mining and manufacturing, and for transmitting solar energy to earth suggests the possibility that significant numbers of people will be working and living under unique conditions in the not-too-distant future (see O'Neill, 1977 and Stine, 1975). It will be interesting to see what changes these new work settings and organizations affect in the theory, data, and practice of I/O psychology in the years to come.

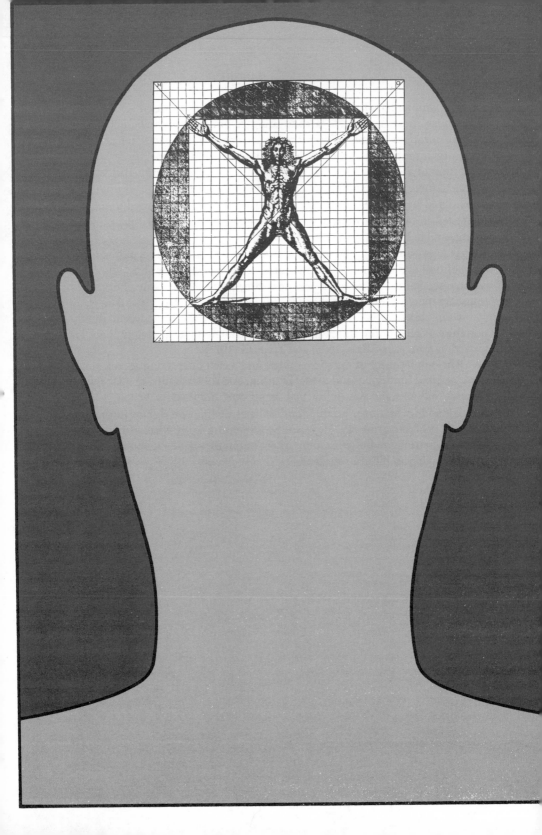

chap. 4

Leisure in the Post-Industrial Society

As participant designers of the sociotechnological systems that make up a post-industrial society, I/O psychologists have a responsibility to approach this process in a systematic, holistic fashion, even when this compels them to extend the boundaries of their discipline to include issues with which they have not traditionally been concerned. These boundaries would not have to be extended too far before the subject of leisure in some form would be encompassed within them, a fact that several leading figures in the field have at various times acknowledged (e.g., Bass, 1972; Dunnette, 1973; Porter, 1966).

There can be little doubt about the growing importance of leisure in our contemporary society—the evidence is all around us. Television commercials and advertisements in magazines and newspapers frantically urge us to buy recreational vehicles, vacation homes, and adult games, or to travel to Europe, Disney World, or the Catskills. Take a walk through a shopping center, try to get a campsite in a national park during the summer, or a ticket to a professional football game in the fall. No wonder, then, that expenditures for leisure-related goods and services now constitute one of the fastest-growing commercial markets today (Culen, 1973).

The time available to consume these goods and services has also increased, although not quite as dramatically. Summarizing statistical trends on the amount of time devoted to nonwork activities, Glickman and Brown (1973) conclude that

> *The patterns in all industrial societies are consistent. Measured in hours per week, or years in a lifetime, the proportion of an individual's time devoted to paid employment consistently declines. Years of formal schooling increase. Entrance to the work force starts later. Hours in the work week decrease. The number of holidays and duration of vacations keeps going up. Retirement starts earlier. (p. 11)*

Several factors suggest that these trends will continue for years to come. Increased longevity could add substantially to the post-retirement years. Even if second career opportunities were more readily available and all mandatory

113

retirement rules eliminated, full-time work until death is not likely to become so widespread as to significantly alter this projection. Continued high rates of unemployment, occasioned in part by the entry of more women into the labor force, would provide an additional impetus to reductions in working time in an effort to spread the available work around (see Levitan and Belous, 1977).

By far the most important factor affecting future growth in both the degree of spending on leisure-related goods and services and the amount of free time available for consuming these goods and services is the continued improvement in the productivity of work organizations, improvements largely made possible in the past by technological innovation and the more efficient organization of work. As we learn more about managing post-industrial age organizations and incorporate information technologies into their operations on a wider scale (see Levitt, 1976), productivity will continue to improve and further increase free time and leisure spending.

We will shortly examine the implications of the growing role of leisure in modern society, particularly its implications for the world of work. First, however, it is important to understand what is meant by the expression ''leisure'' and the various roles it can play in our lives.

The Meaning and Functions of Leisure

Central to all definitions of leisure is the idea that it is free, relatively uncommitted time allowing the exercise of choice. In addition, most contemporary conceptualizations differentiate between ''leisure'' and ''free time'' by attributing some kind of subjective meaning or the experience of a particular quality to the former and not to the latter. The nature of the subjective meanings and experiences usually involves the various functions that leisure is supposed to fulfill. According to Kaplan (1972, 1975) these functions can be summarized by viewing leisure as a merging of two formerly opposed conceptualizations: the classical view and the view based on the Protestant work ethic. The classical concept can be characterized as ''leisure as an end'' and includes such functions as the use of nonwork time for contemplation, scholarship, self-expression, self-realization, and self-development. The second view ''is to look upon leisure as therapy, rest, relaxation, social control, re-creation for subsequent productive effort—and generally, therefore, as instrumental in character'' (Kaplan, 1972, p. 10). Kaplan adds that this latter view has been broadened in the last century to include the dimension identified by economist Thorstein Veblen (Veblen, 1953) of leisure as a symbol of the rich and, more recently, the use of leisure as an instrument of status by the general population.

114

The following quote from Kaplan summarizes the most important charac-teristics of leisure and adds just enough detail to the preceding discussion to provide us with an adequate working definition.

Leisure . . . consists of relatively self-determined activity-experience that falls into one's economically free-time roles, that is seen as leisure by par-ticipants, that is psychologically pleasant in anticipation and recollection, that potentially covers the whole range of commitment and intensity, that contains characteristic norms and constraints, and that provides op-portunities for recreation, personal growth, and service to others. (Kaplan, 1975, p. 26)

Alternative Models for Leisure

The point was made earlier that the factor most instrumental in increasing both nonwork time and expenditures on leisure-related goods and services is produc-tivity. In effect, productivity gains create a choice for workers between higher incomes with the same working hours, the same income with shorter hours, or some compromise between the two. Putting aside the question as to how this choice has been made in the past, economists Juanita Kreps and Joseph Spengler estimate that about two-thirds of this century's productivity gains have been taken as increased income and one-third as free time (Kreps and Spengler, 1966). In more recent years the proportion of the gains taken in in-creased income has been even greater than two-thirds. Moore and Hedges (1971) have estimated that the reduction in hours worked per individual in the 1960s was only 8 percent of the amount made possible by the nation's increased productivity.

Clearly, both free time and money are required by most people to satisfy their leisure needs: that is, money is necessary to make one's free time more comfortable, secure, and enjoyable, while free time is necessary to enjoy the fruits of economic security and the nonessential recreational goods and services purchased by above-subsistence earnings. Nevertheless, there are profound dif-ferences in the kind of leisure activities that follow from the disproportionate preference for income over time described above, and the kind of leisure activi-ties that would result if relatively more of the productivity gains of the future were to be taken as increased free time.

For example, consider the kind of activities that might characterize our lei-sure if historical trends extend into the future. More exotic, sophisticated, and expensive versions of existing amusement parks, night clubs, recreational vehicles, travel clubs, television programs, adult games, and so on would continue to compete for the consumer dollar. No doubt, technological innovations would add unique dimensions to these activities as well as provide new opportunities for inventive entrepreneurs to devise activities, goods, and services of an unprecedented kind. Readers need only use their imaginations to generate some potentially profitable ideas. Failing that, science fiction stories and movies literally abound with novel possibilities for consumer-based leisure.

As fascinating and attractive as these activities might seem at first, a closer examination suggests that we should not rely too heavily on the type of leisure resources just described. There is reason to doubt that these resources can fulfill all of the important leisure functions described earlier. Although they may be adequate modes of entertainment and recreation, it is unlikely that they would serve to enhance personal growth and self-expression. Although it is possible that they *could* be used for those purposes, previous experience with commercially provided leisure—commercial television is a good case in point—would suggest that this is no more likely to be the case in the future than it has been in the past.

Another problem is that many of our leisure resources require the depletion of natural resources. Raw materials make up the goods on which these leisure resources often depend and energy is used to convert these raw materials into the finished product. Energy is also used to power many of these goods—recreational vehicles, for example—and to transport us to vacation spots and areas where these leisure resources can be used.

Yet another problem is that these leisure resources are essentially finite, and the degree to which they can even meet recreational and entertainment needs over the long run must be questioned. How certain can we be that technological innovation and the imagination and expertise of the leisure industries will be able to keep at least one step ahead of the constantly changing needs of an increasingly well-educated, sophisticated, and somewhat jaded populace? Will new entertainments, diversions, and gadgets become passé at ever faster rates?

One last problem is that the consumption of leisure-related goods and services takes time: time spent in gathering information concerning the broad range of goods and services available in order to make a wise purchase decision; maintenance time; time spent in consuming the product; and, of course, work time to earn the money necessary to purchase the product (see Linder, 1970). The end result is that the pursuit of leisure can often be as harried and unleisurely as work and work-related activities. Anyone who has ever waited in a seemingly endless line to get onto a ski lift, into a movie, concert, sporting event, or campground or been stuck in the monstrous summer weekend traffic jams around beach resorts and parks can easily attest to this fact.

116

The problems associated with leisure activities that are so heavily dependent on the consumption of goods and services leads one to ask what alternatives are possible. What if we changed our present preferences for leisure-related goods and services and began to take a larger proportion of our future productivity gains in the form of more nonwork time rather than money? Would there not be a problem trying to find things to do during our increased free time, especially if growth in the availability of leisure-related goods and services does not keep pace? With a few exceptions most people would probably have little trouble occupying themselves with several more hours of unobligated time each week or an extended vacation once every few years (see Klausner, 1968), but substantial gains in free time could create a problem of some magnitude. Clearly, some of this time could be taken up by various educational, athletic, and cultural pursuits. But if these activities cannot sufficiently compensate for the decreased emphasis on leisure-related goods and services what other alternatives could there be?

Fortunately, there is an alternative that could help to solve the "problem" of leisure, an alternative often overlooked by those who define their leisure in terms of consumer products. What I have in mind is the kind of self-generated activity that is relatively independent of private goods and services and requires little more than an individual's own imagination and spontaneity and the abundant stimulation offered by the presence of other people and the natural and constructed environment. Thought processes such as daydreaming, problem solving, and self analysis represent one form of self-generated leisure that requires nothing more than time, peace and quiet, and one's own imagination. Interaction with other people can also be entertaining, increase the diversity of the activities in which we engage, provide additional sources of stimulation and knowledge, and offer valuable social feedback that can be used to increase self-awareness and satisfaction in interpersonal relations. Hiking and camping in the natural environment is yet another relatively inexpensive leisure activity that is essentially self-generated. Constructed environments such as cities can also be valuable leisure resources as the following quote from Paul and Percival Goodman's classic work *Communitas: Means of Livelihood and Ways of Life* so aptly illustrates.

> *A man suddenly withdrawn in will and schedule from the general economy, and with a lot of time on his hands, might begin to look at the immense activity of others as at the objects in a great zoo or museum: a sociological garden abounding in its tame and savage ways. . . .*
> *Thus a man may have nothing but pleasant memories of New York or Paris, even during the summer season. He speaks of the variety of the city, its easy gait, its shops, parks, markets, and animated streets. And the*

fact is that he stayed in these places during the years that he did not have to work for a living, he was perhaps a student on a scholarship. Therefore he saw the variety and the out-of-the-way places that busy people do not stumble on. (1960, p. 215)

Comparing the Two Alternatives

Closer examination of the two models reveals their fundamental distinguishing characteristics. Basically, the role of the participant in "entertainment/consumption" activities is passive since he or she is usually dependent upon external agents such as TV sets, vehicles, devices, or rules. The activities are structured *for* individuals rather than *by* them and there is relatively little need for self-generated, original, and spontaneous activity. On the other hand, the alternative, "human potential" model suggests activities that are more spontaneous, self-initiated, and self-directed. In this case the individual is responsible for creating whatever structure is necessary, and the locus of control is within the individual rather than imposed from without. Because of the locus of control and the source of the activity, the individual need not rely on external means and, consequently, is more flexible in the use of his or her leisure. In effect, the person is the creator of his or her own leisure.

One way to differentiate conceptually between these two models is to think of them in terms of "play" and "games," a distinction made in another context by social critic and historian Theodore Roszak. He describes "games" as

human activity that absorbs people in the orderly pursuit of arbitrary—usually competitive—goals according to arbitrary rules. . . . "Game" is the word we reserve for . . . <u>organized</u> play. But it is not always to the regularity and orderliness of a game that play gives itself. Playing is clearly a much more generalized and lawless form of activity. Babies and animals "play" in a perfectly chaotic fashion. In fact, playful babies have very little patience with rules and regulations. They <u>play</u> quite naturally, but they must be taught their <u>games</u>. (1966, pp. 26–27)

The important distinction for our purposes is that *"games" are more highly structured and the source of this structure is external to the individual, while the relatively little structure present in play is generated by the "players" themselves.* This distinction can be applied to the two leisure activity models described earlier, the one defined by the consumption of leisure-related, technology-dependent goods and services and the other by nonconsumptive, self-generated leisure activities. Until now we have assumed that the important difference between the two is the fact that the first is associated with increased income and leisure-related spending while the second would be made possible, even necessary, by a decision to take a larger proportion of future productivity gains in the form of increased free time. At this point, we can begin to see an even more fundamental difference underlying the two classes; that is, the *degree and source of the structure, which is the usual, but not necessarily the inevitable result of the commercialization of technological change.* This is the most important basic difference, and the one that will be stressed in this chapter.

So that we may better understand this important distinction, the significance of play in human functioning, and the possible advantages of leisure resources modeled after play, we now examine the concept of play in more detail.

Play as a Model for Leisure

The subject of play has received considerable attention from varied perspectives over the years. Dutch historian Johann Huizinga (1950) treats play as a central element in the development of human culture, an element of such importance that he adds the expression *homo ludens*, Man the Player, to the expression *homo sapiens*, Man the Knower, and *homo faber*, Man the Maker, as designations for the human species. For philosopher Barry Sadler (1969), play is an important outlet for the expression of individuality and creativity. For Jean Piaget (1962), intellectual and cognitive development is very much dependent on play during infancy and childhood. Most relevant to our purposes, however, are the various psychological theories in which the concept of play is not only an important element, as in Piaget's theoretical formulations, but is the actual primary topic of concern.

According to psychologist Brian Sutton-Smith, one of the leading researchers on this topic, there are two classic approaches represented in the psychological theories of play (Sutton-Smith, 1972). One emphasizes play as a function of the stimulus qualities of the environment and the other deals with it in terms of qualities internal to the organism, particularly the types of rule systems that govern the behavior of the player. Here we will examine an example of each approach and then draw some conclusions from a comparison of the two.

One of the best examples of the first approach, play as a function of the stimulus qualities of the environment, views play as arousal or stimulus-seeking behavior. Several psychologists have argued that there is an optimal level of arousal below which organisms will be motivated to seek the stimulation necessary to increase their arousal to this optimum level (see Berlyne, 1961; Fiske and Maddi, 1961). In this formulation, play does not necessarily serve any immediate extrinsic function but is seen, instead, as the principal means for producing the novelty and complexity needed to maintain arousal. In the process, players also learn about their environment, their potential for interacting effectively with it, and, at the same time, they develop a capacity for adaptation to change and unpredictable situations (Ellis, 1972 and 1973). That play is viewed as being structured by the individual and not organized from without can be seen in the following quote.

[Play] is a personal process in that what is new, complex, or dissonant can only be so in relation to the previous experience of the individual. . . . It is not play if the course of the behavior is determined entirely by a leader. Play comes from the individual exercise of options among opportunities to complexify a private world. (Ellis, 1972, p. 4)

One of the best examples of the second approach described by Sutton-Smith (i.e., play as a function of the qualities of the organism) is the work conducted by Sutton-Smith himself. Like Ellis, he views play as being structured by the individual rather than by external sources.

For me, play is what a person does when he can choose the arbitrariness of the constraints within which he will act or imagine. . . . The player substitutes his own conventions and his own energies for those of society and nature. (1972, p. 6)

In addition, play is marked by the emergence of novel responses, responses that have no specific and immediate extrinsic purpose.

If this extraordinary variety of actions . . . is of any evolutionary significance, then it must be to bring these responses into a state of readiness for potential usage, not for specific immediate needs. Play prepares for the unforeseeable future, not the forseeable one. . . . It produces an array of responses of potential value. (Sutton-Smith, 1973, pp. 4–5)

In the process, players develop the capacity to deal with change and learn about their environment and their ability to control it.

Clearly, although the two approaches have different emphases, there is substantial agreement between them concerning several of its most important

120

aspects. First, in dealing with play as behavior organized *by* the individual and not *for* the individual and as having no immediate extrinsic function, it would appear that both approaches are essentially in agreement with Roszak. Second, both approaches also appear to agree on the ultimate function and result of play behavior: the ability to adapt to change, awareness of capabilities and potentials, and knowledge of the world of which the individual is part.

By now, the relevance of play to our earlier discussion of the two alternative models of leisure should begin to become apparent. If not, perhaps the following quote from Sutton-Smith will help to clarify this relationship.

Other things being equal, there is some optimal level of play participation, which contributes to the subject greater autonomy, greater enjoyment of life, a greater potential repertory of responses, and a greater potential flexibility in the use of these resources. (1972, p. 7)

Elaborating on the above, we could say that to the extent that leisure is play-like it will be intrinsically more satisfying and better fulfill its intended functions, particularly those described by Kaplan as ''leisure as an end,'' that is, the use of leisure for self-expression and personal development. According to this view, ''playful'' leisure can lead to increased knowledge about the world and our abilities to deal with it as well as aid in the further development of our adaptability, spontaneity, independence, and imagination.

In addition, play-like leisure activities place less of a burden on the resources of society—energy and materials, commercial ingenuity, technology—to provide new and continually increasing outlets for the leisure needs of its citizens. The spontaneous ability to generate novel and absorbing activities, perspectives, and experiences suggests a leisure resource of almost limitless variation. In effect, the whole world, internal and external, can serve as a potential leisure resource to the person with the flexibility and imagination to take advantage of it.

Although we have described leisure activities as falling into two distinct classes, it should be apparent that the line of demarcation between the two is not always a sharp one. Under certain conditions many of the examples presented in the context of the entertainment/consumption model could have been presented within the context of the human potential/play model. For example, can we classify *all* TV and movie watching as entertainment or diversion? What about those programs that require or invite an active mental involvement on the part of the viewers to interpret, analyze, and find meaning relevant to their own experience? Travel is another example. Travelers can always insulate themselves by interacting exclusively with fellow tourists and

121

viewing the travelscape through the windows of a tour bus, an experience not unlike watching a travelogue. On the other hand, one can also travel in a far less structured fashion, experiencing diverse natural and cultural environments on their own terms. The point is that the difference between one class and the other is *a difference in degree*. It may even be possible to dispense with the two classes of leisure resources altogether. It is not so much an issue of what we do with leisure so much as the way we do it. The important difference is in the attitude and the state of mind with which we go about our leisure, that is, our ability to play *with and within* the structures that arise from our own limitations and the external environment *rather than being restricted by them.*

A similar point can be made with respect to our earlier distinction between the leisure activities typically associated with the consumption of goods and services and those that could help to fill large blocks of free time. To consume goods and services in pursuit of leisure does not necessarily preclude participation in more active, less structured activities and in some cases might even make it easier. For example, to take advantage of the leisure resources available within the city, one can spend relatively small amounts for admissions to museums, zoos, and cultural events, fares for public transportation, and for the diverse ethnic foods for which most of the major cities of the world are known. Similarly, the exploration of wilderness areas is made considerably more comfortable and enjoyable by the purchase of good equipment. Once again it is a matter of degree; that is, the activities associated with the alternative class of leisure resources generally requires *relatively* less spending than the more common forms of commercially dependent leisure activities. In addition, it is often the case that more highly structured activities also tend to be more expensive. Compare, for example, the cost of a daydream with the cost of a TV set!

Summary: Ellis (1973) describes three criteria for playful behavior identified by Neumann (1971) in an unpublished doctoral dissertation. By reviewing these criteria we can summarize the key points made in the preceding several pages.

Neumann's first criterion of playful behavior, as described by Ellis, is that the locus of control be vested in the individual.

Children are playing when control of the content of their behavior is largely under their control. . . . In general, play has been characterized as behavior in which the player is freed as far as possible from constraints imposed upon which response is to be made to a given set of antecedent events. . . . The degree to which control is passed to an outside agent determines the degree to which the behavior is not playful. (pp. 123–124)

The second criterion requires that the behavior be intrinsically motivated.

The child is playing when the motive for the behavior is intrinsic to the process of the behavior itself and there are no critical deferred or immediate rewards imposed from outside. . . . The player is emitting the behavior for the rewards associated with the processes of its emission rather than with the end product. (pp. 123-124)

The third criterion is the player's transcending of the "immediate constraints of the reality of the situation" (p. 123).

If the player could suspend some of the external realities of the situation and was allowed to behave to some extent independently of those constraints, then the behavior would be playful. Make-believe suspension of some of the constraints of reality makes for play. (p. 124)

Most important for our purposes is Ellis' conclusion that common to all three criteria is the assumption that for play to occur, the player—whether child or adult—should be as free from external constraint as possible. In other words, *play-like leisure and its advantageous consequences are a function of the degree of structure imposed on the individual by his or her leisure activities, facilities, and environments—with less external structure leading to more play, and vice-versa.*

In the abstract, this conclusion leaves many practical questions unanswered. How can "structure" be measured and used to guide the design of such leisure resources as parks, toys, cities, media, and playgrounds? Would the increased availability of unstructured leisure options automatically lead to play-like leisure—do people have the capacity to use these options in this manner? If they do not, how can this capacity be developed? Is education the answer? In other words, how can we get from our present reliance on highly structured materials and experiences to a society where leisure is essentially self-created and self-directed?

As important as these issues may be, they are somewhat peripheral to the principal focus of I/O psychology and, therefore, will not be directly addressed in the remainder of this book (however, some relevant comments and suggestions for further reading can be found in the Notes section of this chapter; further discussion of these issues can be found in Mankin, 1976). But several related issues that arise from the inherent connections between work and leisure have profound implications for the future of work, organizations, and society and are, as a result, more relevant to our concerns.

Work and Leisure

Work and leisure are related in several important ways. First, one is frequently defined as the negation of the other, an overly simplistic practice that often leads to distortion, confusion, and interpretive difficulties in discussions concerning these topics. Second, as pointed out earlier, the time, resources, and opportunities typically associated with contemporary leisure are a direct result of the organization of work into more efficient forms and the application of new technologies to work processes. Third, one of the primary functions of leisure is to provide the rest needed to restore a worker's energy for further productive work.

Finally, and most important for our purposes, are the ways in which the conditions, activities, and attitudes experienced in one sphere can influence those experienced in the other. This general issue manifests itself in several different but related forms. At the purely pragmatic level are the occurrences in one sphere of activity (work or leisure) that may have a significant impact on the other. There are also theories that postulate psychological and sociological connections between work and leisure of a more abstract nature, and a considerable amount of research has been conducted to examine these connections. A third manifestation of this issue is essentially a normative one; that is, it focuses primarily on the desirability of particular kinds of work-leisure connections and recommends policy and programs for facilitating these connections.

The *pragmatic, theoretical/empirical, and normative perspectives* on work-leisure relationships overlap to a certain extent. Both the *pragmatic* and *normative* perspectives are effectively action-oriented and tend to emphasize the implementation of programs and policies. They differ, however, in scope, level, and rationale, with the pragmatic focusing primarily on specific organizational programs for dealing with issues of immediate and practical concern, while the normative involves recommendations for more extensive and longer range organizational reform and public policy. Nonetheless, normative recommendations for social policy should and often do include the more specifically focused pragmatic strategies.

The *theoretical/empirical* and *normative* perspectives also overlap since the latter perspective is frequently based on assumptions and interpretations of the research that arise with respect to the former. In fact, there is often confusion between the two in that a particular theoretical position held by an indi-

124

vidual may be influenced more by ideological views (the normative perspective) than by the available evidence.

Finally, although most pragmatic programs are implemented to address a particular issue in one sphere of activity, they usually have at least an indirect impact on the other. To be consistent with the systems frame of reference, their impact on and relationship to both work and leisure should be considered. Anticipating and planning for this impact would profit from an understanding of the theoretical issues and empirical data. Occasionally these *theoretical/empirical* perspectives are incorporated into the development of *pragmatic* programs although one can reasonably argue that this occurs less frequently than it should.

Although all of the perspectives overlap, the discussion to follow is partitioned into three separate sections. It is important to keep in mind, however, that the distinctions are somewhat arbitrary and are made primarily for the purposes of explication. Furthermore, some of the issues discussed in one section will also come up in the other although the context and rationale will vary in each case. All of the points of overlap, as well as the distinctions, should become clearer as we proceed.

The Pragmatic Perspective

The four issues to be discussed in this section—industrial recreation, alternative work schedules (AWSs), adjusting to retirement, and avocational counseling and design—reflect the traditional aims and activities of I/O psychology. To be more specific, work organizations were initially interested in the first two issues, industrial recreation and AWSs, because they expected them to have a positive effect on productivity. The leisure-related aspects of industrial recreation are generally regarded as a means to serve these traditional ends, and the impact of AWSs on leisure behavior was initially considered to be an attractive but secondarily important result of efforts to serve these same ends. The third issue, adjusting to retirement, appears to reflect the more recent concern of work organizations for the overall welfare of their employees, while the fourth, avocational counseling, is more appropriately regarded as an application of the data and methodology of I/O psychology to problems not usually included within its domain. These points will become clearer as we deal with each issue in turn.

Industrial Recreation: Many companies provide a wide variety of recreational programs and facilities for employees, their families, and the local community. Examples include social, travel, special interest, and hobby clubs; athletic facilities and teams; amateur theater groups; company sponsored excur-

125

sions and trips; employee country clubs and parks; calisthenic work breaks; and, more recently, educational and community service programs.

The reasons typically given for industrial recreation are almost as diverse as the kinds of offerings provided; to attract better workers, improve employee and community relations, increase loyalty to the company, enhance quality of life of employees and the community, and to lower absenteeism and turnover and raise productivity by improving worker morale and physical health are among those most frequently mentioned (see *Top Management Speaks on the Value of Recreation Programs in Industry*, 1976).

It is difficult to evaluate the success of industrial recreation in meeting these goals because systematic well-controlled experimental studies of their effects are difficult to find. Most of the evidence consists of company reports, testimonials by corporate executives, and journalistic accounts of particular programs. Furthermore, the little evidence that is available is generally outdated (e.g., Creed, 1946).

In any case, the increased importance of leisure in the post-industrial society and the developing interest of work organizations in the overall welfare of their employees may lead many companies to become more concerned about recreational opportunities for their employees. Two recent trends may augment this concern, particularly with respect to the subject of employee health. The first is the soaring cost of employee medical insurance and the other is the growing recognition of the potential effect of tension, fatigue, and health on job performance. Fitness and stress and tension control programs that include physical exercise, nutrition and life style counseling, and such psychological techniques as meditation and relaxation training appear especially promising because of their integrated, systematic approach and their emphasis on teaching individuals how to influence their own physical and mental health. The author awaits scientific evaluation of these programs with considerable interest.

Alternative Work Schedules: Although most of the earlier interest in AWSs can be traced back to the publication of the book *4 days, 40 hours: Reporting a revolution in work and leisure* (Poor, 1970), several other proposals and programs deviating from the standard 5 day, 8 hour work shift have also begun to receive considerable attention in the past several years. Among them are:

1. The compressed work week—includes the four day, 40 hour work week and other variations on this theme (e.g., the "3 + 12", 3 days of 12 hours of work apiece).

2. Flexitime—an AWS variation in which workers choose their arrival and departure times within certain limits. Typically, the only restrictions are that

workers be on the job during a designated "core" period (e.g., from 10 a.m. to 4 p.m.) and that they work a prescribed number of hours per day (e.g., 8 hours). In some plans, workers may work less on any given day as long as they make up this time on other days.

3. Part-time work—an AWS option that may be most appropriate for students, retirees, and couples with young children.

4. Shared work—a group of employees share responsibility for a job. Several variations are possible within this format; for example, each person may work part-time, or if the job is large enough full-time workers can decide among themselves when each will work, as long as all of them put in a prescribed amount of time per day, week, month, or even a year (see Olmsted, Meier, and Smith, 1977).

5. Self-designed schedules—some proposals expand the degree of worker discretion by permitting them to design their own schedules, within limits imposed by organizational requirements. For example, Best (1973b) suggests that workers could submit their preferences for both the number of work hours they desire and the scheduling of these hours to their employers or supervisors a few days prior to each week. Computers would then be used to integrate individual schedules similar to the way they are now used to allocate classrooms in large universities and to reserve airline seats. Alternative preferences would also be submitted in case first choices cannot be accommodated.

Other proposals for self-designed work scheduling do not restrict the time frame within which the self scheduling can occur. For example, some proposals would permit workers to design their own schedules over a month, a year, or even a lifetime (Bosserman, 1971). Kaplan (1971) proposes that banks, in conjunction with industry, loan "free hours" as they now loan money to be repaid by work at some later date.

6. Other—Bass and Ryterband (1973) suggest the possibility of equalizing work by having people who do unpleasant work spend fewer hours at it than white-collar and professional workers spend at theirs (also see Bluestone and England, 1973). Porter (1973) proposes that the accrual of time off be used as a reward for satisfactory work performance.

As with the topic of industrial recreation, interest in the AWS was initially spurred by its expected impact on work; specifically, it was believed that rearranged schedules would lead to less turnover and absenteeism, more job satisfaction, increased production, and decreased operating costs (e.g., those costs associated with starting up and closing down a plant four days a week instead of five). More recently, the potential impact of AWSs on leisure has begun to attract a greater share of the attention. In particular, most of the AWSs that have either been implemented or proposed redistribute and combine formerly fragmented pieces of free time into larger, more meaningful chunks, effectively increasing the number of leisure options available to the worker. Consider, for example, the additional possibilities provided by a three-day weekend as opposed to a two-day weekend in which the loss of two hours of free time over four days of the week is more than made up by the opportunities provided by an extra day off per week. The longer the time frame over which work can be distributed, the more options are created, and when combined with such other developments as longer vacations, early retirement, and worker sabbaticals, the limits on leisure imposed by the availability of large blocks of free time could all but disappear. Of course, the potential has yet to be realized since most of these developments have not been implemented on a large scale.

There are several other possible effects that are worthy of note. A wider variety of schedules for the work force in general could lead to more efficient utilization of transportation and recreational facilities by equalizing demand for these facilities over time. More workers would have the opportunity to acquire further education. Flexible work scheduling and the increased availability of part-time work would allow people to enter the work force who would not otherwise be able to (e.g., women with children, the elderly, the handicapped). Husbands and wives would be able to coordinate their work schedules so that they can spend more time together (or apart, for that matter), and distribute homemaking and child-rearing responsibilities more equitably. Widespread use of part-time workers would create a readily available reserve of labor for unexpected workloads and times of emergency (Best, 1973b). And, finally, the potential savings in fuel consumption and commuting costs created by a shift to a shorter work week should not be overlooked.

Clearly, several factors can limit the situations in which AWSs can work. In organizations where people must work in concert, a wide variety of AWSs could interfere with the smooth flow of work. Organizations must also consider whether their new work schedules will fit into the larger business system within which they operate.

Other factors can act in a more general fashion to limit the spread of AWSs. Union opposition is one of these factors. Although the unions have shown more concern in recent years for the nonwork lives of their members—by pushing such nontraditional bargaining issues as early retirement, longer vacations, and the elimination of compulsory overtime—they have not looked favorably upon the AWS. The reason is that many of the AWSs presently under consideration require workers to put in more than eight hours a day, a standard for which the unions had worked long and hard. The possible fatigue associated with a ten-hour day, for example, cannot be compensated for, in the opinion of many union leaders, by an extra day off per week. In addition, there is the fear that some forms of the AWS could lead to a reduction in such widely accepted benefits as overtime, holidays, premium pay for night shifts, personal leave, and sick pay. Therefore, organized labor's efforts have generally been directed toward maintaining the 8-hour day and shortening the work week—e.g., to "4 + 32,"—a thrust spurred in part by a desire to create more job openings for the unemployed (see Raskin, 1976).

A number of legal technicalities could also block the proliferation of AWSs. For example, some states still have laws that limit the number of hours women can work per day (however, these laws conflict with federal regulations concerning sex discrimination and are therefore unenforceable). A more difficult problem is presented by state laws that set maximum hours of work beyond which overtime must be paid.

None of these factors appear insurmountable. The problem of intra- and interorganizational coordination means that there is no set plan appropriate for all companies and situations. Each organization is unique and has to develop work schedules to meet its specific needs and demands. No doubt the problems of coordination will for some time preclude the adoption of AWSs by many organizations, but as flexible work schedule options proliferate throughout the work world and new technologies are used in innovative ways to reduce the need to adhere to one work schedule, this obstacle to the further spread of AWSs should lessen considerably. Union opposition and legal restrictions may also change if it can be demonstrated that the benefits of the AWS concept outweigh the costs.

At this time, it is difficult to determine unequivocally whether the AWS concept has lived up to expectations since implementation of the concept is not yet sufficiently widespread, nor in operation long enough where it has been implemented. Nevertheless, from the limited data available it does seem that, in general, AWSs can have a positive impact on employee attitudes, absenteeism, lateness, traffic congestion, and utilization of equipment and facilities without adversely affecting productivity. Problems with scheduling and coordinating work and arranging overtime indicate that AWSs are not applicable in all situations. When they are applicable, they should be implemented with careful planning and consideration of the particular needs, characteristics and situations of individual organizations and the additional support programs and interventions needed to supplement work schedule revisions (Evans, 1975; Golembiewski and Hilles, 1977; Golembiewski, Hilles, and Kagno, 1974; Golembiewski, Yeager, and Hilles, 1975; Goodale and Aagaard, 1974; Haldi Assoc.,

Inc., 1978; Hartley, 1976; Hedges, 1977; Hopp and Sommerstad, 1977; Ivancevich, 1974; Mueller and Cole, 1977; Nord and Costigan, 1973; Owen, 1977; Schein, Maurer, and Novak, 1977; Swerdloff, 1975).

Research also indicates that AWSs can significantly affect family life and recreational activities, but the specific nature of these effects is a function of the particular AWS form adopted, the individual characteristics of the workers involved and the compatibility of the schedule with the worker's environment (e.g., work schedules of friends and spouses, local climate, operating hours and availability of recreational facilities and community services) (Dunham, 1977; Haldi Associates, Inc., 1978; Macklan, 1977; Nord and Costigan, 1973). Some research also suggests that widespread adoption of AWSs could have a number of important societal impacts but, once again, the specific nature of these impacts is subject to the influence of several other factors, including urban policy, geographical location, fuel costs, and the particular AWS form most widely adopted (Haldi Associates, Inc., 1978)—for example, continued deterioration of urban centers, a mild climate, minimal increases in the price of gasoline, and compressed work weeks would tend to increase camping in state and national parks.

Of the two AWS forms most frequently considered, flexitime and the compressed work week, the greater flexibility inherent to flexitime would appear to make this approach more generally acceptable. Indeed, the response to flexitime has been almost universally positive, while reaction to the compressed work week has been mixed. The biggest problem seems to be that the longer work days associated with compressed work weeks create difficulties for some workers, especially when the work is fatiguing (Goodale and Aagard, 1974; Haldi Associates, Inc., 1978). Fewer working hours in the week (e.g., a four day, 32 hour week) would no doubt increase the acceptability of the compressed work week.

It would seem fair to conclude that the AWS concept shows considerable promise. As with any other technology, however, it should be implemented with planning and careful consideration of the goals to be served, the specific conditions under which it will operate, and the particular form most appropriate to these goals and conditions. The unique advantages it offers for our work and our leisure depends on a recognition of both its potential and its limitations.

Adjusting to Retirement: One of the more salient manifestations of the recent interest in the problems of the elderly has been the increased attention to the difficulties workers may face in making the transition from a long and active work life to a relatively less active period of retirement. Although it appears that most workers will have little difficulty in adjusting to retirement (Atchley,

1971; Thompson, 1973), especially if their more immediate concerns for financial security and health are adequately met (Boyack, Brenner, Chapman, Linnell, Manion, Mulanaphy and Peterson, 1976), the abrupt changes in role, habit, and life style that retirement frequently entails can be, and often are, problems for many. The source of the problem might be the retiree's lack of experience with leisure skills and activities and their forced withdrawal from a satisfying job and their long-standing social relationships with their co-workers. They may also have difficulty in adjusting to the unaccustomed degree of autonomy associated with extended leisure or to functioning in an essentially "nonproductive" capacity for the first time since their childhood. The apparent incompatibility between their former work role and the demands of their new, often involuntary leisure role may prevent many retirees from enjoying what should be a pleasant reward for a lifetime of labor.

As with many of the other proposals described throughout this book there are two levels—the organizational and societal—at which programs can be implemented to facilitate the smooth transition from work to retirement. Probably the most important resource that organizations can provide is money, not only in the usual form of retirement pensions but for tuition aid and cost of living stipends to workers who wish to pursue further education. To be truly useful for workers facing retirement, these tuition plans should not be limited to only those courses that are relevant to jobs performed within the sponsoring company but should include "life-enrichment" and leisure education, as well as retraining for second-careers. A recent review of corporate preretirement programs indicates a growing acceptance of this departure from standard practice for company sponsored tuition-aid programs (O'Meara, 1974).

Time off from work is another resource that organizations can and frequently do provide to help prepare their employees for their eventual retirement; time off to take advantage of the educational opportunities described above and to perform community services. In addition, gradually decreased work hours and longer vacations can help older workers develop outside interests and acclimate themselves to extended periods of nonwork. Programs offering extended leaves of absence for continuing education and community service might also have to guarantee that employees will be able to return to their previous jobs or to similar jobs that offer approximately the same pay, status, and advancement opportunity.

Since preretirement counseling and planning assistance are related to positive attitudes and better adjustment to retirement (Atchley, 1976; Palmore, 1977) and are frequently cited by retirees as an important element in retirement preparation (Kalt and Kohn, 1975), these programs should also be considered by organizations concerned with the welfare of their older workers. In

131

addition to providing the employee with information on their retirement benefits, these programs often include counseling on financial planning (family
budgeting, estate planning, investment counseling, tax considerations, savings
plans), health care (medical benefits, physical problems of aging, diet, physical
examinations), legal matters, and housing advice (location and climate, costs of
renting and purchasing, retirement communities). Less frequently included are
counseling on subjects related to leisure activities, second career opportunities
(skill assessments, retraining programs, starting small businesses), the psychological problems and life style adjustments of retirement, the life planning
skills of self diagnosis, problem solving, and decision making, and the development of attitudes conducive to autonomy and adaptation to the relatively unstructured conditions of nonwork. There has been, however, increased interest
in incorporating these subjects into a more comprehensive approach to preretirement counseling (see Bartlett, 1974; Boyack et al., 1976; Ludlow, 1973;
O'Meara, 1974; Pyron, 1969). Program formats run the gamut from standardized company brochures and other literature to individual counseling and
group sessions that can even include the spouses of retiring employees (Boyack
and Tiberi, 1975; O'Meara, 1974; Pellicano, 1977).

A further organizational initiative would involve extending the role of organizations as communities in-and-of-themselves to include retirees by allowing them continued use of facilities, creating social clubs for retirees, employees
near retirement, and other interested persons, and generally maintaining links
between the organization and the retiree. In some cases, it might even be possible for the organization to provide part-time work tailored to the needs, experience, and skills of retirees.

Finally, an approach that does not appear to have received due consideration would be to make work and the work environment as much like nonwork
as is reasonably possible. The rationale for doing this is relatively straightforward. If a person's work experiences are meaningfully similar to his or her nonwork experiences, it would stand to reason that the transition from one to the
other should be relatively smooth and uneventful. Following the human poten-
tial/play model, one might hypothesize that by reducing the degree of structure imposed by the design of the work itself, its scheduling, and the environment in which it is embedded, and generally allowing and encouraging more
self-direction (autonomy) on the part of the worker, employees would be better
prepared for a less structured, more active retirement. While the studies cited
in Chapter 3 (p. 72) concerning the educative effect of work autonomy on nonwork do not specifically address the issue of retirement, extrapolations from this
research suggest that this hypothesis may indeed be valid. Noting that interpersonal skills—skills that appear to be particularly important in retirement

132

(McAvoy, 1977; Peppers, 1976)—also carry over from the job, Atchley (1976) reaches a similar conclusion concerning the role of job characteristics in preparing workers for retirement. He believes that "to the extent that jobs teach people self-direction, intellectual flexibility or sociability, they in effect prepare people for the demands of retirement" (p. 28).

Various extraorganizational developments, the societal level approaches referred to earlier, could supplement these organizational programs in several important ways. For example: (1) individuals exposed in their work years to the kind of unstructured leisure proposed in this chapter might be better prepared to make the transition to retirement; (2) by providing new career opportunities and supporting volunteer community service activities by retirees (see Chapter 2), federal, state, and local governments would create alternatives to mandatory leisure for active senior citizens who desire to maintain productive work roles; (3) improved public transportation systems and telecommunications-based substitutes, coupled with the widespread use of part-time work and decentralized work organizations, would also make it easier for retirees to remain at least somewhat active in the world of work (Chapter 3); (4) an educational system that was flexible, easily accessible, and facilitated the development of broader values than those based on traditional definitions of productivity (Chapter 2) would serve as a valuable leisure resource for retired workers, and ease transitions between work and leisure; (5) public policy initiatives to insure the "portability" of pension funds from one organization to another as workers change jobs throughout their work lives and legislation to allow older workers to reduce their work hours and draw partial pensions, as has recently been implemented in Sweden (see Bratthall, 1976), are additional examples of the mutually supportive relationships between societal and organizational level programs that can significantly improve the situation for retired workers.

All of these programs or some combination thereof would help transform what is too frequently a traumatic experience for many workers into an additional opportunity for growth and change. Because a growing number of individuals will face this transition in the years to come, this issue should be given a particularly high priority by I/O psychologists interested in the emerging problems of the post-industrial society.

Avocational Counseling and Design: Counseling on possible leisure activities is an important part of any program aimed at preparing people for retirement. Others, too, could benefit from a service of this sort. Prison inmates, ex-convicts, delinquent youth, hospital patients, former drug addicts, alcoholics and those seeking rehabilitation, the physically and mentally handicapped, the culturally disadvantaged, and even many people in the mainstream of society, including workers in organizations adopting alternative work schedules (e.g., see Nord and Costigan, 1973) and the temporarily unemployed all might find avocational counseling to be of some use at one point or other. Indeed, anyone whose leisure opportunities are constrained by circumstance, condition or ability is a potential client for a service of this sort.

Ideally, avocational counseling should provide individuals with the assistance they need to make free and intelligent use of their nonwork time. It can function as an information and referral service by assessing clients' recreational habits, needs, and skills and making them aware of compatible and available leisure options among which they can choose.

Avocational counseling is a relatively new field and as a result there is not a great deal of reported research or information on actual programs and services. However, one established program that is particularly worthy of comment is the avocational counseling project conducted by the Milwaukee public schools. The stated goals of this project are:

1.   To "open doors" for people in the mainstream of life who, for important and personal reasons, seek to raise the level of their potential through recreation/education outlets that are available locally.

2.   To ease the transition of temporarily sheltered persons who take the last step away from public institutional care and the first step back into community living.

3. To provide counseling and opportunities for leisure rehabilitation for persons who are on the fringe of the mainstream but need special assistance. (Milwaukee Public Schools, p. 1)

To meet these goals, a computerized classification system has been developed to match avocational interests, as indicated by an empirically derived "interest finder," with available recreational resources and activities in the community. The community activities are continually and systematically inventoried, updated, and filed.

Obviously there is a parallel between the preceding material and the discussion of the personnel counseling and placement system in Chapter 2, a parallel that is more than just coincidental. In effect, the program described above is also a personnel counseling and placement system, but instead of trying to match people with jobs it is concerned with matching people to avocational activities and resources. The overriding, generalized goal in each case is the same: to achieve a good match between people and the activities in which they are engaged.

This parallel suggests how the concepts, tools, and procedures of I/O psychology can be applied to subjects not usually included within its domain. The parallel is illustrated by the work of Robert P. Overs and his associates at the Curative Workshop of Milwaukee—work that has overlapped the activities of the Milwaukee Public Schools project (Overs, 1975; Overs, O'Connor, and DeMarco, 1974; Overs, Taylor, and Adkins, 1974). Specifically, Overs adapts the concepts, tools, and techniques of personnel psychology and vocational counseling for use in avocational counseling and, in the process, deals with several issues similar to those discussed in Chapter 2. For example, he notes that avocational counseling, like any other kind of counseling, is based on the notion of *individual differences* (Overs, 1975). He also discusses the *relative advantages of nonverbal instruments over paper-and-pencil inventories,* the *standardization* problems of paper-and-pencil inventories, and the development of *classification systems for avocational activities,* to mention just a few.

In light of these similarities, it would appear that I/O psychologists could help develop instruments for assessing recreationally relevant interests, skills, and personality characteristics, and for describing avocational environments, activities, and resources in terms of their psychological and psychosocial characteristics. Furthermore, the experience that many I/O psychologists have with the research strategies for matching individuals to jobs should be transferable to the development of more effective procedures for matching avocational interests and abilities.

The applications of I/O psychology to avocational counseling can be carried even further by proposing the development of a system for the design of individualized avocational activities similar to the job design technology called for in Chapter 3. Instead of focusing on personnel placement, job training, the individualization of existing jobs, and the design and synthesis of new careers, the proposed system would attempt to provide clients with compatible recreational opportunitites by recommending the acquisition of new skills and putting them in touch with the means for acquiring them, suggesting appropriate modifications that could be made in existing activities, and even synthesizing new activities when necessary.

Of course, the recommendations that arise from the counseling and design should be considered as just that—recommendations, not prescriptions. Clients would choose among alternatives and improvise to suit themselves. Indeed, to avoid overdependence on the structure inherent in a counselor-client relationship, clients should be encouraged to use the suggested or created activities and experiences as a foundation to be modified or built upon. The ultimate goal should be for individuals to develop enough initiative, imagination, spontaneity, adaptability, and independence to enable them to generate and direct their own leisure. In theory, effective avocational counseling and design should eliminate the need for the same in the future.

Considering the conceptual similarity between the system of individualized job design suggested in Chapter 3 and the system being proposed here, it might even be possible to develop a single, integrated system to deal with both work and leisure by reducing many of the present distinctions between them and concentrating on achieving satisfaction irrespective of the traditionally defined nature and functions of the resources, activities, preparation and facilities involved.

This brings us to the last topic to be discussed in this chapter, a topic that has already been referred to both implicitly and explicitly several times throughout this book and one which, in effect, now emerges as its overriding concern, the desirability of merging work and leisure in the post-industrial society and the various means at our disposal for accomplishing this end.

Theoretical/Empirical Perspective

Included within this perspective are the theories and models that postulate various relationships between work and leisure and the research that has been conducted to examine these theories. The two principal types of theories start with the assumption that work is the central focus of most people's lives and, therefore, exerts a strong influence on other aspects of their lives, particularly their leisure. Different hypotheses concerning the specific nature of this influence distinguish the two views. In the "spillover" theories the individual is pictured as transferring behavior, skills, and attitudes appropriate to, or acquired in their work to their nonwork. Advocates of this view often contend that "alienated" work leads to alienated leisure; for example, they might argue that because of the nature of their work, assembly-line workers will spend much of their nonwork time in activities that require little involvement, self-expression, imagination, and skill. The work alienation theories described in Chapter 3 exemplify this view, and the suppositions they make about the social and personal consequences of overly restrictive work (also described in Chapter 3) are examples of the hypotheses that arise from the spillover theories.

On the other hand, others have argued that workers "compensate" for unpleasant work experiences by engaging in nonwork activities that offer what they lack on the job (e.g., Friedmann, 1961). Using the example of assembly-line workers, a compensation theorist might predict that their leisure activities

136

will reflect the need fulfillment they have little opportunity to experience at work. Do-it-yourself home craftsmanship is an example of such compensation.

At least two other theories concerning the work-leisure relationship have also been suggested. One postulates no significant relationship between work and leisure (e.g., Roberts, 1970), and the other argues that the causal link is not from work to leisure but from leisure to work (e.g., Anderson, 1961; Dumazedier, 1967).

For several reasons, none of these theoretical positions is unequivocally supported by the research literature. On the one hand, conceptual confusion and value judgments have made it difficult to define operationally the various hypotheses that follow from the theories and to interpret the research. For example, as we saw in Chapter 3 it is not clear how the consumption-oriented values of those workers who express little desire for challenge and autonomy on their jobs should be classified in terms of the various work-leisure theories. That is, while some theorists and researchers might view consumption as appropriate compensation for work that offers little opportunity for higher-order need satisfaction (e.g., Faunce and Dubin, 1975), others might view consumption as an example of the overemphasis on the satisfaction of "false" needs that they feel is so characteristic of work in modern industrial societies (e.g., Marcuse, 1964).

On the other hand, the nature of a person's work is apparently not the only factor that influences their nonwork activities, or vice-versa. The role of such variables as age, sex, social class, personality characteristics and the various meanings different individuals may attribute to the same or similar activities can all moderate the relationship between work and leisure (Champoux, 1974; Kando and Summers, 1971).

For these reasons, the relationships observed between work and leisure are increasingly interpreted as reflecting a process far more complex than implied by either of the theoretical positions alone. In addition to the reciprocal effects of work and nonwork on each other, the observed relationships are also a function of individual differences in values, personality, and previous experience, the particular behavior or attitudes under consideration, and various factors that may not be directly related to work. Much of the recent theory and research has concentrated on the conditions under which work may influence nonwork in particular ways, or not at all; or for that matter, the conditions under which the direction of the relationship is in the opposite direction, from leisure to work, a situation that could become more common if the importance of leisure continues to grow in years to come (Champoux, 1974; Faunce and Dubin, 1975; Kando and Summers, 1971; Parker and Smith, 1976).

The relationships between work and leisure have been examined from another perspective as well. Although spillover/compensation theories are attempts to characterize the experience of individuals, this other perspective focuses on the nature of contemporary and future societies. The main controversy concerns the issue of "fusion" versus "polarity." According to Parker (1971) both the fusion and polarity positions are based on perceived changes in the content, organization, and setting of work in modern industrial societies. On the one hand, there are those who argue that the distinction between work and leisure has become blurred. For example, sociologist Harold Wilensky, one of the first to examine this issue in detail (Wilensky, 1960 and 1964) views the long coffee break, the business lunch, the do-it-yourself movement, and the golf game among business associates as evidence for a trend toward work-leisure fusion. On the other hand, Parker notes that some social observers dismiss these developments as unimportant when considered within the context of the main structures of modern industry and see, instead, a growing split between the various spheres of contemporary life, with work and leisure becoming more sharply differentiated and polarized.

Parker describes the parallel between spillover/compensation (he uses the expressions "extension" and "opposition"), and fusion/polarity as follows:

Extension of work into leisure in the life of the person is paralleled by fusion of work and leisure spheres in the society as a whole. Individual opposition of work and leisure is matched by polarity of spheres in society. (1971, p. 102)

Parker also describes the relationship between the two levels.

This is not to say that the societal arrangements for work and leisure necessarily impose themselves on every aspect of our personal lives. But it is obviously easier to sustain a personal pattern that is in line with the pattern of society in which we move. For example, if we want to keep work and leisure as distinctly opposite parts of our lives we shall find it easier to do so in a society that keeps places of work free from the influence of leisure and places of leisure free from the taint of work. (p. 102)

Resolving the fusion vs. polarity controversy on the basis of empirical evidence alone is difficult since there appears to be little systematic evidence from which definite conclusions can be drawn. In fact, it is not at all clear that either position is even amenable to experimental verification. Depending on

138

which aspects of work and leisure one examines, either position is potentially supportable. For example, increasing interest in longer vacations, worker sabbaticals, and alternative work schedules suggest fusion while the continued growth of large "multi-equal" institutions separated in time and space and with highly specialized well-defined functions (Dubin, 1973)—for example, work organizations, educational institutions, consumer groups, or labor unions—seems to be consistent with the separate spheres of activity postulated by the supporters of the polarity position. As with the spillover vs. compensation controversy, the best conclusion appears to be one that acknowledges that either fusion or polarity, or both, is occurring, depending on how we define the terms and on the particular circumstances under consideration.

Thus, in some respects we are moving toward a fusion of work and leisure, and in other respects toward a polarity. However, given the alternative futures perspective of this book and the social activism this perspective implies, *where we are going is less an issue than where we want to go and how we get there.* For our purposes, it would be more appropriate to ask which of the two situations, fusion or polarity, is desirable and what are the conditions that will bring each of them about. If a decision can be made concerning the first question, the task then becomes to design the mechanisms and policies that will produce the conditions amenable to the particular outcome we desire. This is where the normative perspective on work-leisure relationships enters the picture.

Normative Perspective

Parker (1971) uses the expressions "holists" to describe those people who advocate policies that would increase the interdependence of work and leisure and "segmentalists" to describe those who advocate keeping them apart. For Parker the difference between this controversy and the fusion/polarity and spillover/compensation issues to which it corresponds is that Parker's terms describe philosophies of life rather than issues that can be resolved by the weighing of evidence in favor of the competing theories. Nonetheless, the philosophy of life frequently reflects beliefs concerning the theoretical/empirical issues, with segmentalists tending to accept the compensation and polarity arguments while the holists generally go along with the spillover and fusion theses. To understand better the nature and implications of the two positions and the recommendations for social policy that flow from each, let us examine each of them in more detail.

Two basic assumptions underlie the segmentalist position. First, the spheres of work and leisure in modern industrial societies are relatively separate

139

LEISURE IN THE POST-INDUSTRIAL SOCIETY

and do not, as the polarity theorists argue, influence each other in any significant way. Second, leisure is rapidly gaining on work as a central life interest in modern societies. From these assumptions, segmentalists generally conclude that it would be easier to enhance quality of life, at least in the short run, by focusing our energies on the creation of more opportunities for satisfaction in leisure than by concentrating on improving work. In other words, segmentalists tend to believe that workers can and should *compensate* for alienating jobs by engaging in nonwork activities that offer the satisfaction they cannot derive from their jobs. As a result, segmentalists often recommend increased pay as a solution to the problem of alienating work.

Wilensky presents another argument commonly used to support the segmentalist position, an argument to which he does not necessarily subscribe, as we will see shortly.

> *Theorists of political pluralism . . . argue that . . . segmentation strengthens social stability or a democratic political order or both. Segmental participation in diverse spheres means limited commitment to each. Limited commitment blocks susceptibility to manipulation. Segmental and limited attachments to secondary organizations and the State leave the person free, and constrain tendencies to mass behavior. (1960, p. 546)*

Holists, on the other hand, tend to believe that because work spills over into leisure, fulfilling leisure cannot occur unless work is also fulfilling.

> *It might be easier to make leisure more meaningful if one at the same time could make work more demanding. . . . It may be slightly less demanding to reorganize work routines so that they become less routine, more challenging, and hence more instructive, than to cope all at once with the burdens placed on leisure by the evaporation of the meaning of work. . . . I believe that we cannot take advantage of what remains of our pre-industrial heritage to make leisure more creative, individually and socially, if work is not creative, too. (Riesman, 1958, pp. 370-371).*

In this view, efforts to improve experiences in one sphere affect and are in turn affected by circumstances in the other. Leisure cannot act as a substitute for work and therefore we must, it is argued, focus on both spheres at once, particularly on work, to make any real improvement in the overall quality of life. Parker also maintains that an integration of work and leisure may be "a more stable situation and easier to maintain than a split consciousness" (1971,

140

p. 123) and that segmentalist solutions tend to be shorter in range and smaller in scale and, as a result, ultimately less adequate than holistic solutions. Finally, in the following Wilensky presents the counterargument to the position he described in the quote several paragraphs earlier that segmentation increases social stability.

Some argue that segmental, and hence weak, attachments to various spheres of private life mean stronger attachments to remote symbols of nation, race, and class, which are expressed in hyperpatriotism, racism, extremist politics and fear of conspiracy. The root difficulty is assumed to lie in the failure of individuals and groups to integrate their diverse behavior into a coherent pattern—one which promotes and reflects healthy mastery of self and social environment. The resulting quest for role integration within the fragmented person easily becomes the collective quest for moral certainty in the community. (1960, pp. 545–546)

Clearly, the policies and programs advocated throughout this book are holistic in nature. The basis for this holism does not derive, however, from an unqualified acceptance of the spillover and fusion positions. It rests, instead, upon the following: (1) jobs can and frequently do influence an individual's nonwork behavior and attitudes; (2) similarly, work-related conditions and programs at the organizational and societal levels often have significant nonwork implications; (3) the converse is also true, that nonwork attitudes, considerations, and policies can at times influence the world of work; (4) satisfaction in both work and leisure are possible for most people and are, therefore, reasonable goals for which to strive; and (5) the policies and programs that have been recommended throughout this book to achieve relatively pragmatic and non-ideological goals are ultimately holistic in nature since they tend to reduce the distinctions between work and nonwork.

To elaborate on this last and particularly crucial point, let us again examine some of these recommendations and the goals they were designed to achieve.

1. *The counseling, placement, organizational support services and job creation schemes described in Chapter 2* can maximize the utilization of human resources by removing unneccessary barriers to employment and providing individuals with more work options and information that would enable them to choose wisely among these options.

2. *The technology-based educational system described in Chapter 2* can provide a flexible and accessible system capable of preparing people for work,

citizenship, and leisure in accord with their individual needs, circumstances, and desires.

3. *The job and organizational design proposals made in Chapter 3* can increase work satisfaction, organizational effectiveness, and the quality of life by giving workers more control over their work and greater opportunity to choose among a wider range of job contents.

4. *The spatial integration of work and nonwork via urban clustering or work decentralization as described in Chapter 3* can reduce travel time, costs, and other constraints associated with the journey to work, thereby generally increasing the accessibility of various job alternatives.

5. *The expanded use of emerging technologies to provide more flexibility in work content, scheduling, and location also described in Chapter 3* can increase worker control over their jobs and their ability to integrate them into their lives.

6. *The increased emphasis on self-generated, playlike leisure and the variety of proposals for bringing this about described earlier in this chapter* can provide more alternatives to the leisure resources and activities that presently dominate modern industrialized societies.

7. *The alternative work schedules, retirement programs, and avocational counseling services also described in this chapter* can provide more leisure options and enable workers to integrate their work and nonwork more effectively.

Taken as a whole, these recommendations for policy and programs would expand the availability of varied work, leisure, and educational options, and enable individuals to exercise more discretion in choosing among them as well as in determining the context and nature of the options themselves. In other words, these policies and programs would introduce more *"play,"* in the sense used here, into people's lives by removing some of the constraints typically associated with their work and education and sometimes even with their leisure. That is, they would increase the degree of *"autonomy"* people would experience in all three aspects of their lives. In effect, these aspects would become more alike in a particularly significant way, and the distinctions between them would be reduced.

Work, education, and leisure would resemble each other in yet another way. Each would provide individuals with opportunities to use and develop valued skills in the decision making, judgment, self-discipline, and responsibility inherent to the exercise of autonomy itself, as well as in the increased availability of more challenging work, education, and leisure options. Of course this does not mean that everyone at all times would or should seek challenge; even the most active and ambitious of individuals need to relax from time to time. The point is that there would be greater *opportunity* to select more challenging options.

Reducing the formal distinctions between work, education, and leisure would create, in turn, more opportunity for flexible life styles in which individuals could make easier transitions among all three. In other words, to end this discussion on the theme with which we began, their life styles and society would be *"holistic"* in the most important sense of the expression.

Conclusion

Perhaps it might even be possible to eliminate the distinctions between work, education, and leisure by characterizing them in terms of their underlying psychological dimensions. That is, in place of "leisure" we could talk about the discretion, choice, and personal control—in other words, the autonomy—that seems to be the essence of the concept of leisure and is apparently the one characteristic common to just about all its definitions. In place of "work" and "education," we could refer to the use and development of valued skills—the "growth" often associated with satisfying and satisfactory learning and performance. And the principal characteristic inherent to the concept of "job" would be the financial remuneration we receive for what would otherwise be referred to as work.

With this classification scheme it would be possible to avoid the frequently artificial and confusing distinctions we now make between many activities and deal with them in more meaningful terms. Table 3 illustrates this scheme by indicating the author's impressions of the relative degree to which the three characteristics of autonomy, growth, and extrinsic rewards can be found in a wide range of activities. For example, an army private generally has little opportunity for personal discretion once he or she decides to enter this line of work, but often has the opportunity to develop and use valued skills and receives the extrinsic rewards of moderate pay, substantial job security, housing, food, clothing, and inexpensive recreational and consumer benefits. Nonorganized amateur sports such as tennis, rock climbing, golf, and jogging are high in autonomy (assuming that the person is not subject to excessive social pressures to pursue these activities from business associates, friends, and spouses) and growth but, of course, provide no direct financial rewards.

The purpose of this table is to illustrate the proposed characterization scheme and not to suggest a definitive analysis of the listed activities. A more

143

Table 3. Proposed Characterization Scheme as Applied to Various Activities

Activities	Autonomy	Growth	Pay and Benefits
	Characteristic Dimensions		
Professional, administrative, and high-level technical work	+	+	+
Nonprofessional individual sports, chess, some educational experiences	+	+	−
"Goofing-off"	+	−	−
Necessary and repetitious housework and maintenance chores	−	−	−
Army private	−	+	+
Assembly-line work	−	−	+
High school football (particularly offensive interior lineman)	−	+	−
Night watchman	+	−	+

accurate characterization of each activity would require a closer examination of the subjective meanings attributed to these activities by the individuals who engage in them. For example, a night watchman might use the relatively unstructured circumstances (autonomy) of his or her job to study, read, or develop and practice other skills. Similarly, one could argue that "goofing-off" is very important to the development of the ability to relax—a particularly important skill in the fast-paced, high-pressure modern world. Or an assembly-line worker who "doubles-up" with a co-worker by taking turns doing both jobs while the other rests or who engages in occasional acts of industrial sabotage may be doing so to demonstrate and use his or her skills (imagination and ability to "beat the system") and exert some control over a highly structured and restrictive work situation. In essence, he or she is "playing" on and with a job.

By dealing with work, education, and leisure in these terms, it would no longer be necessary to distinguish between personnel selection and avocational counseling, job design and its avocational counterpart, and job training and education. Instead, these processes would all be part of an integrated, holistic approach to matching activities and their social, organizational, and physical environments to the needs and characteristics of individuals. Social policy and organizational programs could then be guided by criteria that are more directly related to the day-to-day experiences by which we assess the elusively subjective quality of our lives. The opportunity for autonomy and growth in more than just our jobs, together with a sustainable level of material comfort, are the goals toward which a post-industrial psychology can strive with a reasonable expectation of success. The potential payoffs associated with the fulfillment of these goals would appear to justify the effort.

Summary

Although it appears unlikely that we will soon become a leisure-centered society, the growing importance of leisure in our lives is, nevertheless, unmistakable. However, the possibility that we may not be able to rely as heavily on the consumption of leisure-oriented goods and services as we do at present, points to the need for alternative activities and resources. The concept of play and the psychological theories and research on this phenomenon suggest a more unstructured, self-generated and self-directed model for leisure that might be more compatible with the conditions and demands of the post-industrial age.

This concept also has implications for the relationship between work, leisure, and education. By emphasizing increased opportunities for autonomy and challenge in these three aspects of our lives, the policies and programs advocated throughout this book are consistent with the concept of play as interpreted here. Furthermore, the implementation of these proposals could lead to the integration of all three aspects of our lives and a more holistic approach to dealing with the problems that might arise in these traditionally separate contexts.

Notes and Suggestions for Further Reading

Among the many *general references* available on the subject of leisure, the author recommends the classic work by Huizínga (1950), the book by de Grazia (1964) covering a wide range of issues related to the subject, and Pieper's (1963) presentation of the classical interpretation of the concept. Kaplan (1975) and Neulinger (1974) offer comprehensive sociological and psychological perspectives on leisure including their own theoretical formulations, reviews of the research, and discussions of the societal implications.

Some interesting speculations on the *future of leisure* based on historical economic and demographic trends are offered by Johnston (1975) and Owen (1976). Specifically, the two articles taken together suggest that the recent

145

decline in birth rates could reduce the portion of a family's income traditionally expended on child-rearing, increasing their discretionary income in the process, and lead many families to defer further substantial increases in income in favor of more leisure time (e.g., by one of the partners only working part-time).

On the other hand, recent research suggests that *working women* may realize few if any of these leisure gains since the sum total of their paid work hours and housework frequently adds up to a net loss in free time (women with full-time jobs still end up doing most of the housework) (Berheide, Berk, and Berk, 1976; Fullerton and Byrne, 1976; Kreps, 1976; Vanek, 1974).

For a discussion of the possibilities of *future scarcities in leisure resources* see Dunn (1974). The potential *problems associated with the increased use of capital-intensive (i.e., technology-dependent) products in outdoor recreation* are discussed by Harry (1976).

In spite of the different emphases of the psychological theories of play described in this chapter, play is clearly a function of both the environment and of the individual's characteristics and abilities. The different emphases are useful, nonetheless, for identifying important issues and potential societal implications. For example, an emphasis on the individual's capacity for play draws attention to the issue of how *to prepare people for playlike leisure.* Some of the *educational implications* of this issue were discussed in Chapter 2. Caplan and Caplan (1974), Ellis (1973), and Green (1968) also address various aspects of this issue. Furthermore, the educational alternatives that stress relatively unstructured approaches to learning would appear to be relevant as well (e.g., Bremer and Bremer, 1972; Holt, 1970; Kohl, 1970; Neill, 1960 and 1966). The humanistic psychology and "human potential" movement suggests a less formal approach that might be more appropriate for adults. By focusing on personal responsibility, self-expression, interpersonal sensitivity, spontaneity, and awareness of ongoing experience, some of the philosophies and techniques that have been associated with this movement are apparently consistent with the model of playlike leisure proposed here (see Buhler and Allen, 1972; Saltman and Bernardi, 1972).

The environmental emphasis in play theories, on the other hand, draws attention to issues concerning *the design of environments, facilities, and resources to allow and encourage playlike leisure.* The proposals for the design of urban parks made by Gold (1975) and Jacobs (1961) are relevant to this issue. Jacobs also discusses the importance of and means for generating and maintaining a diversity of life styles, cultures, architectural traditions, and experiences in urban environments. As such, her recommendations appear to be particularly pertinent to leisure especially in light of the importance she attributes to the

146

mixing of functions (work, residence, leisure, shopping, etc.) within a relatively small geographical area. (e.g., a neighborhood).

The implications of the play model for *the design of playgrounds* is another case in point. The well-defined and inflexible shapes, arrangements, and functions of standard playground equipment would seem to be the very antithesis of play as it is viewed here. On the other hand, such recent innovations as the "adventure" or "junk" playground would appear to be more promising. Using some basic tools and building materials and an assortment of recycled junk that may include old tires, abandoned mattresses, empty cable reels, and so on, children can work with knowledgeable supervisors and essentially create their own play environments. In effect, play occurs during the construction of the playground itself as well as in its use. The adventure playground might also help to prepare children for adult leisure and work because it provides more opportunity for the experience of autonomy and challenge (for more discussion of adventure and junk playgrounds see Allen, 1968; Bengtsson, 1972; Hayward, Rothenberg, and Beasley, 1974; Hewes, 1974).

The use of technology-dependent consumer products in the design of leisure resources does not always impose unnecessary structure on the nature of these activities, and can even be a catalyst for imagination and spontaneity. For example, the development of relatively inexpensive, flexible, and compact portable videotape systems has increased the accessibility of this medium of expression to those who lack the training for operating more sophisticated equipment. Shamberg (1971) discusses the innovative use of this technology for education and community service as well as for leisure. This example also illustrates Davis and Taylor's point about the myth of "technological determinism" that was discussed in Chapter 3. That is, it is not the technology itself but the assumptions about human nature that guide the specific designs and uses of the technology—in the present context, via the consumer goods which are frequently so conducive to a passive, overly structured leisure. One could view the portable videotape system as a small-scale, relatively labor-intensive "appropriate technology" (see Notes for Chapter 1) that can be used to facilitate rather than repress autonomy and creativity.

For an annotated bibliography on the subject of *industrial recreation* see Schott and Crapo (1973). *Recreation Management: The Journal of Employee Recreation, Health and Education* is a valuable source for up-to-date information on this topic (available from the National Industrial Recreation Association, 20 N. Wacker Drive, Chicago, Ill. 60606). Two recent articles from this journal are particularly relevant to this text; Pfeiffer and Cohen (1977) describe a relaxation training program for employees and Rentz (1977) describes a proj-

147

ect in which disadvantaged youth were hired and trained by a local industry to build recreational facilities for their employees.

A comprehensive, nontechnical overview of different approaches to *alternative work schedules* with case studies can be found in Robison (1976).

Additional resource material on *retirement* include: Carp (1972), an overview of theory and research (also see Atchley, 1976); O'Meara (1977), an extensive practical summary of trends, issues, problems, and programs; Manion (1974), a brief discussion of preretirement education; Kelleher and Quirk (1974), an annotated bibliography of the literature on preparing for retirement; Barfield and Morgan (1974), a report of a research project on early retirement plans, attitudes, and experiences; Shelley and Shelley (1976), a proposal for a "retirement index" that could be used to determine when an individual is ready for retirement; and Palmore (1977), a research report on the development and evaluation of a comprehensive retirement planning program.

For descriptions of an *avocational counseling project for the elderly* see Overs, Taylor, Cassell, and Chernov (1977), and for the *handicapped* see Overs, DeMarco, and O'Connor (1974).

The concept of *intrinsic motivation* is as central to the subject of play as it is to work, indicating once more the inherent relationship between the two. For further discussion of the role of intrinsic motivation in play see Barnett (1976), Csikszentmihalyi (1975 and 1976), and Lepper and Greene (1975). The review of the theory and research on play and exploratory behavior by Weisler and McCall (1976) is also relevant as are the references on intrinsic motivation and work cited in Chapter 3.

Clearly, other dimensions could be added to the *characterization scheme* illustrated in Table 3 such as interpersonal relations, status, and physical activity. Or the existing dimensions might be profitably broken down into more specifically defined components. For example, it is tempting to split the "growth" dimension into two separate dimensions—the use of valued skills ("work") on the one hand, and the further development of these skills or the acquisition of new ones ("education"), on the other—but it is difficult to think of an activity high on one dimension and low on the other. The difficulty in separating the two might arise from the fact that using a skill leads to its further development just as physical exercise can lead to greater strength and coordination. Perhaps the split should be made between the use and further development of a valued skill, on the one hand, and the acquisition of new skills, on the other.

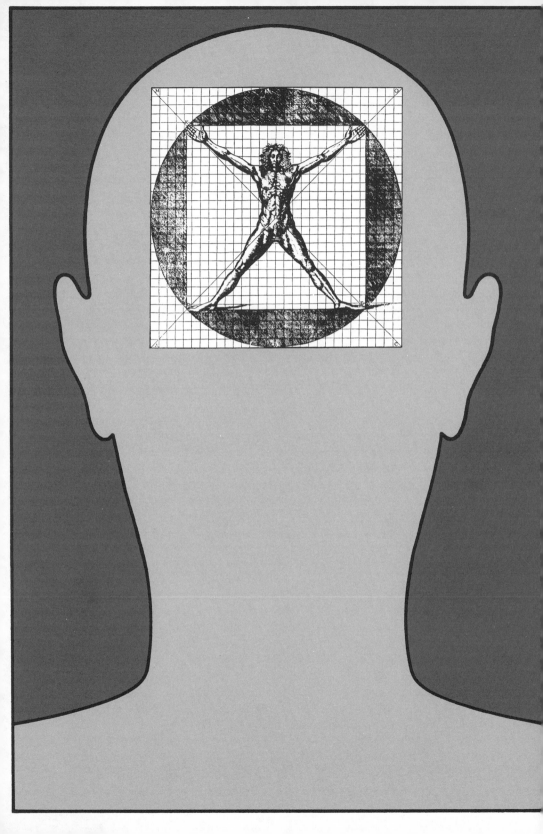

chap. 5

Conclusion:
The Sociotechnological Context for a Post-Industrial Psychology

Just as the first four chapters reflected an orientation somewhat different in emphasis from that found in most I/O psychology text books, the orientation of the present chapter differs from those preceding. In effect, all three orientations represent different points of observation. The more traditional orientation typically focuses on intraorganizational processes, issues, and problems, indicating a point of observation that lies *within the boundaries of the organization.* In contrast, the preceding chapters of this book were more characteristic of an ''open systems'' orientation (after Katz and Kahn, 1966) where the primary emphasis is on the interactions between organizations and their environments, and the point of observation is at the *organization-environment interface.* To illustrate the difference between these two orientations, the relationship between job design and its social and organizational context is an example of the first orientation while the interactions between job design and societal values, resource shortages, transportation, and sociopolitical attitudes are examples of the second.

The present chapter reflects a third orientation, an orientation that is well represented by Kenyon De Greene's book *Sociotechnical Systems* (1973). As the following quote shows, De Greene's use of the term ''sociotechnical system'' implies something considerably different from what was originally intended by those who coined it.

> *The term ''sociotechnical system'' of course had a very specific meaning as originally defined and used by Emery and Trist of the Tavistock Institute in London. In this book the original concept is greatly extended to include not only intraorganizational and organizational problems, but even more important, large-scale societal problems and political behavior in technological societies. Herein we deal more with high-level management situations than with work situations as was the case of most of the Tavistock writings. (p. xiv)*

Throughout his book De Greene uses the expression ''to cover a broad assemblage of theory, dynamic forces, practice, applications, and management concepts'' (p. 347) for dealing with ''the macrosystems of society, and with the identification of problems and design of techniques for the better management of society'' (p. 348). Since the original use of the expression ''sociotechnical systems'' is more consistent with the first (traditional) orientation of I/O psychology, the expression ''sociotechnological'' will be used to refer to the orientation of this last chapter. The connection between the three orientations, the paradigms described in Chapter 1 and the nature and focus of the activities I/O psychologists might perform with respect to these orientations are summarized in Table 4.

Table 4 The Relationship Between the Orientations Described in Chapter 5, the Paradigms of Chapter 1, and the Corresponding Foci for the Activities of I/O Psychologists

Examples	Paradigm	Orientation	Focus of I/O Psychology
—	''Scientific management''	—	On financial incentives and the physical conditions of work
Most standard texts in I/O psychology	''Social/organizational''	''Sociotechnical''	On the social and organizational context, in addition to the above
Present text (Chapts. 1–4)	''Post-industrial''	''Open systems''	On the interactions between organizations and society (the organizational response to societal trends and public policy, and, conversely, on the development of public policy directly impacting on work and organizations)
Present text (Chapt. 5)		''Sociotechnological''	On the societal context (on public policy issues relating to quality of life in general)

Although the issues discussed in this chapter have little *direct* relevance to the relationship between people, their work, and the organizations of which they are part—the usual purview of I/O psychology—they are nonetheless important since they provide the societal context, the infrastructure, within which the post-industrial psychology that has been described throughout this book can flourish.

The Information Utility

To realize the tremendous social and economic potential of a society in which the production, distribution, and processing of information is one of the most important activities, several writers in recent years have proposed the development of an "information utility" to provide a wide variety of information-based services to individuals and public and private institutions (e.g., Nanus, 1972; Parker, 1976; Parker and Dunn, 1972). This utility could be created by combining and elaborating upon many existing computer and telecommunications systems to form a vast communications network that would be available throughout the nation just as gas and electric utilities are today.

In addition to facilitating the job placement, educational, and "telecommutation" functions described in Chapters 2 and 3, an information utility could provide many other valuable services to individual and institutional users. For example, a family doctor or medical paraprofessional located in a remote area could use a combined two-way television and computer terminal linked with a distant hospital to consult with medical specialists and gain access to their diagnostic services. Terminals located in the home would enable citizens to instantaneously express their opinion on political issues presented via televised debates and town meetings. These same home terminals could also be used for shopping, paying bills, entertainment, household planning, and as a general information and library service.

Perhaps the most important social benefit to be derived from an information utility would be the opportunity it could provide to all persons for equal access to public information about jobs, education, consumer products and services, governmental processes, and virtually every other aspect of contemporary society. Given the growing importance of information and its increasingly profound impact on our daily lives, this is an opportunity that can hardly be taken lightly. As Parker and Dunn (1972) note:

If access to these information services is not universally available throughout the society, then those already "information-rich" may reap the benefits while the "information-poor" get relatively poorer. A widening of this "information gap" may lead to increased social tensions. On the other hand, policies stimulating universal availability may permit those presently economically or culturally deprived to gain information that could help them narrow the gap in economic and political power between themselves and the rest of society. (p. 1396)

153

As with all technologies, however, the potential social benefits are counterbalanced by potential social costs. For example, as Katzman (1974) points out, equal access does not necessarily mean equal use.

The problem is that economically and socially deprived individuals are also handicapped by motivational factors and other aspects of their psychological environments. Someone with the ability to make full use of communication technology may not want to bother with it when his environment is not supportive. Someone with marginal ability may be spurred to use new techniques by a supportive environment. The question has been misstated. It is not, "How can we provide equal access?" Rather, it is, "How can we insure equal use?" The answer to the former is not automatically the answer to the latter. (p. 130)

Unless means are developed to encourage and facilitate its use by individuals in all social strata, an information utility will only increase further the already large opportunity gap between the "information-rich" and the "information-poor."

An additional potential cost is the possible use of the information utility by those who might gain control of its channels and content to invade privacy and, even more serious, to manipulate people.

To safeguard against these abuses, to insure equal access, and to encourage and facilitate its use by all, this utility must serve and be accountable to the public interest. Furthermore, the needs to be met by this utility cannot be limited to those upon which a profit can be made. Finally, the necessity of coordinating and interconnecting the different uses, formats, and hardware systems that would make up this utility, coupled with the unique nature of the "commodity" it would provide, suggests that cooperation among information industries is more appropriate than competition (Parker, 1976).

These considerations, among others, point to the role of the federal government in establishing public policies and developing plans for the implementation, direction, and regulation of this utility. A similar conclusion has been at least implicit in several of the other proposals discussed throughout this book and the need to integrate and coordinate these complementary programs, including the information utility, further reinforces this conclusion. Since this issue lies at the heart of one of the most important and fiercely debated controversies of our time, the next several pages will summarize the issue, discuss its relevance to the themes of this book, and describe the characteristics and elements of its emerging resolution.

154

Planning the Future

The increasingly interrelated problems of unemployment, inflation, pollution, resource scarcities, the proliferation of ever more powerful technologies, the growing demands for equal opportunity and the wider availability of basic human services—indeed, the growing complexity of the post-industrial age in general—have led many people to call for the creation of more effective mechanisms for long-range social and economic planning. Remedial, piecemeal responses to problems as they arise are inappropriate, they argue, where the complexity of the problems and of societies requires coordinated, comprehensive action. Furthermore, the time delays between recognition of a problem and the impact of ameliorative steps indicate a need for foresight, readiness, and rapid response. Merely maintaining the status quo and proffering short-term solutions to existing problems is felt by some people to be less than what is ultimately possible and is, therefore, not enough. They urge, instead, that we strive toward a more ambitious, perhaps utopian, ideal of creating a more desirable future by explicating goals and by consciously planning the sociotechnological interventions needed to achieve these goals. The consequence of not doing so, they argue, is at best the failure to achieve desired objectives and at worst the fulfilling of goals nobody wants. This position is succinctly presented by Donald Michael, a prominent advocate of long-range social planning, in his critique of the long held belief that "what is missed by one disjointed and incremental action will be attended to by another" (1973, p. 4).

While there is little question that "disjointed incrementalism" . . . typifies the way organizations have behaved, many observers are pointing out that this is a major reason why the plight of the society is increasingly desperate. If there is to be an effective allocation of intellectual, psychological, and material resources and humane results from these allocations . . . something radically different [from] policies based on reflexive mini-twitches [will be required].

For many, then, the evidence seems overwhelming that disjointed incrementalism is profoundly inadequate for dealing with the present and the conjectured future. Indeed, much of the rapidly accumulating social mess can be seen as the legacy of an indifference to the future that resided in past applications of disjointed incrementalism to the production of knowledge as well as the governance of society. In an important sense, that approach worked so well in a simpler society that it produced, either through oversight or indifference, a state of affairs that may well be unmanageable now. . . . My position is simply that evidence seems to be accumulating that the traditional approaches are not working well enough to keep society from being overwhelmed by the pile-up of old and new problems, and that it is necessary to take new kinds of risks in the direction of [long-range social planning] rather than assume that liv-ing with the old risks of incrementalism will finally carry the day. (pp. 4–5)

The goals and plans presented throughout this book are similar in intent to the goals and plans proposed by those who advocate a more conscious and explicit process for planning the future; specifically, better means for developing and utilizing human resources, giving individuals more control over their lives, providing an adequate level of income and public services, and guaranteeing fundamental rights and freedoms (e.g., Ginzberg, 1976; Humphrey, 1975; Loebl, 1976; Okun, 1975; O'Toole, 1977). The specifics of the goals, planning mechanisms, and social interventions they propose may differ widely but they are in agreement in one important respect: the federal government must take a more active role in solving present and anticipated problems, providing and guaranteeing access of all citizens to essential human services, and generally guiding the future course of society.

On the other hand, the growing support for more planning is tempered by strong reservations that have arisen about this process from even its most outspoken advocates. These reservations derive from a recognition of the dangers inherent to this activity, the inadequacies of most conventional planning models, the inappropriateness of the systems used in other countries to the United States, and the distinct advantages associated with the traditional emphasis in this country on private enterprise, the free market, and the limited power of the federal government. Fortunately, these concerns have not dampened interest in planning so much as spurred imagination and thoughtful consideration of the ways in which it can be done more effectively and "liberally."*

An Emerging Model for Planning

Although the specifics of these more effective and liberal planning models are still very much a subject of debate, a consensus has begun to emerge on their

---

*In the sense used here, "liberally" means favoring "the freedom of individuals to act or express themselves in a manner of their own choosing" (from *The American Heritage Dictionary of the English Language*, 1975, p. 753).

general outline and characteristics. In particular, most of these models emphasize a democratic, decentralized, and flexible approach to goal setting and planning in contrast to the more authoritarian, centralized, and restrictive approaches that have been used in countries with dictatorial forms of government.

With respect to goals, this means that the role of the planner is not to impose his or her goals on the public but to inform citizens as to the range of alternative futures that are reasonably possible and help them to establish feasible objectives in light of these possibilities. This also implies that specific, fixed, collective goals that restrict individual options should be subordinated, whenever possible, to those that encompass and facilitate a wide range of personally defined objectives. The aim is to plan and create diverse opportunities for personal fulfillment, not to force conformity to a narrowly prescribed set of alternatives. Furthermore, chosen goals are not to be viewed as fixed ends but rather as guidelines that can be altered as the scope of possibilities and public values, wants, and needs change with time and circumstance.

Once goals have been established, government planning agencies would have the responsibility for formulating alternative plans for achieving these goals and presenting them to the public or their representatives along with a description of their potential consequences and associated costs and benefits. As with the process by which the goals are selected, the plans that would be ultimately adopted should reflect public discussion, democratic choice, and, if necessary, political compromise.

The implications of these plans for individual behavior also parallel those described with respect to the nature of the goals. In the words of Friedrich A. Hayek, renowned libertarian and critic of authoritarian planning: "the holder of coercive power should confine himself in general to creating conditions under which the knowledge and initiative of individuals are given the best scope so that *they* can plan most successfully" (1944, p. 35).

Finally, the performance of the plans should be continually evaluated to assess their effectiveness and their context monitored to identify previously unforeseen trends and developments. If this information indicates that the plans are ineffective or that the present and future societal context may not conform to what was previously expected, these plans can be modified or replaced.

This ability to learn from planning successes and failures, and to modify plans and goals accordingly, is one of the most important characteristics of many of the recently proposed models for societal guidance. Given our rudimentary knowledge of complex societal processes and our rather limited experience with the technology of planned social change, developing and implementing nontrivial social interventions with expectations and promises of unmitigated success is a naive and inevitably frustrating business. We must

157

learn to expect many partial successes and more than occasional failure, and to systematically use this information to improve upon our planning efforts.

An important corollary is that it is only through action that we can generate the knowledge and refine the techniques needed for social reform. Delaying innovation until we have all the necessary information only postpones change indefinitely and deprives us of the most effective means for acquiring this information, via the laboratory of the real world. If we recognize the unavoidably exploratory and risky nature of the venture, design the programs so that they can be effectively evaluated and modified, and accept, learn from, and use the experience of failure, a knowledge base will develop upon which more successful future interventions can be built.

While the planning model outlined in the last two paragraphs is consistent in some respects with the "incrementalism" that has typified more traditional approaches to social reform, several important differences do exist.

> The learning approach . . . is of course incremental in the sense that experiments and program and goal alterations proceed step-wise. But the philosophy and the consequences of its application are the antithesis of what is called for and follows from disjointed incrementalism as conventionally described and justified. The "increments" involved in [long-range social planning] are defined by deliberate choices of goals; they are future-oriented, innovative, and implemented even though outcomes are uncertain; they are articulated rather than disjointed; and they are responsible and responsive to environmental needs at least as much as to considerations of organizational survival and aggrandizement. (Michael, 1973, p. 63)

The final characteristic of the proposed planning models to be discussed here is the emphasis they place on integrating planning with the more traditional market system by selecting and trying to find the optimal combination of both approaches. Rather than setting production quotas and prices and tightly controlling the operations of individual organizations in the economy, as is frequently done in centrally planned societies, the planners in a mixed system would rely heavily on private enterprise to help perform many of the functions described in the preceding paragraphs. This could be accomplished by providing resources, guidance, and enabling mechanisms for business while selectively using incentives, government contracts, regulations and indirect interventions into the economy. Government planners would also be responsible for developing social programs to supply the goods and services that cannot be profitably and effectively provided by private enterprise and for coordinating the activities of individual organizations and industries and the public and private sectors. In effect, the relationship between the planners and the organizations that comprise the economy (including such essentially noneconomic entities as consumer groups and minority rights lobbies) would be similar in nature to the relationship between supervisors and work groups in technologically advanced organizations, that is, facilitating, boundary controlling, linking, and coordinating.

In conclusion, whether or not there will be government planning in the United States is a moot point since it is clear that a fair degree of planning is already taking place and has been for some time. Government intervention and regulation in the form of minimum wage laws, occupational safety and health standards, affirmative action guidelines, welfare programs, pollution standards, agricultural price supports, and regulation of public utilities are just a few examples. Some writers even claim that the largest corporations, because of their size and the resources at their disposal, wield enough power to manage a substantial portion of the economy in service of their own interests (e.g., Galbraith, 1975). The problem is that these efforts lack the degree of focus, coordination, comprehensiveness, public accountability, and long-range perspective needed to guide us through an uncertain and hazardous future. As Nobel Prize-winning economist and advocate of national planning Wassily Leontief argues:

> The real trouble at present is that the government not only does not know what road it wants to follow, but does not even have a map. To make things worse . . . one member of the crew in charge presses down the accelerator, another pumps the brakes, a third turns the wheel, and the fourth sounds the horn. Is that the way to reach your destination safely? (1976, p. 10)

And, we might add, the passengers rarely know what is going on and would have little opportunity to influence the process even if they did.

The issue is no longer planning vs. no planning, but rather what kind of planning. *Learning how* to develop a comprehensive democratic system for planning which expands opportunities for self-development could be the highest priority of a humane post-industrial society and the goal of our initial, tentative efforts to do the same.

Summary and Conclusions

The policies and programs recommended throughout this book comprise only a portion of a comprehensive system for increasing the control individuals can ex-

159

ert over their lives and the opportunities they have for self development. Instituting the policies and programs described here (as well as those that would complete the picture but necessarily lie outside the scope of the present book) would not be possible without the development of an appropriate societal infrastructure. One element of this infrastructure is the creation of a new public utility to facilitate the most equitable and socially beneficial use of information and its associated technology. A more effective planning mechanism would also be needed to develop and oversee this utility and the other policies and programs recommended in the preceding chapters.

The aim of this book has been to explore the ways in which I/O psychology could reflect the changing conditions of society and intentionally create change toward an image of a preferred future. As was pointed out in Chapter 1 this process is necessarily a subjective one, because of the uncertainties associated with projecting the future and the personal values inherent in any vision of what "should be." Since the future will ultimately be shaped by many events and human actions, both anticipated and unforeseen, the range of possible future alternatives goes beyond the views that have been presented here. Consequently, many may not agree with the recommendations expressed herein. Fine! The point was to make them explicit and overt so that they could be discussed and compared with the alternatives.

The active participation of I/O psychologists in the process of creating a future that provides every individual with the opportunity to find fulfillment in all aspects of their lives has never before been so necessary nor potentially rewarding. With foresight, intelligence, and a willingness to accept the risks associated with the uncertainty of the outcome, we can help develop the sociotechnological designs needed to achieve this ambitious but worthwhile goal. In other words, we must begin to move *toward a post-industrial psychology*. This book represents one approach to this end; clearly, there are many others. Indeed, the success of this book will rest, in part, on the extent to which it encourages the introduction of these views, their implications, and the values they reflect into the arena of professional and public debate.

Notes and Suggestions for Further Reading

The original emphasis of *sociotechnical systems theory* was on intraorganizational processes, particularly the interrelations between the technological and social aspects of work systems. As such, it reflected the traditional orientation described in the opening paragraph of this chapter. More recently, two of the researchers who played a central role in the early development of sociotechnical systems theory, Frederick E. Emery and Eric L. Trist, have written a book (Emery and Trist, 1973) that extends their earlier work to encompass the socio-technological framework described in this chapter.

Comprehensive discussion of the *pros and cons of planning* can be found in Galbraith, Wallich, Ulmer, and Weidenbaum (1976), Schuck (1976), and Weidenbaum and Rockwood (1977). Musgrave (1977) and the comments on his article by Fromm (1977) and Sweezy (1977) also deal with this issue as well as the collateral issue of the mixed economy. Similarly, Bell (1975), DiQuattro (1975), Etzioni (1976b), Harman (1974), Henderson (1976), Humphrey (1975), the Initiative Committee for National Economic Planning (1975), Loebl (1976), and Okun (1975) offer proposals that fall at various points on the continuum that lies between the poles of capitalism and socialism in their "purest" forms. Overviews of planning theory with more emphasis on the social than the economic dimensions can be found in Galloway and Mahayni (1977) and Michael (1973, Chapters 1 and 2). This last reference is particularly useful for its presentation of the emerging views of the meaning and purposes of long-range social planning.

In spite of the conventional wisdom that social programs rarely work, there is reason to believe that some recent *government efforts to alleviate social problems* have been more successful than previously thought (Ginzberg and Solow, 1974; Levitan and Johnson, 1976; Levitan and Taggert, 1976).

The notion of *planning as a learning process* where social programs are first implemented as pilot projects and then revised, expanded, or dropped on the basis of an evaluation of their effectiveness is developed in detail by Donald T. Campbell in his classic papers on the "experimenting society" (1969 and 1971). This theme is also central to Michael's view (1973) of the planning process. Other writers have extended the learning principle even further by arguing that the appropriate goal of planning should be to develop an adaptive capacity for rapid response whenever action needs to be taken, regardless of what the future has in store (Ackoff, 1970; Weick, 1969). This idea has been most frequently applied to corporate planning, but it would seem relevant to social planning as well.

Evaluating the performance of social plans and programs requires a means for assessing this performance. Economic performance can be measured in dollars and cents, but social performance cannot be expressed in such obvious, easily quantifiable terms. The growing interest in the nonmaterial aspects of the quality of life has led to a considerable amount of recent activity aimed at the development of *social indicators* for assessing existing conditions of an essentially noneconomic nature and the effectiveness of programs aimed at improving upon these conditions. For general information on this topic see Bauer

161

(1966), Campbell (1976), Campbell, Converse, and Rodgers (1976), Gross and Straussman (1974). Biderman (1971) proposes the use of communications media for conveying social indicator information to the public, while Krendall (1970) and Zapf (1974) discuss the possibility of using the public to provide information in the other direction, to the planners, as "monitors" and indicators of their own quality of life.

Umpleby (1972) carries these proposals a step further by suggesting the use of two-way telecommunications for *direct citizen participation in planning and decision making* via instantaneous public opinion polling and referendums and electronic town meetings. He notes further that this system could be coupled with computer-based simulations that would demonstrate to the citizenry the possible consequences of alternative policies. Citizens would then have the opportunity to express their opinions or even vote on these policies in light of the anticipated outcomes generated by the computer model.

One of the most promising developments in recent years has been the growing interest in *technology assessment* and the development of mechanisms for incorporating this information into public policy and decision making. Technology assessment, an essential element of any effective social planning process, is the attempt to systematically identify and evaluate the direct and indirect economic, social, institutional, and environmental impacts of the use of new technologies and the expansion of existing technologies. For more information on technology assessment see Coates (1971 and 1974).

The *corporate social audit* is an organizational level counterpart to the concept of social indicators. Briefly, corporate social auditing is an attempt to measure the effects of an organization's operation on society. Environmental pollution, compliance with equal employment regulations, occupational safety and health records, job satisfaction, and product safety are some of the factors that would enter into the assessment of an organization's social performance. For more information see Bauer and Fenn (1972) and Seidler and Seidler (1975). One manifestation of the corporate social audit that is particularly relevant to this book is the use of *human resource accounting*, a process for measuring the cost or value of a firm's human capital, to assess an organization's contribution to the development and utilization of its employee's skills (see Flamholtz, 1974; Rhode and Lawler, 1973).

Concern for corporate social performance grows out of the larger issue of *corporate social responsibility*. This issue is at least indirectly reflected throughout much of this book. Davis (1973) and Sethi (1974) provide good overviews of this issue.

A particularly intriguing way that *I/O psychology could precipitate social change* is illustrated by the recent research on work motivation. If one makes the admittedly oversimplified assumption that the image of human nature upon which capitalism is based emphasizes the role of immediate self-interest and financial incentives in human behavior (an essentially Paradigm I perspective), and that socialism emphasizes the importance of collectivism and social motivation (Paradigm II), what kind of socioeconomic system and institutions would be most consistent with a view that stressed the role of intrinsic motivation? Some interesting points of departure and source ideas can be found in Chomsky (1972, 1973), Claiborne (1971), Deci (1975a), DiQuattro (1975) and Herrnstein (1972, 1973).

References

Abdel-Halim, A. A. and K. M. Rowland. Some personality determinants of the effects of participation: A further investigation. *Personnel Psychology*, 1976, *29*, 41–45.

Abt Associates, Inc. *Telecommunications and education* (Report No. 73–145). Cambridge, Mass.: Abt Associates, 1974.

Ackoff, R. A concept of corporate planning. *Long Range Planning*, 1970, *3*, 2–8.

Agassi, J. B. The quality of women's working life. In L. E. Davis and A. B. Cherns (Eds.), *The quality of working life* (Vol. 1). New York: The Free Press, 1975.

Allardt, E. Work and political behavior. In R. Dubin (Ed.), *Handbook of work, organization and society*. Chicago: Rand-McNally, 1976.

Allen, Lady, of Hurtwood. *Planning for play*. Cambridge, Mass.: MIT Press, 1968.

Alpert, D. and D. C. Bitzer. Advances in computer-based education. *Science*, 1970, *167*, 1582–1590.

Altimus, C. A. and R. J. Tersine. Chronological age and job satisfaction: The young blue-collar worker. *Academy of Management Journal*, 1973, *16*, 53–66.

American Psychological Association. *The bylaws of the Division of Industrial and Organizational Psychology*. Washington, D.C.: APA, 1977.

Anderson, N. *Work and leisure*. London: Routledge, 1961.

Andrisani, P. J. and R. C. Miljus. Individual differences in preferences for intrinsic versus extrinsic aspects of work. *Journal of Vocational Behavior*, 1977, *11*, 14–30.

Argyris, C. *Integrating the individual and the organization*. New York: Wiley, 1964.

Argyris, C. *On organizations of the future*. Beverly Hills, Ca.: Sage Publications, 1973.

Astin, A. W. A manpower placement system for APA. *American Psychologist*, 1972, *27*, 479–481.

Atchley, R. C. Retirement and leisure participation: Continuity or crisis. *Gerontologist*, 1971, *11(1)*, 13–17.

Atchley, R. C. *The sociology of retirement*. New York: Wiley, 1976.

Barbash, J. Humanizing work: A new ideology. *AFL-CIO American Federationist*, 1977, *84(7)*, 8–15.

Barfield, R. E. and J. N. Morgan. *Early retirement: The decision and the experience and a second look.* Ann Arbor, Mich.: Institute for Social Research, University of Michigan, 1974.

Barnett, L. Play and intrinsic rewards: A reply to Csikszentmihalyi. *Journal of Humanistic Psychology*, 1976, *16(3)*, 83–87.

Barrett, G. V. and B. M. Bass. Cross-cultural issues in industrial and organizational psychology. In M. D. Dunnette (Ed.), *Handbook of industrial and organizational psychology.* Chicago: Rand-McNally, 1976.

Bartlett, D. M. Retirement counseling: Making sure employees aren't dropouts. *Personnel*, 1974, *51(6)*, 26–35.

Bass, B. M. Interface between personnel and organizational psychology. *Journal of Applied Psychology*, 1968, *52*, 81–88.

Bass, B. M. Organizational life in the 70's and beyond. *Personnel Psychology*, 1972, *25*, 19–30.

Bass, B. M. Self-managing systems, Z.E.G. and other unthinkables. In H. Meltzer and F. R. Wickert (Eds.), *Humanizing organizational behavior.* Springfield, Ill.: Charles C. Thomas, 1976.

Bass, B. M. and G. V. Barrett. *Man, work, and organizations: An introduction to industrial and organizational psychology.* Boston: Allyn and Bacon, 1972.

Bass, B. M. and R. Bass. Concern for the environment: Implications for industrial and organizational psychology. *American Psychologist*, 1976, *31*, 158–166.

Bass, B. M. and E. C. Ryterband. Work and organizational life in 2001. In M. D. Dunnette (Ed.), *Work and nonwork in the year 2001.* Monterey ,Ca.: Brooks/Cole, 1973.

Batten, M. D. and S. Kestenbaum. Older people, work and full employment. *Social Policy*, 1976, *7(3)*, 30–33.

Bauer, R. (Ed.). *Social indicators.* Cambridge, Mass.: MIT Press, 1966.

Bauer, R. A. and D. H. Fenn, Jr. *The corporate social audit.* New York: Russell Sage Foundation, 1972.

Baxter, N. Job-Flo: How to learn if there's a job in Dallas when you're jobless in Des Moines. *Occupational Outlook Quarterly*, 1976, *20(2)*, 2–7.

Beer, M. The technology of organization development. In M. D. Dunnette (Ed.), *Handbook of industrial and organizational psychology.* Chicago: Rand-McNally, 1976.

Beer, M. and J. W. Driscoll. Strategies for change. In J. R. Hackman and J. L. Suttle (Eds.), *Improving life at work.* Santa Monica, Ca.: Goodyear, 1977.

166

Bell, D. *The end of ideology*. Glencoe, Ill.: Free Press, 1960.

Bell, D. Labor in the post-industrial society. *Dissent*, Winter 1972, 103–189.

Bell, D. *The coming of post-industrial society*. New York: Basic Books, 1973.

Bell, D. *The cultural contradictions of capitalism*. New York: Basic Books, 1975.

Bem, S. L. and D. J. Bem. Does sex-biased job advertising "aid and abet" sex discrimination? *Journal of Applied Psychology*, 1973, *3*, 6–18.

Bengtsson, A. (Ed.). *Adventure playgrounds*. New York: Praeger, 1977.

Bennis, W. G. Organizational developments and the fate of bureaucracy. *Industrial Management Review*, 1966, 7, 41–55.

Bennis, W. G. *Organization development: It's nature, origins, and prospects*. Reading, Mass.: Addison-Wesley, 1969.

Berg, I. *Education and jobs: The great training robbery*. Boston: Beacon Press, 1971.

Berg, I. and M. Freedman. The American work place: Illusions and realities. *Change*, 1977, *9(11)*, 24–30; 62.

Berger, B. "People work": The youth culture and the labor market. *Public Interest*, Spring 1974, *(35)*, 55–66.

Berheide, C. W., S. F. Berk, and R. A. Berk. Household work in the suburbs: The job and its participants. *Pacific Sociological Review*, 1976, *19*, 491–518.

Berlyne, D. E. *Conflict, arousal and curiosity*. New York: McGraw-Hill, 1961.

Best, F. (Ed.) *The future of work*. Englewood Cliffs, N.J.: Prentice-Hall, 1973a.

Best, F. Flexible work scheduling: Beyond the forty-hour impasse. In F. Best (Ed.), *The future of work*. Englewood Cliffs, N.J.: Prentice-Hall, 1973b.

Best, F. and B. Stern. Education, work, and leisure: Must they come in that order? *Monthly Labor Review*, 1977, *100(7)*, 3–10.

Bezdek, R. and B. Hannon. Energy, manpower, and the highway trust fund. *Science*, 1974, *185*, 669–675.

Biderman, A. D. Kinostatistics for social indicators. *Educational Broadcasting Review*, 1971, *5(5)*, 13–19.

Biderman, A. D. and T. F. Drury (Eds.). *Measuring work quality for social reporting*. New York: Wiley, 1976.

Blauner, R. *Alienation and freedom: The factory worker and his industry*. Chicago: University of Chicago Press, 1964.

Blaxall, M. and B. Reagan (Eds.). *Women and the workplace*. Chicago: University of Chicago, 1976.

Blood, M. R. Job samples: A better approach to selection testing? *American Psychologist*, 1974, *29*, 218–219.

Blood, M. R. and C. L. Hulin. Alienation, environmental characteristics, and worker responses. *Journal of Applied Psychology*, 1967, *51*, 284–290.

Bluestone, B. and R. England. Equality at work: The effects of a guaranteed income. *Working Papers for a New Society*, 1973, *1(3)*, 40–47.

Bluestone, I. Worker participation in decision-making. *The Humanist*, Sept./Oct. 1973, 11–15.

Blum, M. L. and J. C. Naylor. *Industrial psychology: Its theoretical and social foundations* (Rev. ed.). New York: Harper & Row, 1968.

Blumberg, P. and J. M. Murtha. College graduates and the American dream. *Dissent*, Winter 1977, 42–53.

Boehm, V. R. Negro–white differences in validity of selection procedures. *Journal of Applied Psychology*, 1972, *56*, 33–39.

Boguslaw, R. *The new utopians: A study of system design and social change.* Englewood Cliffs, N.J.: Prentice-Hall, 1965.

Bosserman, P. Implications for youth. In M. Kaplan and P. Bosserman (Eds.), *Technology, human values and leisure.* Nashville, Tenn.: Abingdon Press, 1971.

Bouvin, A. New Swedish legislation on democracy at the workplace. *International Labour Review*, 1977, *115(2)*, 123–143.

Bowen, H. R. *Investment in learning: The individual and social value of American higher education.* San Francisco: Jossey-Bass, 1977.

Bowen, H. R. and G. L. Mangum (Eds.). *Automation and economic progress.* Englewood Cliffs, N.J.: Prentice-Hall, 1966.

Bowles, E. Older persons as providers of services: Three federal programs. *Social Policy*, 1976, *7(3)*, 81–88.

Boyack, V., H. Brenner, C. Chapman, R. H. Linnell, U. V. Manion, J. Mulanaphy and J. Peterson. *Pre-retirement planning programs.* Paper presented at Conference on Academic Planning for the Eighties and Nineties, University of Southern California, January 1976.

Boyack, V. L. and D. M. Tiberi. *A study of pre-retirement education.* Paper presented at the 28th Annual Gerontological Society Meeting, Louisville, Kentucky, October 1975.

Bratthall, K. Flexible retirement and the new Swedish partial-pension scheme. *Industrial Gerontology*, 1976, *3*, 157–165.

Brayfield, A. H. and W. H. Crockett. Employee attitudes and employee performance. *Psychological Bulletin*, 1955, *52*, 415–422.

Bremer, A. and T. Bremer. *Open education: A beginning.* New York: Holt, Rinehart and Winston, 1972.

Brenner, H. *Estimating the social costs of national economic policy: Im-

plications for mental and physical health and criminal aggression (Joint Economic Committee Paper No. 5). Washington, D.C.: U. S. Government Printing Office, 1976.

Brief, A. P. and R. J. Aldag. Employee reactions to job characteristics: A constructive replication. *Journal of Applied Psychology*, 1975, *60*, 182–186.

Brief, A. P. and R. J. Aldag. The intrinsic-extrinsic dichotomy: Toward conceptual clarity. *Academy of Management Review*, 1977, *2*, 496–500.

Broedling, L. A. The uses of the intrinsic-extrinsic distinction in explaining motivation and organization behavior. *The Academy of Management Review*, 1977, *2*, 267–276.

Brousseau, K. R. *Effects of job experience on personality* (Technical Report No. 14). New Haven, Conn.: Yale University, School of Organization and Management, January 1977.

Buckley, W. (Ed.). *Modern systems research for the behavioral scientist: A sourcebook*. Chicago: Aldine, 1968.

Buhler, C. and M. Allen. *Introduction to humanistic psychology*. Monterey, Ca.: Brooks/Cole, 1972.

Campbell, A. Subjective measures of well-being. *American Psychologist*, 1976, *31*, 117–124.

Campbell, A., P. E. Converse, and W. L. Rodgers. *The quality of American life*. New York: Russell Sage, 1976.

Campbell, D. Reforms as experiments. *American Psychologist*, 1969, *24*, 409–429.

Campbell, D. *Methods for the experimenting society*. Paper presented at the meeting of the American Psychological Association, Washington, D.C., September 1971.

Campbell, J. P. Personnel training and development. *Annual Review of Psychology*, 1971, *22*, 565–602.

Caplan, F. and T. Caplan. *The power of play*. Garden City, N.Y.: Anchor Press, 1974.

Caplan, N. *Competency among hard-to-employ youths*. Ann Arbor: University of Michigan, Center for Research in the Utilization of Scientific Knowledge, 1973.

Caplan, R. D., S. Cobb, V. R. P. French, Jr., R. Van Harrison, S. R. Pinneau, Jr. *Job demands and worker health* (HEW Publication No. (NIOSH) 75–160). Washington, D.C.: U. S. Government Printing Office, 1975.

Carey, M. L. Revised occupational projections to 1985. *Monthly Labor Review*, 1976, *99(11)*, 10–22.

Carnegie Commission on Higher Education. *The fourth revolution: Instruc-*

tional technology in higher education. New York: McGraw-Hill, 1972.

Carnegie Commission on Higher Education. *Toward a learning society: Alternative channels to life, work, and service.* New York: McGraw-Hill, 1973.

Carp, F. M. *Retirement.* New York: Behavioral Publications, 1972.

Cass, E. L. and F. G. Zimmer (Eds.). *Man and work in society.* New York: Van Nostrand, 1975.

Cavanagh, G. Humanizing influences of blacks and women in the organization. In H. Meltzer and F. R. Wickert (Eds.), *Humanizing organizational behavior.* Springfield, Ill.: Charles C. Thomas, 1976.

Champoux, J. E. *Work and nonwork: A review of theory and empirical research.* Unpublished manuscript, University of New Mexico, 1974.

Chomsky, N. The fallacy of Richard Herrnstein's IQ. *Social Policy*, 1972, *3(3)*, 19–25.

Chomsky, N. Comments on Herrnstein's response. *Cognition*, 1973, *1*, 407–418.

Churchman, C. W. *The systems approach.* New York: Delacorte Press, 1968.

Clague, E. and L. Kramer. *Manpower policies and programs: A review, 1935-75.* Kalamazoo, Mich.: W. E. Upjohn Institute, 1976.

Claiborne, R. Review of R. Titmuss, *The Gift Relationship. Washington Post*, May 9, 1971, p. 4.

Coates, J. F. Technology assessment: The benefits . . . the costs . . . the consequences. *The Futurist*, 1971, *5*, 225–231.

Coates, J. F. Some methods and techniques for comprehensive impact assessment. *Technological Forecasting and Social Change*, 1974, *6*, 341–357.

Conference Board. *Employing the disadvantaged: A company perspective.* New York: The Conference Board, 1972.

Conference Board. *Challenge to leadership: Managing in a changing world.* New York: The Free Press, 1973.

Coolican, D. M. *Self-planned learning: Implications for the future of adult education* (Educational Policy Research Center, Working draft 7402). Unpublished manuscript, Syracuse University Research Corporation, April 1974.

Cooper, R. and M. Foster. Sociotechnical systems. *American Psychologist*, 1971, *26*, 467–474.

Creed, E. C. The relationship of recreational participation to industrial efficiency. *Research Quarterly*, 1946, *17*, 193–203.

Crites, J. O. Career counseling: A comprehensive approach. *Counseling Psychologist*, 1976, *6(3)*, 2–12.

Crooks, L. A. (Ed.). *An investigation of sources of bias in the prediction of job performance: A six-year study.* Princeton, N. J.: Educational Testing Service, 1972.

Csikszentmihalyi, M. Play and intrinsic rewards. *Journal of Humanistic Psychology*, 1975, *15(3)*, 41–63.

Csikszentmihalyi, M. Replay to Barnett. *Journal of Humanistic Psychology*, 1976, *16(3)*, 89–91.

Culen, E. Leisure activities and spending. *The Conference Board: Road Maps of Industry* (No. 1712). April 15, 1973.

Davis, K. The arguments for and against corporate social responsibility. *Academy of Management Journal*, 1973, *16*, 312–322.

Davis, L. E. and A. B. Cherns (Eds.). *The quality of working life* (Vol. 1). New York: The Free Press, 1975a.

Davis, L. E. and A. B. Cherns (Eds.). *The quality of working life* (Vol. 2). New York: The Free Press, 1975b.

Davis, L. E. and J. C. Taylor (Eds.). *The design of jobs.* Middlesex, England: Penguin, 1972.

Davis, L. E. and J. C. Taylor. Technology effects on job, work, and organizational structure: A contingency view. In L. E. Davis and A. B. Cherns (Eds.), *The quality of working life* (Vol. 1). New York: The Free Press, 1975.

Davis, L. E. and J. C. Taylor. Technology, organization and job structure. In R. Dubin (Ed.), *Handbook of work, organization and society.* Chicago: Rand-McNally, 1976.

Day, L. H. Social consequences of zero economic growth. In A. Weintraub, E. Schwartz, and J. R. Aronson (Eds.), *The economic growth controversy.* White Plains, N. Y.: International Arts and Science Press, 1973.

Deci, E. L. *Intrinsic motivation.* New York: Plenum, 1975a.

Deci, E. L. Notes on the theory and meta theory of intrinsic motivation. *Organizational Behavior and Human Performance*, 1975b, *15*, 130–145.

de Grazia, S. *Of time, work, and leisure.* Garden City, N. Y.: Anchor Books, 1964.

De Greene, K. B. *Sociotechnical systems: Factors in analysis, design, and management.* Englewood Cliffs, N. J.: Prentice-Hall, 1973.

De Greene, K. B. Technological change and manpower resources: A systems perspective. *Human Factors*, 1975, *17*, 52–70.

Delworth, U. The paraprofessionals are coming! *Personnel and Guidance Journal*, 1974, *53*, 250.

DeMaria, A. T., D. Tarnowieski, and R. Gurman. *Manager unions? An AMA research report.* New York: American Management Association, 1972.

den Hertog, F. J. Work structuring. In P. Warr (Ed.), *Personal goals and work design.* New York: Wiley, 1976.

Dermer, J. The interrelationship of intrinsic and extrinsic motivation. *Academy of Management Journal,* 1975, *18,* 125–129.

Dickson, P. *The future of the workplace.* New York: Weybright and Talley, 1975.

DiQuattro, A. Market socialism and socialist values. *Review of Radical Political Economics,* 1975, *7(4),* 76–90.

Drucker, P. F. *The new society: The anatomy of industrial order.* New York: Harper & Row, 1962 (originally published 1949).

Drucker, P. F. *The age of discontinuity.* New York: Harper and Row, 1968.

Dubin, R. Work and nonwork: Institutional perspectives. In M. D. Dunnette (Ed.), *Work and nonwork in the year 2001.* Monterey, Ca.: Brooks/Cole, 1973.

Dubin, R. (Ed.). *Handbook of work, organization and society.* Chicago: Rand McNally, 1976.

Dubin, R. and J. E. Champoux. Central life interests and job satisfaction. *Organizational Behavior and Human Performance,* 1977, *18,* 366–377.

Dumazedier, J. *Toward a society of leisure.* New York: Collier-Macmillan, 1967.

Dunham, R. B. Reactions to job characteristics: Moderating effects of the organization. *Academy of Management Journal,* 1977a, *20,* 42–65.

Dunham, R. B. Shift work: A review and theoretical analysis. *Academy of Management Review,* 1977b, *4,* 624–634.

Dunn, D. R. Anticipating leisure resource scarcity. *Quest,* 1974, *21,* 41–45.

Dunnette, M. D. *Personnel selection and placement.* Belmont, Ca.: Wadsworth, 1966.

Dunnette, M. D. *Work and nonwork in the year 2001.* Monterey, Ca.: Brooks/Cole, 1973.

Dunnette, M. D. Aptitudes, abilities and skills. In M. D. Dunnette (Ed.), *Handbook of industrial and organizational psychology.* Chicago: Rand-McNally, 1976.

Dunnette, M. D., L. Hough, H. Rosett, E. Mumford, and S. A. Fine. Work and nonwork: Merging human and societal needs. In M. D. Dunnette (Ed.), *Work and nonwork in the year 2001.* Monterey, Ca.: Brooks/Cole, 1973.

Dyer, L. Implications of new theories of work for the design of compensation systems. In *Proceedings of the 28th Annual Meeting of the Industrial Relations Research Association.* Madison, Wisc.: Industrial Relations Research Association, 1976.

Dyer, L. and D. F. Parker. Classifying outcomes in work motivation research: An examination of the intrinsic-extrinsic dichotomy. *Journal of Applied Psychology*, 1977, *60*, 455–458.

Eberly, D. J. A model for universal youth service. *Social Policy*, 1977, *7(4)*, 43–46.

Elden, M. *Political efficacy at work: More autonomous forms of workplace organization link to a more participatory politics.* Paper prepared for the Seminar on Social Change and Organization Development, Dubrovnik, Yugoslavia, February 1977.

Ellis, M. J. Play: Practice and research in the 1970's. In *Leisure today: Research and thought about children's play.* Washington, D.C.: American Association for Health, Physical Education, and Recreation, 1972.

Ellis, M. J. *Why people play.* Englewood Cliffs, N.J.: Prentice-Hall, 1973.

Ellul, J. *The technological society.* New York: Random House, 1964.

Emery, F. E. *Systems thinking.* Middlesex, England: Penguin Books, 1969.

Emery, F. E. and C. Phillips. *Living at work.* Canberra, Australia: Australian Government Publishing Service, 1976.

Emery, F. E. and E. L. Trist. Sociotechnical systems. In C. W. Churchman and M. Verhulst (Eds.), *Management sciences: Models and techniques.* Oxford, England: Pergamon, 1960.

Emery, F. E. and E. L. Trist. *Towards a social ecology.* New York: Plenum, 1973.

Entine, A. D. The mid-career counseling process. *Industrial Gerontology*, 1976, *3*, 105–111.

Equal employment opportunity and other legal issues in industrial psychology on bias in selection. *Journal of Educational Measurement*, 1976, *13*, 1–99.

Espinosa, J. G. and A. S. Zimbalist. *Economic democracy: Workers' participation in the management of industrial enterprises in Chile, 1970-73.* New York: Academic Press, 1978.

Etzioni, A. National service for youth. *Human Behavior*, August 1976a, 13.

Etzioni, A. *Social problems.* Englewood Cliffs, N.J.: Prentice-Hall, 1976b.

Evans, M. G. A longitudinal analysis of the impact of flexible working hours. *Studies in Personnel Psychology*, 1975, *6(2)*, 1–10.

Fact sheets on Sweden: Swedish labor market policy. Stockholm: The Swedish Institute, March 1976.

Farr, J. L., B. S. O'Leary, and C. J. Bartlett. Ethnic group membership as a moderator of the prediction of job performance. *Personnel Psychology*, 1971, *24*, 609–636.

Faunce, W. A. and R. Dubin. Individual investment in working and living. In L. E. Davis and A. B. Cherns (Eds.), *The quality of working life* (Vol. 1).

New York: The Free Press, 1975.

Fechter, A. *Forecasting the impact of technological change on manpower utilization and displacement: An analytic summary.* Washington, D.C.: The Urban Institute, 1975.

Fein, M. The real needs and goals of blue collar workers. *The Conference Board Record*, February 1973, 26–33.

Feldstein, M. The economics of the new unemployment. *Public Interest*, Fall 1973, *(33)*, 3–42.

Ferrin, R. I. and S. Arbeiter. *Bridging the gap: A study of education-to-work linkages.* Princeton, N.J.: College Board Publications, June 1975.

Fincher, C. Differential validity and test bias. *Personnel Psychology*, 1975, *28*, 481–500.

Fine, S. A. *Guidelines for the design of new careers.* Kalamazoo, Mich.: W. E. Upjohn Institute for Employment Research, 1967.

Fine, S. A. *Guidelines for the employment of the culturally disadvantaged.* Kalamazoo, Mich.: W. E. Upjohn Institute for Employment Research, 1969.

Fine, S. A. Older workers in pursuit of new careers. In H. L. Sheppard (Ed.), *Industrial gerontology*, Cambridge, Mass.: Shenkman, 1970.

Fine, S. A. Functional job analysis: An approach to a technology for manpower planning. *Personnel Journal*, 1974, *53*, 813–818.

Fine, S. A. What's wrong with the hiring system? *Organizational Dynamics*, 1975, *4(2)*, 55–67.

The first national assessment of career and occupational development. Denver: National Assessment of Educational Progress, 1976.

Fiske, D. W. and S. Maddi. *Functions of varied experience.* Homewood, Ill.: Dorsey Press, 1961.

Flamholtz, E. *Human resource accounting.* Encino, Ca.: Dickenson, 1974.

Flanagan, R.,J., G. Strauss and L. Ulman. Worker discontent and workplace behavior. *Industrial Relations*, 1974, *13*, 101–123.

Fleishman, E. A. Toward a taxonomy of human performance. *American Psychologist*, 1975, *30*, 1127–1149.

Ford, R. N. *Motivation through the work itself.* New York: American Management Association, 1969.

Fowles, R. *Handbook of futures research.* Westport, Conn.: Greenwood Press, 1978.

Fox, H. and J. Lefkowitz. Differential validity: Ethnic group as a moderator in predicting job performance. *Personnel Psychology*, 1974, *27*, 209–223.

Foy, N. and H. Gadon. Worker participation: Contrasts in three countries. *Harvard Business Review*, 1976, *54(3)*, 71–83.

174

Frank, H. H. *Women in the organization*. Philadelphia: University of Pennsylvania Press, 1977.

Freedman, J. L. *Crowding and behavior*. New York: Viking, 1976.

Freeman, R. B. *The overeducated American*. New York: Academic Press, 1976.

Friedlander, F. and S. Greenberg. Effect of job attitudes, training and organization climate on performance of the hardcore unemployed. *Journal of Applied Psychology*, 1971, *55*, 287–295.

Friedmann, G. *The anatomy of work*. New York: The Free Press, 1961.

Fromm, G. Discussion: Market and plan; plan and market. *American Economic Review*, 1977, *67(1)*, 68–70.

Fullerton, H. N., Jr. and J. J. Byrne. Length of working life for men and women, 1970. *Monthly Labor Review*, 1976, *99(2)*, 31–35.

The future of computer conferencing: An interview with Murray Turoff. *The Futurist*, 1975, *9*, 182–195.

Galbraith, J. K. *Economics and the public purpose*. New York: New American Library, 1975.

Galbraith, J. K., H. Wallich, M. J. Ulmer, and M. L. Weidenbaum. Discussion: The case for and against national economic planning. *Challenge*, 1976, *19(1)*, 30–38.

Galle, O. R., W. R. Gove, and J. M. McPherson. Population density and pathology: What are the relations for man? *Science*, 1972, *176*, 23–30.

Galloway, T. D. and R. G. Mahayni. Planning theory in retrospect: the process of paradigm change. *American Institute of Planners Journal*, 1977, *43(1)*, 61–71.

Ganz, A. New directions for our cities in the seventies. *Technology Review*, 1974, *76(7)*, 11–19.

Gartner, A., R. A. Nixon, and F. Riessman (Eds.). *Public service employment*. New York: Praeger, 1973.

Ghiselli, E. E. *The validity of occupational aptitude tests*. New York: Wiley, 1966.

Giles, W. F. Volunteering for job enrichment: Reaction to job characteristics or to change? *Journal of Vocational Behavior*, 1977, *11*, 232–238.

Gilmer, B. v. H. *Industrial and organizational psychology*. New York: McGraw-Hill, 1971.

Ginzberg, E. (Ed.). *The future of the metropolis: People, jobs, income*. Salt Lake City, Utah: Olympus, 1974.

Ginzberg, E. *The human economy*. New York: McGraw-Hill, 1976.

Ginzberg, E. and R. M. Solow. Some lessons of the 1960's. *Public Interest*, Winter 1974, *(34)*, 211–220.

Glaser, E. M. *Productivity gains through worklife improvement*. New York:

The Psychological Corporation, 1976.

Glazer, N. *Affirmative discrimination: Ethnic inequality and public policy.* New York: Basic Books, 1975.

Glenn, N. D., P. A. Taylor, and C. N. Weaver. Age and job satisfaction among males and females: A multivariate, multisurvey study. *Journal of Applied Psychology*, 1977, *62*, 189–193.

Glickman, A. S. and Z. H. Brown. *Changing schedules of work: Patterns and implications* (R 73-1). Washington, D. C.: American Institutes for Research, 1973.

Goering, J. M. and E. M. Kalachek. Public transportation and black unemployment. *Society*, 1973, *10(5)*, 39–42.

Gold, S. M. The titanic effect on parks and recreation. *Parks and Recreation*, 1975, *10(6)*, 23–25; 42–43.

Goldstein, I. L. *Training: Program development and evaluation.* Monterey, Ca.: Brooks/Cole, 1974.

Goldthorpe, J. H., D. Lockwood, F. Bechhofer, and J. Platt. *The affluent worker in the class structure.* Cambridge: Cambridge University Press, 1969.

Golembiewski, R. T. and R. J. Hilles. Drug company workers like new schedules. *Monthly Labor Review*, 1977, *100(2)*, 65–69.

Golembiewski, R.T., R. Hilles, and M. Kagno. A longitudinal study of flexi-time effects: Some consequences of an OD structural intervention. *Journal of Applied Behavioral Science*, 1974, *10*, 503–532.

Golembiewski, R. T., S. Yeager, and R. Hilles. Factor analysis of some flexitime effects: Attitudinal and behavioral consequences of a structural intervention. *Academy of Management Journal*, 1975, *18*, 500–509.

Goodale, J. G. Effects of personal background and training on work values of the hard-core unemployed. *Journal of Applied Psychology*, 1973, *57*, 1–9.

Goodale, J. G. and A. K. Aagaard. *Varying reaction to the 4-day work week.* Paper presented at meeting of the American Psychological Association, New Orleans, September 1974.

Goodman, P. and P. Goodman. *Communitas: Means of livelihood and ways of life.* New York: Random House, 1960.

Goodman, P. S. and P. Salipante, Jr. Organizational rewards and retention of the hard-core unemployed. *Journal of Applied Psychology*, 1976, *61*, 12–21.

Goodman, P. S., P. Salipante, Jr., and H. Paransky. Hiring, training, and retaining the hard-core unemployed. *Journal of Applied Psychology*, 1973, *58*, 23–33.

Gorz, A. *Strategy for labor: A radical proposal.* Boston: Beacon Press, 1967.

Gotbaum, V. and E. Barr. On volunteerism. *Social Policy*, 1976, *7(3)*, 50–51.

Gottlieb, D. College youth and the meaning of work. *Vocational Guidance Quarterly*, 1975, *24(2)*, 116–124.

Gough, H. Personality and personality assessment. In M. D. Dunnette (Ed.), *Handbook of industrial and organizational psychology*. Chicago: Rand-McNally, 1976.

Gray, P. *Prospects and realities of the telecommunications/transportation tradeoffs.* Los Angeles: Center for Futures Research, University of Southern California, 1973.

Green, T. E. *Work, leisure, and the American schools.* New York: Random House, 1968.

Gross, B. M. and J. D. Straussman. The social indicators movement. *Social Policy*, 1974, *5(2)*, 43–54.

Grossman, R. and G. Daneker. *Guide to jobs and energy.* Washington, D. C.: Environmentalists for Full Employment, 1977.

Grubb, W. N. and M. Lazerson. Rally 'round the workplace: Continuities and fallacies in career education. *Harvard Educational Review*, 1975, *45*, 451–474.

Guest, A. M. Occupation and the journey to work. *Social Forces*, 1976, *55*, 166–181.

Guion, R. M. *Personnel testing.* New York: McGraw-Hill, 1965.

Guion, R. M. Employment testing and discriminatory hiring. *Industrial Relations*, 1966, *5*, 20–37.

Guion, R. M. Personnel selection, *Annual Review of Psychology*, 1967, *18*, 191–216.

Guion, R. M. Implications for governmental regulatory agencies. In L. A. Crooks (Ed.), *An investigation of sources of bias in the prediction of job performance: A six-year study.* Princeton, N. J.: Educational Testing Service, 1972.

Hackman, J. R. On the coming demise of job enrichment. In E. L. Cass and F. G. Zimmer (Eds.), *Man and work in society.* New York: Van Nostrand Reinhold, 1975.

Hackman, J. R. Personal communication. April 20, 1977.

Hackman, J. R. and E. E. Lawler, III. Employee reactions to job characteristics. *Journal of Applied Psychology*, 1971, *55*, 259–286.

Hackman, J. R. and G. R. Oldham. Development of the job diagnostic survey. *Journal of Applied Psychology*, 1975, *60*, 159–170.

Hackman, J. R. and G. R. Oldham. Motivation through the design of work: Test of a theory. *Organizational Behavior and Human Performance*, 1976, *16*, 250–279.

Hackman, J. R., G. Oldham, R. Janson, and K. Purdy. A new strategy for job enrichment. *California Management Review*, 1975, *17(4)*, 57–71.

Hackman, J. R. and J. L. Suttle (Eds.). *Improving life at work.* Santa Monica, Ca.: Goodyear, 1977.

Haldi Associates, Inc. *New directions in work schedules: User summary.* Washington, D. C.: National Science Foundation, 1977.

Hall, D. T. *Careers in organizations.* Pacific Palisades, Ca.: Goodyear, 1976.

Hammer, T. H. Employee-owned firms: The problems of conversion, industrial democracy and economic survival. *The Industrial Psychologist*, 1977, *14(4)*, 30–31.

Hammond, A. L. Computer-assisted instruction: Two major demonstrations. *Science*, 1972, *176*, 1110–1112.

Hamner, W. G. and L. W. Foster. Are intrinsic and extrinsic rewards additive: A test of Deci's cognitive evaluation theory of task motivation. *Organizational Behavior and Human Performance*, 1975, *14*, 398–415.

Hardin, G. The cybernetics of competition: A biologist's view of society. In W. Buckley (Ed.), *Modern systems research for the behavioral scientist: A sourcebook.* Chicago: Aldine, 1968.

Harkness, R. C. *Telecommunications substitutes for travel.* Unpublished doctoral dissertation, University of Washington, 1973.

Harman, W. W. Humanistic capitalism: Another alternative. *Journal of Humanistic Psychology*, 1974, *14*, 5–32.

Harry, J. E. Technological change and leisure: The case of outdoor recreation. *Humboldt Journal of Social Relations*, 1976, *3(2)*, 54–57.

Hartley, J. Experience with flexible hours of work. *Monthly Labor Review*, 1976, *99(5)*, 41–42.

Hartnett, R. T., M. J. Clark, R. A. Feldmesser, M. L. Gieber, and N. M. Soss. *The British Open University in the United States: Adaptation and use at three universities.* Princeton, N. J.: Educational Testing Service, 1974.

Hayek, F. A. *The road to serfdom.* Chicago: University of Chicago Press, 1944.

Hayward, D. G., M. Rothenberg, and R. R. Beasley. Children's play and urban playground environments: A comparison of traditional, contemporary, and adventure playground types. *Environment and Behavior*, 1974, *6*, 131–160.

Hedges, J. N. Flexible schedules: Problems and issues. *Monthly Labor Review*, 1977, *100(2)*, 62–65.

Henderson, H. The coming economic transition. *Technological Forecasting and Social Change*, 1976, *8*, 337–351.

Henle, P. Worker dissatisfaction: A look at the economic effects. *Monthly Labor Review*, 1974, *97(2)*, 58–59.

Hennig, M. and A. Jardim. *The managerial woman*. New York: Doubleday, 1977.

Herbert, W. Quality of working life: Congress tackles the job. *APA Monitor*, November 1977, pp. 6–7.

Herbst, P. G. *Autonomous group functioning: An exploration in behavior theory and measurement*. London: Tavistock, 1962.

Herbst, P. G. *Socio-technical design*. New York: Barnes and Noble, 1974.

Herrnstein, R. J. Whatever happened to vaudeville? A reply to Professor Chomsky. *Cognition*, 1972, *1*, 301–309.

Herrnstein, R. J. IQ: Social goals and the genetic heresy. *Transaction and Studies*, 1973, *40(4)*, 208–218.

Herzberg, F. *Work and the nature of man*. Cleveland: World, 1966.

Herzberg, F. One more time: How do you motivate employees? *Harvard Business Review*, 1968, *46(1)*, 53–62.

Herzberg, F., B. Mausner, and B. B. Snyderman. *The motivation to work*. New York: Wiley, 1959.

Hewes, J. J. *Build your own playground*. Boston: Houghton Miffin, 1974.

Hiemstra, R. *The older adult and learning*. Unpublished manuscript, University of Nebraska, Lincoln, 1975.

Hilgendorf, E. L. and B. L. Irving. Workers experience of participation: The case of British Rail. *Human Relations*, 1976, *29*, 471–505.

Hiltz, S. R. Computer conferencing: Assessing the social impact of a new communications medium. *Technological Forecasting and Social Change*, 1977, *10*, 225–238.

Holland, J. L. *Making vocational choices: A theory of careers*. Englewood Cliffs, N. J.: Prentice-Hall, 1973.

Holland, J. L. Vocational preferences. In M. D. Dunnette (Ed.), *Handbook of industrial and organizational psychology*. Chicago: Rand-McNally, 1976.

Holt, J. *What do I do Monday?* New York: Dutton, 1970.

Holt, T. A view from Albemarle. *Personnel Psychology*, 1977, *30*, 65–80.

Homans, G. C. *The human group*. New York: Harcourt, Brace, and World, 1950.

Hopp, M. A. and C. R. Sommerstad. Reaction at computer firm: More pluses than minuses. *Monthly Labor Review*, 1977, *100(2)*, 69–71.

House, J. The effects of occupational stress on physical health. In J. O'Toole (Ed.), *Work and the quality of life*. Cambridge, Mass.: MIT Press, 1974.

Howard, A. An assessment of assessment centers. *Academy of Management Journal*, 1974, *17*, 115–134.

Howe, L. K. *Pink Collar workers: Inside the world of women's work*. New York: Putnam, 1977.

Hoyt, K. B., R. N. Evans, E. F. Mackin, and G. L. Mangum. *Career education: What it is and how to do it.* Salt Lake City: Olympus, 1972.

Huber, J. Toward a socio-technological theory of the women's movement. *Social Problems*, 1976, *23*, 371–388.

Huizinga, J. *Homo ludens: A study of the play element in culture.* Boston: Beacon Press, 1950.

Hulin, C. L. and M. R. Blood. Job enlargement, individual differences, and worker responses. *Psychological Bulletin*, 1968, *69*, 41–45.

Humanist manifesto II. *The Humanist*, Sept./Oct. 1973, 4–9.

Humphrey, H. H. The U. S. Government's planning efforts: A criticism and a proposal. *World Future Society Bulletin*, 1975, *9(5)*, 3–10.

Hunnius, G., G. D. Garson, and J. Case. *Workers' control.* New York: Vintage books, 1973.

Hunt, R. G. *Interpersonal strategies for system management.* Monterey, Ca.: Brooks/Cole, 1974.

Hutchins, R. M. *The learning society.* New York: Mentor, 1968.

Initiative Committee for National Economic Planning. For a national economic planning system. *Social Policy*, 1975, *5(6)*, 17–19.

Ivancevich, J. M. Effects of the shorter workweek on selected satisfaction and performance measures. *Journal of Applied Psychology*, 1974, *59*, 717–721.

Jacobs, J. *The death and life of great American cities.* New York: Random House, 1961.

Jakubauskas, E. B. and N. A. Palomba. *Manpower economics.* Reading, Mass.: Addison-Wesley, 1973.

Jeffery, L. R. Computers and communications: Providing professional skills to serve society. *Matrix*, 1975, *8(1)*, 2–27.

Jenkins, D. *Job power: Blue and white color democracy.* New York: Doubleday, 1973.

Jennings, K. The problem of employee drug use and remedial alternatives. *Personnel Journal*, 1977, *56*, 554–578.

Jensen, A. R. How much can we boost I.Q. and scholastic achievement? *Harvard Educational Review*, 1969, *39*, 1–123.

Jewish Employment and Vocational Service. *Work-sample program: Experimental and demonstration project.* Philadelphia: JEVS, 1968.

Johansen, R. Social evaluations of teleconferencing. *Telecommunications Policy*, 1977, *2*, 395–419.

Johansen, R., R. DeGrasse, Jr., and T. Wilson. *Group communication through computers: Effects on working patterns* (Vol. 5). Menlo Park, Ca.: Institute for the Future, 1978.

Johansen, R., J. Vallee, and M. Palmer. *Computer conferencing: Measurable effects on working patterns.* Paper prepared for the National Telecommunications Conference of the Institute for Electrical and Electronic Engineers, Dallas, November 1976.

Johnston, D. F. *The future of work and leisure.* Paper presented at the Second General Assembly of the World Future Society, Washington, D.C., June 1975.

Kahn, H. *The future of the corporation.* New York: Mason and Lipscomb, 1974.

Kahn, R. L. The meaning of work: Interpretation and proposals for measurement. In A. Campbell and P. E. Converse (Eds.), *The human meaning of social change.* New York: Russell Sage, 1972.

Kahn, R. L. The work module: A tonic for lunchpail lassitude. *Psychology Today*, February 1973, 55.

Kalt, N. C. and M. H. Kohn. Pre-retirement counseling: Characteristics of programs and preferences of retirees. *Gerontologist*, 1975, *15*, 179–181.

Kando, T. M. and W. C. Summers. The impact of work on leisure: Toward a paradigm and research strategy. *Pacific Sociological Review*, 1971, *14*, 310–327.

Kanter, R. M. *Men and women of the corporation.* New York: Basic Books, 1977a.

Kanter, R. M. *Work and family in the U.S.: A critical review and agenda for research and policy.* New York: Russell Sage, 1977b.

Kaplan, M. A life of leisure. *Industrial Design*, 1971, *18(4)*, 17–18.

Kaplan, M. New concepts of leisure today. In *Leisure today: Changing concepts of leisure.* Washington, D.C.: American Association for Health, Physical Education, and Recreation, 1972.

Kaplan, M. *Leisure: Theory and policy.* New York: Wiley, 1975.

Karasek, R. A. *The impact of the work environment on life outside the job.* Institute for Social Research, Stockholm University, Stockholm, 1976.

Kassalow, E. M. White-collar unions and the work humanization movement. *Monthly Labor Review*, 1977, *100(5)*, 9–13.

Katz, D. and R. L. Kahn. *The social psychology of organizations.* New York: Wiley, 1966.

Katzell, M. E. and W. C. Byham. *Women and the work force.* New York: Human Sciences Press, 1972.

Katzell, R. A. and F. J. Dyer. Differential validity revived. *Journal of Applied Psychology*, 1977, *62*, 137–145.

Katzell, R. A. and D. Yankelovich. *Work, productivity and job satisfaction.*

New York: The Psychological Corporation, 1975.

Katzman, N. The impact of communication technology: Some theoretical premises and their implications. *Ekistics*, 1974, *225*, 125–130.

Kelleher, C. H. and D. A. Quirk. Preparation for retirement: An annotated bibliography of literature 1965–1974. *Industrial Gerontology*, 1974, *1*, 49–73.

Kemble, F. *Our national education and work policy: Pitfalls and possibilities.* Washington, D. C.: American Federation of Teachers, 1976.

Kirchner, W. K. Some questions about "Differential validity: Ethnic group as a moderator in predicting job performance." *Personnel Psychology*, 1975, *28*, 341–343.

Kirkpatrick, J. J., R. B. Ewen, R. S. Barrett, and R. A. Katzell. *Testing and fair employment.* New York: New York University Press, 1968.

Klausner, W. J. An experiment in leisure. *Science Journal*, 1968, *4(6)*, 81–85.

Koch, J. L. Employing the disadvantaged: Lessons from the past decade. *California Management Review*, 1974, *17*, 68–77.

Kohl, H. R. *Open classroom.* New York: Random, 1970.

Kohn, M. L. *Class and conformity: A study in values.* Homewood, Ill.: Dorsey, 1969.

Kohn, M. L. Occupational structure and alienation. *American Journal of Sociology*, 1976, *82*, 111–130.

Kohn, M. L. and L. Schooler. Class, occupation, and orientation. *American Sociological Review*, 1969, *34*, 659–678.

Kohn, M. L. and L. Schooler. Occupational experience and psychological functioning: An assessment of reciprocal effects. *American Sociological Review*, 1973, *38*, 97–118.

Korman, A. K. *Industrial and organizational psychology.* Englewood Cliffs, N. J.: Prentice-Hall, 1971.

Kornhauser, A. *Mental health of the industrial worker.* New York: Wiley, 1965.

Kremen, B. No pride in this dust. *Dissent*, Winter 1972, 21–28.

Krendall, E. A case study of citizen complaints as social indicators. *IEEE Transactions on Systems Science and Cybernetics*, 1970, *6*, 265–272.

Kreps, J. M. (Ed.). *Women and the American economy.* Englewood Cliffs, N. J.: Prentice-Hall, 1976.

Kreps, J. M. and R. Clark. *Sex, age and work: The changing composition of the labor force.* Baltimore: Johns Hopkins Press, 1975.

Kreps, J. M. and J. L. Spengler. The leisure component of economic growth. In H. R. Bowen and G. L. Mangum (Eds.), *Automation and economic progress.* Englewood Cliffs, N. J.: Prentice-Hall, 1966.

Kuhn, T. S. *The structure of scientific revolutions.* Chicago: University of Chicago Press, 1970.

Landy, F. J. and D. A. Trumbo. *Psychology of work behavior.* Homewood, Ill.: Dorsey, 1976.

Lawler, E. E., III. Job design and employee motivation. *Personnel Psychology,* 1969, *22,* 426–435.

Lawler, E. E., III. *Motivation in work organizations.* Monterey, Ca.: Brooks/ Cole, 1973a.

Lawler, E. E., III. *What do employees really want?* Paper presented at the meeting of the American Psychological Association, Montreal, August 1973b.

Lawler, E. E., III. *Can we legislate the quality of work?* Paper presented at the meeting of the American Psychological Association, New Orleans, September 1974.

Lawler, E. E., III. Individualizing organizations: A needed emphasis in organizational psychology. In H. Meltzer and F. R. Wickert (Eds.), *Humanizing organizational behavior.* Springfield, Ill.: Charles C. Thomas, 1976a.

Lawler, E. E., III. Quality of work life: Divergent viewpoints. *The Industrial-Organizational Psychologist,* 1976b, *13(4),* 38–39.

Lawrence, J. E. S. Science and sentiment: Overview of research on crowding and human behavior. *Psychological Bulletin,* 1974, *81,* 712–720.

Leavitt, H., L. Pinfield, and E. Webb. *On organizations of the future: Interaction with the external environment.* New York: Praeger, 1974.

Lefkowitz, J. and H. Fox. Some answers to "Some questions about Differential validity: Ethnic group as a moderator in predicting job performance." *Personnel Psychology,* 1975, *28,* 345–349.

Lekachman, R. Toward equality through employment. *Social Policy,* 1974, *5(3),* 6–11.

Leontief, W. National economic planning: Methods and problems. *Challenge,* 1976, *19(3),* 6–11.

Lepper, M. R. and D. Greene. Turning play into work: Effects of adult surveillance and extrinsic rewards on children's intrinsic motivation. *Journal of Personality and Social Psychology,* 1975, *31,* 479–486.

Levine, C. C. Occupational outlook handbook in brief: 1976–77 edition. *Occupational Outlook Quarterly,* 1976, *20(1),* 2–27.

Levitan, S. A. and R. S. Belous. *Shorter hours, shorter weeks: Spreading the work to reduce unemployment.* Baltimore: Johns Hopkins University Press, 1977.

Levitan, S. A. and B. H. Johnson. *The Job Corps: A social experiment that works.* Baltimore: Johns Hopkins Press, 1976.

183

Levitan, S. A. and W. B. Johnston. *Work is here to stay, alas.* Salt Lake City, Utah: Olympus, 1973.

Levitan, S. A., G. L. Mangum, and R. Marshall. *Human resources and labor markets.* New York: Harper and Row, 1976.

Levitan, S. A. and R. Taggart. *The promise of greatness.* Cambridge, Mass.: Harvard University Press, 1976.

Levitan, S. A. and R. Taggart. *Jobs for the disabled.* Baltimore: Johns Hopkins Press, 1977.

Levitt, T. The industrialization of service. *Harvard Business Review*, 1975, *54(5)*, 63–74.

Levitt, T. Management and the "post-industrial" society. *Public Interest*, Summer 1976, *(44)*, 69–103.

Levy, S. J. Drug abuse in business: Telling it like it is. *Personnel*, 1972, *49(5)*, 8–13.

Likert, R. *New patterns of management.* New York: McGraw-Hill, 1961.

Linder, S. B. *The harried leisure class.* New York: Columbia University Press, 1970.

Livingston, D. *Intermediate technology and the decentralized society.* Paper presented at the meeting of the American Psychological Association, Washington, D. C., May 1976.

Locke, E. A. The nature and causes of job satisfaction. In M. D. Dunnette (Ed.), *Handbook of industrial and organizational psychology.* Chicago: Rand-McNally, 1976a.

Locke, E. A. The case against legislating the quality of work life. *The Personnel Administrator*, 1976b, *21(5)*, 19–21.

Locke, E. A. Legislating the quality of work life: Locke's reply to Lawler's rebuttal. *The Industrial-Organizational Psychologist*, 1976c, *14(1)*, 24.

Loebl, E. *Humanomics.* New York: Random House, 1976.

Lopez, F. M., Jr. Current problems in test performance of job applicants: I. *Personnel Psychology*, 1966, *19*, 139–150.

Ludlow, H. T. Thinking about retirement—Do we know how? *The Conference Board Record*, 1973, *10(4)*, 48–62.

Maccoby, M. Changing work: The Bolivar project. *Working Papers for a New Society*, 1975, *3(2)*, 43–55.

Mackinnon, D. W. *An overview of assessment centers* (Technical Report No. 1). Greensboro, N. C.: Center for Creative Leadership, 1975.

Maier, N. R. F. *Psychology in industrial organizations* (4th ed.). Boston: Houghton Mifflin, 1973.

Maklan, D. M. How blue-collar workers on 4-day workweeks use their time. *Monthly Labor Review*, 1977, *100(8)*, 18–26.

Mangum, G. I. and J. Walsh. *A decade of manpower development and planning.* Salt Lake City: Olympus, 1973.

Manion, U. V. Issues and trends in preretirement education. *Industrial Gerontology,* 1974, *1(4),* 28–36.

Mankin, D. A. Leisure in a steady-state society. *Society and Leisure,* 1976, *8(3),* 97–103.

Marando, V. L. Metropolitanism, transportation, and employment for the central-city poor. *Urban Affairs Quarterly,* 1974, *10,* 158–169.

Marcuse, H. *One-dimensional man: Studies in the ideology of advanced industrial society.* Boston: Beacon Press, 1964.

Marien, M. The two visions of post-industrial society. *Futures,* 1977, *9,* 415–431.

Maslow, A. H. *Motivation and personality.* New York: Harper & Row, 1954 (2nd ed., 1970).

Maslow, A. H. *Eupsychian management: A journal.* Homewood, Ill.: Dorsey Press, 1965.

McAvoy, L. H. Needs of the elderly: An overview of the research. *Parks and Recreation,* 1977, *12(3),* 31–35.

McCall, M. W., Jr. and E. E. Lawler, III. High school students' perceptions of work. *Academy of Management Journal,* 1976, *19,* 16–24.

McClean, A. A. Job stress and the psychosocial pressures of change. *Personnel,* 1976, *53(1),* 40–49.

McCormick, E. J. Job and task analysis. In M. D. Dunnette (Ed.), *Handbook of industrial and organizational psychology.* Chicago: Rand-McNally, 1976.

McCormick, E. J. and J. Tiffin. *Industrial psychology* (6th ed.). Englewood Cliffs, N. J.: Prentice-Hall, 1974.

McGregor, D. *The human side of enterprise.* New York: McGraw-Hill, 1960.

Meadows, D. H., D. L. Meadows, J. Randers, and W. W. Behrens. *The limits to growth.* New York: Universe Books, 1972.

Meissner, M. The long arm of the job: A study of work and leisure. *Industrial Relations,* 1971, *10,* 239–260.

Meltzer, H. and F. R. Wickert (Eds.). *Humanizing organizational behavior.* Springfield, Ill.: Charles C. Thomas, 1976.

Mesthene, E. G. *Technological society: Its impact on man and society.* New York: New American Library, 1970.

Michael, D. The individual: Enriched or impoverished? Master or slave? In *Information technology: Some critical implications for decision makers.* New York: The Conference Board, 1972.

Michael, D. N. *On learning to plan—and planning to learn.* San Francisco: Jossey-Bass, 1973.

Michael, D. N. On growth and the limits of organizational responsiveness. *Technological Forecasting and Social Change*, 1977, *10*, 1–14.

Milkovich, G. T. and L. R. Gomez. Day care and selected employee work behaviors. *Academy of Management Journal*, 1976, *19*, 111–115.

Milwaukee Public Schools. *Leisure counseling media kit.* Division of Municipal Recreation and Adult Education, Milwaukee, Wisc.

Mirengoff, W. and L. Rindler. *The Comprehensive Employment and Training Act: Impact on people, places, programs.* Washington, D. C.: National Academy of Sciences, 1976.

Molnar, A. R. *Viable goals for educational technology efforts: Science education and the new technological revolution.* Paper presented at the meeting of the American Association for the Advancement of Science. New York, January 1975.

Moore, G. H. and J. N. Hedges. Trends in labor and leisure. *Monthly Labor Review*, 1971, *94(2)*, 3–11.

Moos, R. H. and P. M. Insel. *Work environment scale: Technical report.* Palo Alto, Ca.: Social Ecology Laboratory, Department of Psychiatry, Stanford University, 1974.

Morgan, R. P. *Technology and telecommunications in education.* Unpublished manuscript, Washington University, 1976.

Moses, J. L. *The technical assistance program: A review of the Public Policy and Social Issues Committee in action.* Paper presented at the meeting of the American Psychological Association, Washington, D.C., September 1976.

Moses, J. L. and W. C. Byham (Eds.). *Applying the assessment center method.* New York: Pergamon Press, 1977.

Mueller, O. and M. Cole. Concept wins converts at federal agency. *Monthly Labor Review*, 1977, *100(2)*, 71–74.

Mumford, L. *The myth of the machine: The pentagon of power.* New York: Harcourt Brace Jovanovich, 1970.

Münsterberg, H. *Psychology and industrial efficiency.* Boston: Houghton Mifflin, 1913.

Munts, R. and I. Garfinkel. *The work disincentive effects of unemployment insurance.* Kalamazoo, Mich.: W. E. Upjohn Institute for Employment Research, 1974.

Musgrave, R. A. National economic planning: The U. S. case. *American Economic Review*, 1977, *67(1)*, 50–54.

Nanus, B. Managing the fifth information revolution. *Business Horizons*, 1972, *15(2)*, 5–13.

Nanus, B. The future-oriented corporation. *Business Horizons*, 1975, *18(1)*, 5–12.

186

National Commission for Manpower Policy. *Proceedings of a conference on public service employment.* Washington, D. C.: NCMP, May 1975.

National Commission for Manpower Policy. *An employment strategy for the United States: Next steps.* Washington, D. C.: NCMP, 1976.

National Manpower Policy Task Force. *The best way to reduce unemployment is to create more jobs.* Washington, D. C.: NMPTF, June 1975.

Neff, W. S. *Work and human behavior.* New York: Atherton Press, 1968.

Neill, A. S. *Summerhill: A radical approach to child rearing.* New York: Hart, 1960.

Neill, A. S. *Freedom—not license!* New York: Hart, 1966.

Neugarten, B. L. The future and the young-old. *The Gerontologist,* 1975, *15(1),* 4–9.

Neulinger, J. *The psychology of leisure.* Springfield, Ill.: Charles C. Thomas, 1974.

Neumann, E. A. *The elements of play.* Unpublished doctoral dissertation, University of Illinois, 1971.

Nicholson, N., C. A. Brown, and J. K. Chadwick-Jones. Absence from work and job satisfaction. *Journal of Applied Psychology,* 1976, *61,* 728–737.

Nieva, V. F. and B. A. Gutek. Women and work: A bibliography of psychological research. JSAS *Catalog of Selected Documents in Psychology,* 1976, *6,* 50. (Ms. No. 1257).

Nilles, J. M., F. R. Carlson, P. Gray, and G. J. Hanneman. *The telecommunications-transportation tradeoff: Options for tomorrow.* New York: Wiley, 1976.

Nord, W. R. The failure of current applied behavioral science—a Marxian perspective. *Journal of Applied Behavioral Science,* 1974, *10,* 557–579.

Nord, W. R. *Dreams of humanization and the realities of power.* Paper presented at the meeting of the American Psychological Association, Washington, D. C., Sept. 1976.

Nord, W. R. Job satisfaction reconsidered. *American Psychologist,* 1977, *12,* 1026–1035.

Nord, W. R. and R. Costigan. Worker adjustment to the four-day week: A longitudinal study. *Journal of Applied Psychology,* 1973, *58,* 60–66.

Notz, W. W. Work motivation and the negative effects of extrinsic rewards: A review with implications for theory and practice. *American Psychologist,* 1975, *9,* 884–891.

Novick, M. R. and D. D. Ellis, Jr. Equal opportunity in educational and employment selection. *American Psychologist,* 1977, *32,* 306–320.

Obradovic, V. Participation and work attitudes in Yugoslavia. *Industrial Relations,* 1970, *9,* 161–169.

187

Oettinger, A. G. *Run, computer, run: The mythology of educational innovation.* New York: Macmillan, 1971.

Okun, A. M. *Equality and efficiency: The big tradeoff.* Washington, D. C.: The Brookings Institute, 1975.

Oldham, G. R. Job characteristics and internal motivation: The moderating effect of interpersonal and individual variables. *Human Relations*, 1976, *29*, 559–569.

Oldham, G. R., J. R. Hackman, and J. L. Pearce. Conditions under which employees respond positively to enriched work. *Journal of Applied Psychology*, 1976, *61*, 395–403.

O'Leary, L. R. Fair employment, sound psychometric practice, and reality: A dilemma and a partial solution. *American Psychologist*, 1973, *28*, 147–150.

Olmsted, B., G. Meier, and S. Smith. *Job sharing.* Palo Alto, Ca.: New Ways to Work, 1977.

O'Meara, J. R. Retirement—the eighth age of man. *The Conference Board Record*, 1974, *11(10)*, 59–64.

O'Meara, J. R. *Retirement: Reward or rejection?* New York: The Conference Board, 1977.

O'Neill, G. K. *The high frontier: Human colonies in space.* New York: Morrow, 1977.

O'Toole, J. (Ed.). *Work and the quality of life.* Cambridge, Mass.: MIT Press, 1974.

O'Toole, J. The reserve army of the underemployed: I—The world of work. *Change*, May 1975, 26–33; 63.

O'Toole, J. *Energy and social change.* Cambridge, Mass.: MIT Press, 1976.

O'Toole, J. *Work, learning and the American future.* San Francisco: Jossey-Bass, 1977.

Overby, C., J. Hutchison, and R. Wiercinski. *Transportation-communications tradeoffs: Some employment implications for homebound persons—vocational prostheses.* Paper presented at Seventh International Symposium on Human Factors in Telecommunications, Montreal, September 1974.

Overs, R. P. Avocational counseling: Gateway to meaningful activity. *Counseling and Values*, 1975, *20(1)*, 36–41.

Overs, R. P., E. O'Connor, and B. DeMarco. *Avocational activities for the handicapped: A handbook for avocational counseling.* Springfield, Ill.: Charles C. Thomas, 1974.

Overs, R. P., S. Taylor, and C. Adkins. *Avocational counseling in Milwaukee.* Milwaukee: Curative Workshop of Milwaukee, 1974.

Overs, R. P., S. Taylor, E. Cassell, and M. Chernov. *Avocational counseling for the elderly*. Sussex, Wisc.: Avocational Counseling Research, Inc., 1977.

Owen, J. D. Workweeks and leisure: An analysis of trends, 1948–75. *Monthly Labor Review*, 1976, *99(8)*, 3–8.

Owen, J. D. Flexitime: Some problems and solutions. *Industrial and Labor Relations Review*, 1977, *30*, 152–160.

Owens, W. A., and D. O. Jewell. Personnel selection. *Annual Review of Psychology*, 1969, *20*, 419–446.

Palmore, E. Predicting longevity: A follow-up controlling for age. *Gerontologist*, 1969, *9*, 247–250.

Palmore, E. A practical experiment in preretirement planning. *Advances in Research*, 1977, *1(3)*, 1–5.

Paper session: Career trends, personality, and life satisfaction. Presented at the meeting of the American Psychological Association, Washington, D. C., September 1976.

Parker, E. B. Social implications of computer/telecoms systems. *Telecommunications Policy*, 1976, *1*, 3–20.

Parker, E. B. and D. A. Dunn. Information technology: Its social potential. *Science*, 1972, *176*, 1392–1399.

Parker, S. R. *The future of work and leisure*. New York: Praeger, 1971.

Parker, S. R. and M. A. Smith. Work and leisure. In R. Dubin (Ed.), *Handbook of work, organization, and society*. Chicago: Rand-McNally, 1976.

Parsons, H. M. What happened at Hawthorne? *Science*, 1974, *183*, 922–932.

Pascal, A. H., D. Bell, L. A. Dougharty, W. L. Dunn, and V. M. Thompson. *An evaluation of policy related research on programs for mid-life career redirection: Major findings* (Vol. 2). (R-1582/2-NSF). Santa Monica, Ca.: Rand Corporation, February, 1975.

Pateman, C. *Participation and democratic theory*. Cambridge, England: Oxford University Press, 1970.

Pateman, C. A contribution to the political theory of organizational democracy. *Administration and Society*, 1975, *7(1)*, 5–26.

Patrick, R. A. Everybody wins with van pooling. *Transportation USA*, 1976, *1(4)*, 12–15.

Patten, T. H., Jr. *Manpower planning and the development of human resources*. New York: Wiley, 1971.

Payne, R. and D. S. Pugh. Organizational structure and climate. In M. D. Dunnette (Ed.), *Handbook of industrial and organizational psychology*. Chicago: Rand-McNally, 1976.

Payton-Miyazaki, M. and A. H. Brayfield. The good job and the good life: Relation of characteristics of employment to general well-being. In A. D.

189

Biderman and T. F. Drury (Eds.), *Measuring work quality for social reporting*. New York: Wiley, 1976.

Pellicano, D. F. Overview of corporate pre-retirement counseling. *Personnel Journal*, 1977, *56(5)*, 235–236; 255.

Peppers, L. G. Patterns of leisure and adjustment to retirement. *Gerontologist*, 1976, *16*, 441–446.

Perry, W. *The open university: History and evaluation of a dynamic innovation in higher education*. San Francisco: Jossey-Bass, 1977.

Pfeiffer, G. J. and M. D. Cohen. Relaxation training in a corporate environment. *Recreation Management*, 1977, *20(5)*, 12–15.

Piaget, J. *Plays, dreams and imitation in childhood*. New York: Norton, 1962.

Pieper, J. *Leisure: The basis of culture*. New York: New American Library, 1963.

Pinder, C. C. Additivity versus nonadditivity of intrinsic and extrinsic incentives: Implications for work motivation, performance, and attitudes. *Journal of Applied Psychology*, 1976, *61*, 693–700.

Piovia, E. S., R. B. Hill, and W. Leigh. *Journey to work patterns of transportation consumers among the urban disadvantaged*. (DOT-05-10191). Washington, D. C.: National Urban League, December 1973. (NTIS No. PB-230 704).

Poor, R. (Ed.). *4 days, 40 hours: Reporting a revolution in work and leisure*. Cambridge, Mass.: Bursk and Poor, 1970.

Porat, M. U. *The information economy* (Vol. 1). Unpublished doctoral dissertation. Stanford University, 1976.

Porter, L. W. Personnel management. *Annual Review of Psychology*, 1966, *17*, 395–422.

Porter, L. W. Ad Hoc Committee on Public Policy and Social Issues. *The Industrial Psychologist*, 1971, *8*, 42–43.

Porter, L. W. Turning work into nonwork: The rewarding environment. In M. D. Dunnette (Ed.), *Work and nonwork in the year 2001*. Monterey, Ca.: Brooks/Cole, 1973.

Porter, L. W., E. E. Lawler, III, and J. R. Hackman. *Behavior in organizations*. New York: McGraw-Hill, 1975.

Porter, L. W. and R. M. Steers. Organizational, work, and personal factors in employee turnover and absenteeism. *Psychological Bulletin*, 1973, *80*, 151–176.

Prendergast, C. (Ed.). *Productivity: The link to economic and social progress*. Scarsdale, N. Y.: Work in America Institute, 1976.

Purcell, T. V. What are the social responsibilities for psychologists in industry?

A symposium. *Personnel Psychology*, 1974, *27*, 435–453.

Pyron, H. C. Preparing employees for retirement. *Personnel Journal*, 1969, *48*, 722–727.

Quinn, R. P. and M. S. Baldi de Mandilovitch. *Education and job satisfaction: A questionable payoff.* Ann Arbor, Mich.: Survey Research Center, University of Michigan, 1975.

Quinn, R. P., T. W. Mangione, and M. S. Baldi de Mandilovitch. Evaluating working conditions in America. *Monthly Labor Review*, 1973, *96(11)*, 32–41.

Quinn, R. P., G. L. Staines, and M. R. McCullough. *Job satisfaction: Is there a trend?* (USDOL Manpower Research Monograph No. 30). Washington, D. C.: U. S. Government Printing Office, 1974.

Qvale, T. U. A Norwegian strategy for democratization of industry. *Human Relations*, 1976, *29*, 453–469.

Raskin, A. H. Breakthrough on work hours. *World of Work Report*, 1976, *8(1)*, 4–5.

Ramsay, H. Participation: The shop floor view. *British Journal of Industrial Relations*, 1976, *14(2)*, 129–141.

Rentz, N. J. Community service program nets new recreation facilities. *Recreation Management*, 1977, *20(9)*, 12–15.

Report of the National Advisory Commission on Civil Disorders. New York: Bantam Books, 1968.

Revzin, P. More services are performed by paralegals; attorneys have mixed feeling about trend. *Wall Street Journal*, November 14, 1975, 32.

Rhode, J. G. and E. E. Lawler, III. Auditing change: Human resource accounting. In M. D. Dunnette (Ed.), *Work and nonwork in the year 2001*. Monterey, Ca.: Brooks/Cole, 1973.

Rice, A. K. *Productivity and social organization: The Ahmedabad experiment.* London: Tavistock, 1958.

Rickover, H. C. A humanistic technology. *The Humanist*, Sept./Oct. 1969, 23–24.

Riesman, D. Leisure and work in post-industrial society. In E. Larrabee and R. Meyersohn (Ed.), *Mass leisure*. Glencoe, Ill.: Free Press, 1958.

Riskin, C. Incentive systems and work motivations: The experience in China. *Working Papers for a New Society*, 1974, *1(4)*, 27–33; 77–92.

Ritti, R. R. *The engineer in the industrial corporation.* New York: Columbia University Press, 1971.

Roberts, K. *Leisure.* London: Longmans, 1970.

Robertson, D. E. Update on testing and equal opportunity. *Personnel Journal*, 1977, *56*, 144–147.

Robey, D. Task design, work values, and worker response: An experimental test. *Organizational Behavior and Human Performance*, 1974, *12*, 264–273.

Robison, D. (Ed.). *Alternative work patterns: Changing approaches to work scheduling.* Scarsdale, N. Y.: Work in America Institute, 1976.

Robison, D. Affirmative action: The key issue is proportionate representation. *World of Work Report*, 1977, *2*, 37; 44–45.

Roeber, R. J. C. *The organization in a changing environment.* Reading, Mass.: Addison-Wesley, 1973.

Roethlisberger, F. J. and W. J. Dickson. *Management and the worker.* Cambridge, Mass.: Harvard University Press, 1939.

Rosenthal, N. H. Projected changes in occupations. *Monthly Labor Review*, 1973, *96(12)*, 18–26.

Rosow, J. M. (Ed.). *The worker and the job.* Englewood Cliffs, N. J.: Prentice-Hall, 1974.

Roszak, T. Forbidden games. In *Technology and human values.* Santa Barbara, Ca.: Center for the Study of Democratic Institutions, 1966, 25–32.

Roszak, T. *The making of a counter culture.* Garden City, N. Y.: Anchor Books, 1969.

Rousseau, D. M. Technological differences in job characteristics, employee satisfaction, and motivation: A synthesis of job design research and sociotechnical systems theory. *Organizational Behavior and Human Performance*, 1977, *19*, 18–42.

Ruble, T. L. Effects of one's locus of control and the opportunity to participate in planning. *Organizational Behavior and Human Performance*, 1976, *16*, 63–73.

Rush, H. M. F. and J. K. Brown. The drug problem in business: A survey of business opinion and experience. *The Conference Board Record*, 1971, *8(3)*, 6–15.

Ryterband, E. *A model for managing mid-career crises.* Paper presented at the meeting of the American Psychological Association, Washington, D. C., December 1976.

Sadler, W. A., Jr. Creative existence: Play as a pathway to personal freedom and community. *Humanitas*, 1969, *5*, 57–80.

Salipante, P. and P. Goodman. Training, counseling, and retention of the hard-core unemployed. *Journal of Applied Psychology*, 1976, *61*, 1–11.

Salpukas, A. Unions: A new role? In J. M. Rosow (Ed.), *The worker and the job: Coping with change.* Englewood Cliffs, N. J.: Prentice-Hall, 1974.

Saltman, M. and R. G. Bernardi. *The adult play experience in the hospital set-*

ting. Unpublished manuscript, Center for the Study of Play, Sausalito, Ca., 1972.

Sandler, B. E. Eclecticism at work: Approaches to job design. *American Psychologist*, 1974, *29*, 767–773.

Sawhill, I. V. Perspectives on women and work in America. In J. O'Toole (Ed.), *Work and the quality of life in America.* Cambridge, Mass.: MIT Press, 1974.

Sawyer, J. and H. Schechter. Computers, privacy, and the national data center: The responsibility of social scientists. *American Psychologist*, 1968, *23*, 810–818.

Schein, E. H. *Organizational psychology* (2nd ed.). Englewood Cliffs, N. J.: Prentice-Hall, 1970.

Schein, V. E., E. H. Maurer, and J. F. Novak. Impact of flexible working hours on productivity. *Journal of Applied Psychology*, 1977, *62*, 463–465.

Schmidt, F. L., J. G. Berner, and J. E. Hunter. Racial differences in validity of employment tests: Reality or illusion? *Journal of Applied Psychology*, 1973, *58*, 5–9.

Schmidt, F. L., A. L. Greenthal, J. G. Berner, J. E. Hunter, and F. W. Seaton. *Job sample vs. paper-and-pencil trades and technical tests: Adverse impact and examinee attitudes.* Paper presented at the meeting of the American Psychological Association, Chicago, September 1975.

Schmidt, W. H. *Organizational frontiers and human values.* Belmont, Ca.: Wadsworth, 1970.

Schoenfeldt, L. F. Utilization of manpower: Development and evaluation of an assessment-classification model for matching individuals to jobs. *Journal of Applied Psychology*, 1974, *59*, 583–595.

Schott, R. W. and D. Crapo. *Industrial recreation: An annotated bibliography.* Chicago: National Industrial Recreation Association, 1973.

Schuck, P. H. National economic planning: A slogan without substance. *Public Interest*, Fall 1976, *(45)*, 63–78.

Schultz, D. P. *Psychology and industry today* (2nd ed.). New York: Macmillan, 1978.

Schumacher, E. F. *Small is beautiful.* New York: Harper & Row, 1973.

Schwab, D. P. and H. G. Heneman, III. Age and satisfaction with dimensions of work. *Journal of Vocational Behavior*, 1977, *10*, 212–220.

Scott, W. D. *The theory of advertising.* Boston: Small, Maynard and Company, 1903.

Scott, W. E. The effects of extrinsic rewards on "intrinsic motivation": A critique. *Organizational Behavior and Human Performance*, 1975, *14*,

117–129.

Seashore, S. E. and J. T. Barnowe. Collar color doesn't count. *Psychology Today*, August 1972, 52–54, 80, 82.

Seashore, S. E. and T. D. Taber. Job satisfaction indicators and their correlates. In A. D. Biderman and T. F. Drury (Eds.), *Measuring work quality for social reporting*. New York: Wiley, 1976.

Seidler, L. J. and L. L. Seidler. *Social accounting*. Los Angeles: Melville, 1975.

Sethi, S. P. *The unstable ground: Corporate social policy in a dynamic society*. Los Angeles: Melville, 1974.

Seybolt, J. W. Work satisfaction as a function of the person-environment interaction. *Organizational Behavior and Human Performance*, 1976, *66*, 66–75.

Shamberg, M. *Guerrilla television*. New York: Holt, Rinehart and Winston, 1971.

Sharf, J. Facing reverse discrimination. *APA Monitor*, March 1977, 6:21.

Shelley, E. F. and F. D. Shelley. A retirement index? *Social Policy*, 1976, *7(3)*, 52–54.

Sheppard, H. L. *New perspective on older workers*. Kalamazoo, Mich.: W. E. Upjohn Institute, May 1971.

Sheppard, H. L. and N. Q. Herrick. *Where have all the robots gone? Worker dissatisfaction in 70s*. New York: Free Press, 1972.

Short, J., E. Williams, and B. Christie. *Social psychology of telecommunications*. New York: Wiley, 1976.

Siegel, L. and I. M. Lane. *Psychology in industrial organizations*, Homewood, Ill.: Richard Irwin, 1974. (3rd ed.)

Sirota, D. and A. D. Wolfson. Job enrichment: What are the obstacles? *Personnel*, 1972a, *49(3)*, 8–17.

Sirota, D. and A. D. Wolfson. Job enrichment: Surmounting the obstacles. *Personnel*, 1972b, *49(4)*, 8–19.

Smith, D. H. (Ed.). *Voluntary action research*. Lexington, Mass.: Lexington Books, 1973.

Smith, H. C. and J. H. Wakely. *Psychology of industrial behavior* (3rd ed.). New York: McGraw-Hill, 1972.

Soleri, P. *Arcology, the city in the image of man*. Cambridge, Mass.: MIT Press, 1969.

Special focus: Appropriate technology. *The Futurist*, 1977, *11*, 72–104.

Special issue: Mid-life career change. *Vocational Guidance Quarterly*, 1977, *25(4)*.

Special issue: Paras, peers, and pros. *Personnel and Guidance Journal*, 1974, *53*.

194

Spergel, P. and S. S. Leshner. Vocational assessment through work sampling. *Journal of Jewish Community Service*, 1968, *44*, 225–229.

Srivastva, S., P. F. Salipante, Jr., T. G. Cummings, W. W. Notz, J. D. Bigelow, and J. A. Waters. *Job satisfaction and productivity*. Cleveland, Ohio: Case Western Reserve University, 1975.

Stagner, R. *Humanizing programs: The impact of the affluent society*. Paper presented at the meeting of the American Psychological Association, San Francisco, 1977.

Stevenson, G. Computers launch faster, better matching. *Manpower*, 1976, *7(1)*, 2–8.

Stine, G. H. *The third industrial revolution*. New York: Putnam, 1975.

Stokols, D. The experience of crowding in primary and secondary environments. *Environment and Behavior*, 1976, *8*, 49–86.

Stone, C. H. and F. L. Ruch. Selection, interviewing, and testing. In D. Yoder and H. G. Heneman, Jr. (Eds.), *ASPA handbook of personnel and industrial relations: Staffing policies and strategies*. Washington, D. C.: Bureau of National Affairs, 1974.

Stone, E. F. The moderating effect of work-related values on the job scope—job satisfaction relationship. *Organizational Behavior and Human Performance*, 1976, *15*, 147–167.

Super, D. E. and M. J. Bohn, Jr. *Occupational psychology*. Belmont, Ca.: Wadsworth, 1970.

Susman, G. I. Job enlargement: Effects of culture on worker responses. *Industrial Relations*, 1973, *12*, 1–15.

Sutton-Smith, B. Play as a transformational set. In *Leisure Today: Research and thought about children's play*. Washington, D. C.: American Association for Health, Physical Education, and Recreation, 1972.

Sutton-Smith, B. *Play as adaptive potentiation*. Paper presented at Symposium on Play and Exploratory Behavior, Georgia State University, January 1973.

Swados, H. *On the line*. Boston: Little, Brown, 1957.

Sweezy, P. M. Discussion: Market and plan; plan and market. *American Economic Review*, 1977, *67(1)*, 67–68.

Swerdloff, S. *The revised workweek: Results of a pilot study of 16 firms* (U. S. Dept. of Labor Bulletin 1846). Washington, D.C.: U. S. Government Printing Office, 1975.

Symposium: An assessment center for mid-career and middle life. Presented at the meeting of the American Psychological Association, San Francisco, August 1977.

Symposium: Work as an aspect of human development in midlife years. Presented at the meeting of the American Psychological Association,

Washington, D. C., September 1976.

Tannenbaum, A. S., B. Kavcic, M. Rosner, M. Vianello, and G. Wieser. *Heirarchy in organizations: An international comparison.* San Francisco: Jossey-Bass, 1974.

Taylor, F. W. *Principles of scientific management.* New York: Harper & Row, 1947.

Taylor, J. C. Technology and supervision in the post-industrial era. In J. G. Hunt and L. L. Larson (Eds.), *Contingency approaches to leadership.* Carbondale, Ill.: Southern Illinois University Press, 1974.

TEAM Associates, *An examination of the relationship between psychological well-being and effect of manpower training programs.* (Report #5). (HEW #100-75-0111). Washington, D.C., 1976.

Terborg, J. R. Women in management: A research review. *Journal of Applied Psychology,* 1977, *62*, 647–664.

Terkel, S. A steelworker speaks. *Dissent,* Winter 1972, 9–20.

Terkel, S. *Working.* New York: Pantheon, 1974.

Theobald, R. and J. M. Scott. *Teg's 1994: An anticipation of the near future.* Chicago: Swallow Press, 1972.

Thompson, G. B. Work versus leisure roles: An investigation of morale among employed and retired men. *Journal of Gerontology,* 1973, *28*, 339–344.

Thurow, L. Zero economic growth and the distribution of income. In A. Weintraub, E. Schwartz, and J. R. Aronson (Eds.), *The economic growth controversy.* White Plains, N. Y.: International Arts and Science Press, 1973.

Tichy, N. and M. A. Devanna. *Managing human resources: From style to substance.* Paper presented at Conference on Alternatives to Growth, Woodlands, Tex., October 1977.

Toffler, A. *Future shock.* New York: Bantam Books, 1971.

Toole, D. L., J. F. Gavin, L. B. Murdy, and S. B. Sells. The differential validity of personality, personal history, and aptitude data for minority and non-minority employees. *Personnel Psychology,* 1972, *25*, 661–672.

Top management speaks on the value of recreation programs in industry. Chicago: National Industrial Recreation Association, 1976.

Torbert, W. R. *Being for the most part puppets.* Cambridge, Mass.: Schenkman, 1973.

Triandis, H. C. Work and nonwork: Intercultural perspectives. In M. D. Dunnette (Ed.), *Work and nonwork in the year 2001.* Monterey, Ca.: Brooks/Cole, 1973.

Trist, E. Toward a post-industrial culture. In R. Dubin (Ed.), *Handbook of work, organization, and society.* Chicago: Rand-McNally, 1976.

Trist, E. L. and K. W. Bamforth. Some social and psychological consequences of the longwall method of coal-getting. *Human Relations*, 1951, *4*, 3–38.

Trist, E. L., G. W. Higgin, H. Murray, and A. B. Pollack. *Organizational choice*. London: Tavistock, 1963.

Tyler, L. E. Design for a hopeful psychology. *American Psychologist*, 1973, *28*, 1021–1029.

Tyler, M., M. Katsoulis, and A. Cook. Telecommunications and energy policy. *Telecommunications Policy*, 1976, *1*, 23–32.

Umpleby, S. Is greater citizen participation in planning possible and desirable? *Technological Forecasting and Social Change*, 1972, *4*, 61–76.

Umstot, D. D., C. H. Bell, and T. R. Mitchell. Effects of job enrichment and task goals on satisfaction and productivity: Implications for job design. *Journal of Applied Psychology*, 1976, *61*, 379–394.

Uniform guidelines on employee selection procedures. *Federal Register*, December 30, 1977.

U. S. Congress, Congressional Budget Office. *Temporary measures to stimulate employment: An evaluation of some alternatives*. Washington, D.C.: U. S. Congress, September 2, 1975.

U. S. Department of Labor, Employment and Training Administration. *Sheltered workshop study: A nationwide report on sheltered workshops and their employment of handicapped individuals*. Washington, D. C.: U. S. Government Printing Office, 1977.

U. S. Department of Labor, Manpower Administration. *Dictionary of occupational titles: Definitions of titles* (Vol. 1). Washington, D.C.: U. S. Government Printing Office, 1965.

U. S. Department of Labor, Manpower Administration. *Handbook of Occupational Keywords*. November 1975.

U. S. Department of Labor, Wage and Labor Standards Administration. *Job satisfaction: Thoughts on satisfying human needs through work, as discussed at Airlee House on December 12 and 13, 1968*. Unpublished manuscript, 1968.

Vallee, J., R. Johansen, and K. Spangler. The computer conference. *The Futurist*, 1975, *9(3)*, 116–121.

Van Maanen, J. and E. H. Schein. Improving the quality of work life: Career development. In J. R. Hackman and J. L. Suttle (Eds.), *Improving life in organizations*. Pacific Palisades, Ca.: Goodyear, 1977.

Vanek, J. Time spent in housework. *Scientific American*, 1974, *231(5)*, 116–120.

Veblen, T. *The theory of the leisure class*. New York: Mentor Books, 1953 (originally published in 1899).

Vroom, V. H. *Some personality determinants of the effects of participation*. Englewood Cliffs, N.J.: Prentice-Hall, 1960.

Walker, C. R. (Ed.). *Technology, industry, and man.* New York: McGraw-Hill, 1968.

Walker, C. R. and R. H. Guest. *The man on the assembly line.* Cambridge, Mass.: Harvard University Press, 1952.

Walker, J. M. Organizational change, citizen participation, and voluntary action. *Journal of Voluntary Action Research,* 1975, *4(1)*, 4–27.

Wallick, F. Work with dignity. *The Humanist,* Sept./Oct. 1973; 16–18.

Walters, R. W. and Associates. *Job enrichment for results: Strategies for successful implementation.* Reading, Mass.: Addison-Wesley, 1975.

Wanous, J. P. Individual differences and reactions to job characteristics. *Journal of Applied Psychology,* 1974, *59*, 616–622.

Wanous, J. P. Organizational entry: Newcomers moving from outside to inside. *Psychological Bulletin,* 1977, *84*, 601–618.

Warner, M. Further thoughts on experiments in industrial democracy and self-management. *Human Relations,* 1976, *29*, 401–410.

Warr, P. (Ed.). *Personal goals and work design.* New York: Wiley, 1976.

Weaver, C. N. Job preferences of white collar and blue collar workers. *Academy of Management Journal,* 1975, *18*, 167–175.

Weaver, C. N. Occupational prestige as a factor in the net relationship between occupation and job satisfaction. *Personnel Psychology,* 1977, *30*, 607–612.

Weick, K. *The social psychology of organizing.* Reading, Mass.: Addison-Wesley, 1969.

Weidenbaum, M. and L. Rockwood. Corporate planning versus government planning. *Public Interest,* Winter 1977, *(46)*, 59–72.

Weintraub, A., E. Schwartz, and J. R. Aronson (Eds.). *The economic growth controversy.* White Plains, N. Y.: International Arts and Science Press, 1973.

Weintraub, J. R. and P. C. Smith. *A multivariate examination of an index of heart attack and job attitudes for American industrial workers.* Paper presented at a meeting of the Western Psychological Association, Anaheim, Ca., April 1973.

Weisler, A. and R. B. McCall. Exploration and play: Resume and redirection. *American Psychologist,* 1976, *31*, 492–508.

Wernimont, P. F., and J. Campbell. Signs, samples, and criteria. *Journal of Applied Psychology,* 1968, *52*, 372–376.

Where transit works: Urban densities for public transportaion. *Regional Plan News,* August 1976.

White, B. J. The criteria for job satisfaction: Is interesting work most important? *Monthly Labor Review,* 1977, *100(5)*, 30–35.

Whyte, W. F. *Money and motivation.* New York: Harper & Row, 1955.

198

Wickert, F. R. *Hawthorne and industrial psychology: Views from a one-time insider.* Paper presented at the meeting of American Psychological Association, Chicago, August 1975.

Wilensky, H. L. Work, careers and social integration. *International Social Science Journal*, 1960, *12*, 543–560.

Wilensky, H. L. Mass society and mass culture: Interdependence or independence? *American Sociological Review*, 1964, *29(2)*, 173–197.

Wirtz, W. *The boundless resource: A prospectus for an education/work policy.* Washington, D. C.: New Republic Books, 1975.

Wolforth, J. R. *Residential location and the place of work.* Vancouver, B. C.: Tantalus Research, 1965.

Wool, H. What's wrong with work in America? A review essay. *Monthly Labor Review*, 1973, *96(3)*, 38–44.

Wool, H. *The labor supply for lower level occupations.* (U. S. Department of Labor R & D Monograph No. 42). Washington, D.C.: U. S. Government Printing Office, 1976.

Work in America: Report of a special task force to the Secretary of Health, Education, and Welfare. Cambridge, Mass.: MIT Press, 1973.

Yankelovich, D. *The new morality: A profile of American youth in the 70's.* New York: McGraw-Hill, 1974.

Zaleznik, A., M. F. R. Kets de Vries, and J. Howard. Stress reactions in organizations: Syndromes, causes and consequences. *Behavioral Science*, 1977, *22*, 151–162.

Zanker, A. Jobs: A look at the nation's most nagging problem. *U. S. News and World Report*, February 21, 1977, 54–62.

Zapf, W. The polity as a monitor of the quality of life. *American Behavioral Scientist*, 1974, *17*, 651–675.

Zimbalist, A. The limits of work humanization. *Review of Radical Political Economics*, 1975, *7(2)*, 50–59.

Author Index

Aagaard, A., 129, 130, 176
Abdel-Halim, A.A., 82, 165
Abt Associates, Inc., 51, 165
Ackoff, R.A., 161, 165
Adkins, C., 135, 188
Agassi, J.B., 109, 165
Aldag, R.J., 82, 107, 168
Allardt, E., 71, 165
Allen, L. of H., 147, 165
Allen, M., 146, 169
Alpert, D., 51, 165
Altimus, C.A., 78, 165
American Psychological Association, 15, 165
Anderson, N., 137, 165
Andrisani, P.J., 69, 165
Arbeiter, S., 46, 174
Argyris, C., 63, 110, 198
Aronson, J.R., 110, 198
Astin, A.W., 33, 165
Atchley, R.C., 130, 131, 133, 148, 165

Baldi de Mandilovitch, M.S., 59, 69, 91, 191
Bamforth, K.W., 107, 196
Barbash, J., 108, 166
Barfield, R.E., 148, 166
Barnett, L., 148, 166
Barnowe, J.T., 68, 194
Barrett, G.V., ix, 111, 166
Barrett, R.S., 24, 182
Bartlett, C.J., 24, 173
Bartlett, D.M., 132, 166
Bass, B.M., ix, 16, 17, 104, 110, 111, 113, 127, 166
Bass, R., 17, 166
Batten, M.D., 55, 56, 166
Bauer, R.A., 161, 162, 166
Baxter, N., 55, 166
Beasley, R.R., 147, 178
Bechhofer, F., 74, 176
Beer, M., 86, 109, 166
Behrens, W.W., 43, 185
Bell, C.H., 80, 197

Bell, D., vii, 4, 65, 103, 161, 167, 189
Belous, R.S., 114, 183
Bem, D.J., 22, 167
Bem, S.L., 22, 167
Bengtsson, A., 147, 167
Bennis, W.G., 40, 86, 110, 167
Berg, I., 56, 109, 167
Berger, B., 36, 167
Berheide, C. W., 146, 167
Berk, R. A., 146, 167
Berk, S.F., 146, 167
Berlyne, D.E., 120, 167
Bernardi, R.G., 146, 192
Berner, J.G., 24, 25, 193
Best, F., 56, 107, 127, 128, 167
Bezdek, R., 110, 167
Biderman, A.D., 106, 162
Bigelow, J.D., 69, 195
Bitzer, D.C., 51, 165
Blauner, R., 64, 107, 167
Blaxall, M., 109, 167
Blood, M.R., 25, 82, 83, 167, 168, 180
Bluestone, B., 127, 168
Bluestone, I., 108, 168
Blum, M.L., ix, 1, 4, 16, 53, 168
Blumberg, P., 109, 168
Boehm, V.R., 24, 168
Boguslaw, R., 7, 168
Bohn, M.J., Jr., 55, 195
Bosserman, P., 127, 168
Bouvin, A., 108, 168
Bowen, H.R., 56, 90, 91, 168
Bowles, E., 55, 56, 168
Boyack, V.L., 131, 132, 168
Bratthall, K., 133, 168
Brayfield, A.H., 59, 83, 168, 189
Bremer, A., 146, 168
Bremer, T., 146, 168
Brenner, H., 21, 37, 53, 131, 168
Brief, A.P., 82, 107, 169
Broedling, L.A. 107, 169
Brousseau, K.R., 108, 169

201

Brown, J.K., 71, 192
Brown, Z.H., 113, 176
Byham, W.C., 54, 110, 181
Byrne, J.J., 146, 175
Buckley, W., 17, 169
Buhler, C., 146, 169

Cambell, A., 162, 169
Campbell, D., 161, 169
Campbell, J.P., 25, 169, 198
Caplan, F., 146, 169
Caplan, N., 31, 169
Caplan, R.D., 70, 169
Caplan, T., 146, 169
Carey, M.L., 36, 39, 169
Carlson, F.R., 98, 187
Carnegie Commission on Higher Education, 47, 48, 56, 169
Carp, F.M., 148, 170
Case, J., 78, 180
Cass, E.L., 16, 170
Cassell, E., 148, 189
Cavanagh, G., 53, 170
Champoux, J.E., 82, 137, 170, 172
Chapman, C., 131, 168
Chernov, M., 148, 189
Cherns, A.B., 107, 108, 171
Chomsky, N., 163, 170
Christie, B., 110, 194
Churchman, C.W., 17, 170
Clague, E., 56, 170
Claiborne, R., 163, 170
Clark, M.J., 51, 178
Clark, R., 110, 182
Coates, J.F., 162, 170
Cobb, S., 70, 169
Cohen, M.D., 147, 190
Cole, M., 130, 186
Conference Board, 30, 110, 170
Converse, P.E., 162, 169
Cook, A., 101, 197
Coolican, D.M., 56, 170
Costigan, R., 130, 134, 187
Crapo. D., 147, 193
Creed, E.C., 126, 170
Crites, J.O., 55, 170
Crockett, W.H., 59, 168
Crooks, L.A., 24, 170

Csikszentmihalyi, M., 148, 171
Culen, E., 113, 171
Cummings, T.G., 69, 195

Daneker, G., 11, 110, 177
Davis, K., 162, 171
Davis, L.E., 91, 92, 93, 94, 106, 107, 108, 147, 171
Day, L.H., 110, 171
Deci, E.L., 107, 163, 171
De Grazia, S., 145, 171
De Greene, K.B., 17, 91, 151, 171
Delworth, U., 36, 171
DeMarco, B., 135, 148, 188
De Maria, A.T., 68, 171
Den Hertog, F.J., 108, 172
Dermer, J., 107, 172
Devanna, M.A., 110, 196
Dickson, P., 107, 172
Dickson, W.J., 16, 192
DiQuattro, A., 161, 163, 172
Dougharty, L.A., 40, 189
Driscoll, J.W., 109, 166
Drucker, P.F., 16, 41, 42, 64, 172
Drury, T.F., 106, 167
Dubin, R., 73, 82, 106, 137, 139, 172
Dumazedier, J., 137, 172
Dunham, R.B., 85, 130, 172
Dunn, D.A., 153, 189
Dunn, D.R., 146, 172
Dunn, W.L., 40, 189
Dunnette, M.D., ix, 30, 53, 86, 113, 172
Dyer, F.J., 24, 181
Dyer, L., 85, 107, 172, 173

Eberly, D.J., 34, 173
Elden, M., 72, 173
Ellis, D.D., Jr., 54, 187
Ellis, M.J., 45, 120, 122, 123, 146, 173
Ellul, J., 12, 173
Emery, F.E., 17, 72, 107, 151, 161, 173
England, R., 127, 168
Entine, A.D., 55, 173
Espinosa, J.F., 108, 173
Etzioni, A., 34, 35, 161, 173
Evans, M.G., 129, 173
Evans, R.N., 56, 180
Ewen, R.B., 24, 182

Farr, J.L., 24, 173
Faunce, W.A., 73, 137
Fechter, A., 91, 174
Fein, M., 69, 174
Feldmesser, R.A., 51, 178
Feldstein, M., 90, 174
Fenn, D.H., Jr., 162, 166
Ferrin, R.I., 46, 174
Fincher, C., 24, 174
Fine, S.A., 27, 28, 30, 35, 86, 87, 172, 174
Fiske, D.W., 120, 174
Flamholtz, E., 162, 174
Flanagan, R.J., 68, 174
Fleishman, E.A., 86, 174
Ford, R.N., 79, 174
Foster, L.W., 107, 178
Fowles, R., 17, 174
Fox, H., 24, 174, 183
Foy, N., 108, 174
Frank, H.H., 109, 175
Freedman, J.L., 96, 175
Freedman, M., 109, 167
Freeman, R.B.,. 56, 175
French, V.R.P., Jr., 70, 169
Friedlander, F., 30, 175
Friedmann, G., 64, 107, 136, 175
Fromm, E., 61
Fromm, G., 161, 175
Fullerton, H.N., Jr., 146, 175

Gadon, H., 108, 174
Galbraith, J.K., 159, 161, 175
Galle, O.R., 96, 175
Galloway, T.D., 161, 175
Ganz, A., 110, 175
Garfinkel, I., 90, 186
Garson, G.D., 78, 180
Gartner, A.R., 55, 175
Gavin, J.F., 24, 196
Ghiselli, E.E., 24, 175
Gieber, M.L., 51, 178
Giles, W.F., 86, 175
Gilmer, B.v.H., ix, 16, 175
Ginzberg, E., 110, 156, 161, 175
Glaser, E.M., 109, 175
Glazer, N., 54, 176
Glenn, N.D., 68, 176
Glickman, A.S., 113, 176

Goering, J.M., 110, 176
Gold, S.M., 146, 176
Goldstein, I.L., ix, 176
Goldthorpe, J.H., 74, 82, 83, 176
Golembiewski, R.T., 129, 176
Gomez, L.R., 31, 186
Goodale, J.G., 30, 129, 130, 176
Goodman, P., 97, 117, 176
Goodman, P.S., 30, 176
Gorz, A., 65, 73, 176
Gottlieb, D., 45, 89, 102, 104, 177
Gough, H., 86, 177
Gove, W.R., 96, 175
Gray, P., 98, 100, 177, 187
Green T.E., 146, 177
Greenberg, S., 30, 175
Greene, D., 148, 183
Greenthal, A.L., 25, 193
Gross, B.M., 162, 177
Grossman, R., 11, 110, 177
Grubb, W.N., 56, 177
Guest, A.M., 110, 177
Guest, R.H., 107, 198
Guion, R.M., 24, 27, 177
Gurman, R., 68, 171
Gutek, B.A., 110, 187

Hackman, J.R., 78, 79, 80, 81, 82, 83, 85, 86, 102, 106, 108, 109, 177, 188, 190
Haldi Associates, Inc., 129, 130, 178
Hall, D.T., 55, 178, 195
Hammer, T.H., 108, 178
Hammond, A.L., 51, 178
Hamner, W.G., 107, 178
Hanneman, G.J., 98, 187
Hannon, B., 110, 167
Hardin, G., 10, 11, 178
Harkness, R.C., 101, 178
Harman, W.W., 161, 178
Harry, J.E., 146, 178
Hartley, J., 130, 178
Hartnett, R.T., 51, 178
Hayek, F.A., 157, 178
Hayward, D.G., 147, 178
Hedges, J.N., 115, 130, 178, 186
Henderson, H., 161, 178
Heneman, H.G., III 68, 193
Henle, P., 68, 178

Hennig, M., 109, 179
Herbert, W., 109, 179
Herbst, P.G., 107, 179
Herrick, N.Q., 68, 71, 194
Herrnstein, R.J., 163, 179
Herzberg, F., 63, 76, 179
Hewes, J.J., 147, 179
Hiemstra, R., 56, 179
Higgin, G.W., 107, 196
Hilgendorf, E.L., 108, 179
Hill, R.B., 110, 190
Hilles, R.J., 129, 176
Holland, J.L., 55, 86, 179
Holt, J., 146, 179
Holt, T., 54, 179
Homans, G.C, 63, 179
Hopp, M.A., 130, 179
Hough, L., 30, 172
House, J., 71, 179
Howard, A., 54, 179
Howard, J., 70, 199
Howe, L.K., 109, 179
Hoyt, K.B., 55, 180
Huber, J., 109–110, 180
Huizinga, J., 119, 145, 180
Hulin, C.L., 82, 83, 168, 180
Humphrey, H.H., 156, 161, 180
Hunnius, G., 78, 108, 180
Hunt, R.G., ix, 180
Hunter, J.E., 24, 25, 193
Hutchins, R.M., 51, 180
Hutchison, J., 110, 188

Initiative Committee for National Economic
    Planning, 161, 180
Insel, P.M., 86, 186
Irving, B.L., 108, 179
Ivancevich, U.M., 130, 180

Jacobs, J., 96, 146, 180
Jakubauskas, E.B., 56, 180
Janson, R., 86, 178
Jardim, A., 109, 179
Jeffery, L.R., 110, 180
Jenkins, D., 78, 108, 180
Jennings, K., 71, 180
Jenson, A.R., 23, 180
Jewell, D.O., 26, 189

Jewish Employment and Vocational Service,
    25, 54, 180
Johansen, R., 101, 110, 180, 181, 197
Johnson, B.H., 161, 183
Johnston, D.F., 145, 181
Johnston, W.B., 109, 184

Kagno, M., 129, 176
Kahn, H., 110, 181
Kahn, R.L., 67, 86, 151, 181
Kalachek, E.M., 110, 176
Kalt, N.C., 131, 181
Kando, T.M., 137, 181
Kanter, R.M., 110, 181
Kaplan, M., 114, 115, 121, 127, 145, 181
Karasek, R.A., 70, 72, 181
Kassalow, E.M., 108, 181
Katsoulis, M., 101, 197
Katz, D., 151, 181
Katzell, M.E., 110, 181
Katzell, R.A., 24, 79, 80, 181, 182
Katzman, N., 154, 182
Kavcic, B., 108, 196
Kelleher, C.H., 148, 182
Kemble, F., 56, 182
Kestenbaum, S., 55, 56, 166
Kets de Vries, M.F.R., 70, 199
Kirchner, W.K., 24, 182
Kirkpatrick, J.J., 24, 182
Klausner, W.J., 117, 182
Koch, J.L., 30, 182
Kohl, H.R., 146, 182
Kohn, M.H., 131, 181
Kohn, M.L., 72, 81, 83, 108, 182
Korman, A.K., ix, 16, 182
Kornhauser, A., 70, 71, 82, 182
Kramer, L., 56, 170
Kremen, B., 61, 182
Krendall, E., 162, 182
Kreps, J.M., 91, 110, 115, 146, 182
Kuhn, T.S., 3, 13, 183

Landy, F.J., ix, 183
Lane, I.M., ix, 194
Lawler, E.E., III, ix, 69, 78, 78, 81, 83, 84,
    87, 102, 109, 162, 177, 183, 185, 190, 191
Lawrence, J.E.S., 96, 183
Lazerson, M., 56, 177